Policing a Diverse Society

Policing a Diverse Society

Dr Phil Clements

BA Cert.Ed, MEd, EdD, ILTM
Principal Lecturer, University of Portsmouth

Foreword by Robin Field-Smith MBE

HM Inspector of Constabulary (Personnel, Training and Diversity)

OXFORD
UNIVERSITY PRESS

OXFORD
UNIVERSITY PRESS

Great Clarendon Street, Oxford OX2 6DP

Oxford University Press is a department of the University of Oxford.
It furthers the University's objective of excellence in research, scholarship,
and education by publishing worldwide in

Oxford New York

Auckland Cape Town Dar es Salaam Hong Kong Karachi
Kuala Lumpur Madrid Melbourne Mexico City Nairobi
New Delhi Shanghai Taipei Toronto

With offices in

Argentina Austria Brazil Chile Czech Republic France Greece
Guatemala Hungary Italy Japan Poland Portugal Singapore
South Korea Switzerland Thailand Turkey Ukraine Vietnam

Oxford is a registered trade mark of Oxford University Press
in the UK and in certain other countries

Published in the United States
by Oxford University Press Inc., New York

British Library Cataloguing in Publication Data

Data available

Library of Congress Cataloging in Publication Data

Clements, Phillip Edward.
   Policing a diverse society / Phil Clements ; foreword by Robin Field-Smith.
      p. cm.
   Includes bibliographical references and index.
   ISBN-13: 978–0–19–929135–9
   ISBN-10: 0–19–929135–7
   1. Police—Great Britain. 2. Multiculturalism—Great Britain. 3. Police-community
relations—Great Britain. 4. Discrimination in law enforcement—Great Britain. 5.
Police training—Great Britain. 6. Police administration—Great Britain. I. Title.
   HV8195.A3C54 2006
   363.2′2—dc22

                                                                        2006014405

Typeset by Laserwords Private Limited, Chennai, India
Printed in Great Britain
on acid-free paper by
Ashford Colour Press Limited, Gosport, Hampshire

ISBN 0–19–929135–7   978–0–19–929135–9

10 9 8 7 6 5 4 3 2 1

Foreword

This book is a very timely contribution to the knowledge base and debate on diversity and the police. There is a requirement for all members of our society to ensure they understand what is expected of them in the context of the current and future statutory provision. We already have laws about race relations and gender, and this will shortly be joined by laws on age and disability with faith expected to follow in due course. Ignorance of the law can never be an excuse, but it is not enough just to know the letter. The spirit and wider context must also be grasped. Since we are dealing with people, not machines, we must recognize the emotional, ethical, and moral dimensions. It is not a question of being 'politically correct' but of respect for each and every one of our fellow citizens, our neighbours, near and far, and those with whom we work, play, and communicate.

The police are responsible for ensuring the safety of all those living in, and passing through, our country. In going about their business, police officers and staff do not have the opportunity to exclude, ignore, or give a lesser service, to any individual or group. They have to respect and manage the diversity both within the workforce of police forces and organizations, and in the communities to be policed.

In recent years, there has been a continuing focus on how the police are performing in response to the rich canvas of diversity. Race has been a particular issue, with some high profile cases and stories, some tragic, some commendable. But gender and sexuality have increasingly featured in the national and local news stories, and as, if not more, importantly in the daily life of police personnel. No one should be in any doubt of the scale of the challenge facing the police, and the critical importance of knowing what to do right and getting the right outcomes through intelligent application of skills and attributes.

Phil Clements has written a comprehensive and illuminating book, which will be of interest to the observer, but of real value to those wrestling with the challenges. He draws on his own first-hand experience as a police officer, but sets this within a sound academic and intellectual framework. I commend it to your attention.

Robin Field-Smith MBE MA FCIPD FCMI
HM Inspector of Constabulary (Personnel, Training and Diversity)

Acknowledgements

My journey into diversity and the issues raised has been a long one and spans many years. It has been a journey of learning and I anticipate that it will continue for many years to come. My thanks go to a large number of people who have influenced my thinking; I have learned from all of them. In terms of this book however, I would like to acknowledge some particular people who have above all stimulated critical thinking. My thanks therefore go to Tim Meaklim, Bill Priestley, and Angela Morrell with whom I worked at Centrex and each of whom contributed to my understanding of the issues. I remember with particular fondness members of the then Centrex Lay Advisory Panel for which I provided a secretariat. Those with whom I worked closely included Wycliffe Barrett, Dr Jaslien Singh, Khan Mogul, Inder Singh Uppal, Pete Mercer, Harold Manger, Dr Robin Oakley, and others—to each of them I am grateful for what I learned. I also worked closely with colleagues in the National Black Police Association and the Gay Police Association, and I am grateful for their cooperation and understanding. Since leaving the police, I have continued to work with members of Her Majesty's Inspectorate of Constabulary and others in the service, some of whom have now left, others who are still serving. So my thanks also go to Robin Field-Smith, Scottie Addison, and Philip Rogerson who have all challenged the way I think. Particular thanks go to Richard Martin, at whose suggestion the book was written. I acknowledge the patience of my editor at Oxford University Press, Katie Allan, and the constant friendship and advice of John Jones, Professor Steve Savage, Mike Nash, John Grieve, and others at the Institute of Criminal Justice Studies and my students from whom I learn more than they will probably ever know.

Finally my thanks go to Heather, my wife, friend, and lifelong companion without whose support and love I would never be able to achieve anything.

Phil Clements

Contents

Abbreviations

ACPO	Association of Chief Police Officers
BAWP	British Association of Women in Policing
BCU	basic command unit
CEHR	Commission for Equality and Human Rights
Centrex	Central Police Training and Development Authority
CPS	Crown Prosecution Service
CRE	Commission for Racial Equality
CRR	community race relations
CSO	Community Support Officer
DRC	Disability Rights Commission
EOC	Equal Opportunities Commission
GPA	Gay Police Association
HMIC	Her Majesty's Inspectorate of Constabulary
IAG	independent advisory group
ICT	information and communication technology
IPCC	Independent Police Complaints Commission
IPLDP	Initial Police Learning and Development Programme
LAGPA	Lesbian and Gay Police Association
MCB	Muslim Council of Britain
MPS	Metropolitan Police Service
NBPA	National Black Police Association
NOS	National Occupational Standards
NVQ	National Vocational Qualification
PCSO	Police Community Support Officers
POP	problem oriented policing
SSC	Sector Skills Council
SVQ	Scottish Vocational Qualification

Special Features

The book has been laid out with a number of features to help you access the material more easily and more importantly to assist you, the reader, to think through and reflect on the issues relating to diversity as they relate to the professional practice of a police officer. Whilst the book has been written primarily with the needs of police officers in mind, there are many other members of the 'policing family' for whom the book will be of use. Each chapter is laid out in broadly the same way and will contain all or some of the features shown below.

Chapter outline

This will give an indication of the scope of the chapter and highlight the main areas covered.

Case study examples and exercises

Where these are appropriate, the material in the text will be related to case study examples to give an indication of how the issue relates to the practical business of policing. Some of these are presented as exercises which enable you to apply the principles to a particular case.

Diagrams

Diagrams have been included to help make the text clearer and to provide easier access to the material.

Reflect on practice

This is an important feature of the book. Diversity, it will be argued is not something we merely talk or think about but is something to which we need to respond. This response requires a degree of reflection on your part. Chapter 1 includes some advice on how to reflect effectively. Where you see a 'reflect on practice' section, try to develop the discipline of actually putting reflection into practice. This will pay dividends to you as the reader in terms of making the links with the world as you actually experience it.

Exercises

Throughout the book there are mini-exercises that invite you, the reader to work on a particular issue. In some cases the exercise seeks to establish what you already know and understand about something. In other cases the exercise will help you to apply knowledge to a particular situation. As with the 'reflect on practice' opportunities, try to be disciplined in doing these as they are designed to help you get the most from the book.

Chapter summary

Each chapter concludes with a summary that draws together the key themes.

References

The last section of the book contains details of all the references to other literature that are made in the text.

Using the book

To get the most from working through a book like this, it is probably best not just to read straight through. As you tackle each chapter, look first at the opening chapter outline and then look at the chapter summary at the end. In this way you will get a good sense of what the chapter is about. Then carefully work through the material in the chapter and pay attention to the case study examples and opportunities to reflect on practice. In relation to the case studies, it is always good practice, in addition, to think about your own case study examples as well. This will help you relate the material to your own experience and will probably raise questions in your mind that you can then relate back to the issues discussed in the chapter.

Introduction

The idea of diversity is a given—but responding to that diversity is far from a simple matter and capturing that complexity in a short book is by no means an easy task. When I wrote a book on equal opportunities some years ago I was strongly challenged by a female friend who said that as a man, what could I possibly know about equal opportunities? The same could be said about a book on diversity. I am a white, heterosexual male whose religion sits in the Christian tradition. So what could I possibly know about diversity? It is a reasonable challenge, but it seems to me that responding to diversity places a particular responsibility on people such as me to work through the issues for ourselves and to demonstrate a commitment to a society (and the policing of it) that is free from discrimination, and one where all people of whatever background can live their lives in the way that they want to, free from harassment, and subject only to the law and not others' prejudices.

I was a police officer in London for twenty-five years and only in the last three years have I had the opportunity to fully explore issues of diversity free from the constraints that being a serving police officer impose. But it is inevitable that my police service will impact on the way I think and write. I believe firmly in the principle of democratic policing which is conducted with the consensus of the people that are policed. It seems to me that there is no alternative. I also believe that the vast majority of people in the police family agree—and I am constantly reminded as I engage with police students at my University of the commitment and dedication to justice that most police officers bring to their work.

The idea of this book was to try to bring as many of the issues together into a single source as possible. Even today, there are many texts on specific issues but few that attempt to do what this book is attempting. I have been mindful of two types of reader, as the book has progressed. Firstly, I have tried to bear in mind readers who may have a number of years of service and experience. Secondly, I have tried to reflect the needs of those readers who may be studying for degrees in policing or are working towards an NVQ qualification.

In the years that I have been involved in what might be broadly described as diversity issues, I have learned a great deal from others. One of the most important lessons has been the truth in the phrase that 'you cannot please all of the people all of the time'. So there will undoubtedly be criticism both of what I have decided to include and what I have decided to leave out either wittingly or unwittingly. If you feel that I should have included an issue, or at least dealt with it more fully, and this causes you pain or offence—then I apologize now.

We all live in rapidly changing times and the diversity agenda is moving so swiftly against a backdrop of domestic and international events that it has been necessary in February 2006 to draw a line. Almost every day there is something in the news that seems to impact on the policing of diversity. This makes keeping up with it all both challenging and demanding. I would urge you to take this book as a foundation for your interest and challenge yourself to keep up with events as they unfold.

For more information on police books from Blackstone's, please visit www. blackstonespolicemanuals.com or if you have any comments or questions email police.uk@oup.com.

1

Introducing Diversity

1.1 **Chapter Outline**

In this chapter we will be considering the following issues:

- The concept of diversity
- The difference between diversity and equal opportunities
- The nature of equality
- National Occupational Standards for professionals in criminal justice
- The National Police Learning Requirement for Race and Diversity Training.

1.2 **The Concept of Diversity**

Diversity is a relatively recent concept that as yet does not have a unified theoretical framework. Having said that, there have been a number of attempts to define what is meant by diversity and in this section we will examine some of these definitions. It is also necessary to distinguish notions of diversity from the previously more commonly used term 'equal opportunities'. In the case of the latter, equal opportunities primarily arose as a term to describe the equality of opportunity that people have a right to expect in terms of employment and the provision of goods and services. Diversity on the other hand has come to mean something much wider and cuts to the core of the nature of society and how people respond to rapidly changing ideas and perspectives.

It was the publication of the Stephen Lawrence Inquiry Report in 1999 that led to considerable attention to the way in which discrimination and prejudice may impact on how policing is delivered, particularly in relation to investigation and the way witnesses and families are treated by police. World and UK based events however have broadened the agenda even further. The attack on the World Trade Center in New York on 11 September 2001, for example, led to the so-called 'war on terrorism'. A by-product of this has been increased prejudice and discrimination against Muslims, where the act of a relatively very small number of fundamentalists has led to the stereotyping and labelling, by some, of all members of the Islamic faith. This situation has been exacerbated by the events in London on 7 July 2005 when over fifty people were murdered on the London transport system by four suicide bombers, the latter being a previously unknown phenomenon in the UK. For diversity and the policing of diversity, major debates have arisen for example about the nature and indeed value of the idea of multiculturalism. Voices have been raised against the very nature of multiculturalism and whether in a society which perceives itself to be under threat from terrorist extremists the notion of multiculturalism can be sustained. A particular feature of the attack on London was that the bombers were 'home grown' in the sense that they had lived and been educated in the UK and had come out of the very multicultural society that was meant to embrace and respect the different values and culture that they represented. Later in the book we will look at the impact the bombings in London have had on the debate about diversity. For the time being we will look at some perspectives on diversity.

What then are the key issues that would tend toward the development of a theoretical framework for diversity?

REFLECT ON PRACTICE

Think about how diversity may look in your own context, maybe the police service or some other organization:

- What do you understand diversity to be?
- What diversity amongst the people with whom you work do you recognize?
- What is the range of diversity amongst the people to whom you offer your service—the customers or clients?
- What issues does that diversity raise for you as an individual and for your organization?

Some people will argue somewhat simplistically that diversity is the 'way in which we all differ'. Whilst that view has the attraction of its neatness and simplicity, it is problematic in a number respects. On the one hand, it does nothing to define what difference is relevant for the purpose of the argument. One person may wear glasses another may not, so in that regard they are different—but is that difference relevant for the purpose of thinking about and responding to diversity?

In a recent course on diversity that I ran participants were asked to define diversity in terms of what it meant to them in the workplace. One group came up with the simple statement 'the avoidance of monoculture'. Such a simplistic definition has merit for a number of reasons. Firstly, in referring to 'avoidance' there is an implicit *response* to diversity. Diversity amongst people is a reality that nations, organizations, and communities experience. So just thinking about or trying to define it can be seen as unhelpful. What is necessary is to work out how to respond to the diversity that exists in a way that eliminates unlawful or unethical discrimination, and which actively embraces and works with the benefits that diversity amongst people can offer. The second attractive notion implicit in the statement is that the antithesis of diversity is monoculture. It is not hard to find organizations where there is little overt diversity in the workforce. The temptation in such situations is to come to believe that the prevailing culture is the only one that can effectively deliver the organization's goals. Recruiting, for example may be focused more on whether people will fit in than the skills and attributes that they may potentially contribute to the organization. In a recent article, Chief Constable Peter Fahy, the ACPO lead on diversity, commented that: 'You can advertise, arrange open days and do outreach but you will not attract and retain the right people if you do not tackle the question of organisational culture' (Fahy 2005: 20).

What is needed is a definition that will help to draw us towards the aspects of human difference that are most likely to lead to the experience of prejudice, discrimination, and unfairness. In terms of policing, six strands of diversity are recognized as those in most need of action, namely:

- Race (which is the primary focus)
- Age
- Gender
- Sexual orientation
- Disability
- Faith and belief.

Other commentators have made attempts to delineate what should be included when we refer to diversity. Some examples are given below:

> Diversity refers to much more than skin colour and gender. It can encompass age, race, religious affiliation, economic class, military experience and sexual orientation. (Galagan 1991: 41)

> People are different from one another in many ways—in age, gender, education, values, physical ability, mental capacity, personality, experiences, and the way each individual approaches work. Gaining the diversity advantage means acknowledging, understanding and appreciating these differences and developing a workplace that enhances their value. (Jamieson and O'Mara 1991: 3–4).

> The concept of managing diversity is inclusive—diversity includes white males. Managing diversity does not mean that white males are managing women and minorities, but rather that all managers are managing all employees. The objective becomes that of creating an environment that taps the potential of all employees without any group being advantaged by irrelevant classification or accident of birth. (Hammond and Kleiner, 1992: 7).

What strengths and weaknesses can you see in the attempts to delineate diversity above? One key issue that you may have noted is the separation of employee/employer relations, inter-employee relations and employee/people receiving the service provided. It is important to be clear that diversity relates not only to the relationships that exist within an organization but also to the way that the diversity of the people who receive the service is managed.

The United Nations attempted a definition of diversity in the following terms:

> Diversity takes many forms. It is usually thought of in terms of obvious attributes—age differences, race, gender, physical ability, sexual orientation, religion and language. Diversity in terms of background professional experience, skills and specialization, values and culture as well as social class is a prevailing pattern. (Clements and Jones 2002: 13)

You can immediately begin to see the potential richness of what a definition of diversity may include. There are undoubtedly many aspects of difference between humans that can and do lead to discrimination. Social class, education, even accent would be examples. For the purposes of this book, however, we will try to make the issues more manageable by focusing comment on those aspects of difference where discrimination is prohibited either by either existing or emerging law (race, gender, disability, faith and belief, sexual orientation, and age).

It does need to be noted that in the debate alluded to above, one of the key arguments against the notion of multiculturalism is that stressing the differences between people actually tends to make society more divisive and fragmented. The corollary of this is that the focus should not be on what is different about people but what they have in common. The debate since the events of 7 July has come to include issues around British identity and the commonality of democratic values.

1.3 **The Difference between Diversity and Equal Opportunities**

The last quarter of the twentieth century saw a considerable focus on what came to be called 'equal opportunities', one definition of which was suggested by Collins (1992: 10) 'Equal opportunities is about treating everybody fairly and equally regardless of their background or lifestyle'. It could be argued that if society has a robust and healthy attitude towards diversity and the consequent elimination of prejudice and discrimination between people, then the notion of equal opportunities almost becomes redundant. If people are accepted regardless of their difference then their equal opportunity in society will become automatic. Having said that, British society is far from that position and measures are in place to attempt to ensure the equality of opportunity that people have a right to expect.

A number of agencies—which are now constituted as non-departmental public bodies—were set up by the Government to focus on particular aspects of unfairness that people experience, including discrimination on the grounds of sex, race, and disability.

Each of these organizations currently has a very informative website and you should take the opportunity to visit these sites to get a flavour of the range of work that each of the Commissions undertakes.

	Abbreviation	Website
The Equal Opportunities Commission	EOC	<http://www.eoc.org.uk/>
The Commission for Racial Equality	CRE	<http://www.cre.gov.uk/>
The Disability Rights Commission	DRC	<http://www.drc-gb.org/>

Visits to these websites should make it immediately apparent to you that approaches to diversity in all its forms (see above) are not directly covered by each of the Commissions, or at best they are covered obliquely. In October 2003, the Government announced that the three Commissions were to be merged into a single Commission for Equality and Human Rights (CEHR). This new body will also encompass discrimination on grounds of sexual orientation, religion, or age, together with a brief to promote human rights. Such a merger is not without its critics. One argument that can be levelled against the creation of a CEHR is that in doing so the response to particular aspects of discrimination may well become watered down and consequently the challenge to discrimination in a particular area will be less effective. Time will tell what the strength of this argument is.

'Equal opportunities' generally focuses on aspects of equality that relate to the law relating to employment and employee rights and responsibilities. Diversity on the other hand has come to embrace all the elements of approaches to community and race relations, equal opportunities, race awareness, approaches to sexuality, and other minority issues. Clements and Jones (2002: 30–31) express the differences between equal opportunities and diversity in terms of a continuum. The following is an adaptation of that continuum.

Table 1.1 From Equal Opportunities to Diversity

Main Focus	Description
Basic equal opportunities	The focus is on race, gender, disability, religious belief, and sexual orientation and on the legal requirements in relation to employment and the provision of goods and services with a view to the elimination of unlawful discrimination.
Emerging diversity	The focus is on understanding difference and the implications this might have for issues beyond those relating to employment and the provision of goods and service. Other factors, which could be disadvantageous, are introduced, such as accent, educational background, sexual orientation, and age.
Mainstreaming diversity	In mainstreaming diversity, values are constantly reaffirmed, organizations and society in general becomes supportive of long-term cultural change in terms of the elimination of prejudice and discrimination.

1.4 **The Nature of Equality**

Ashcroft, Bigger, and Coates (1996) identify a number of ways in which equality may be viewed. The most simplistic way of viewing equality is that it means treating everyone the same. They argue that such a view is grounded in the assumption that it is 'best to focus on what people have in common' (p 16).

EXERCISE

- Identify some ways in which treating people the same may actually lead to treating them unequally.

A striking example of how treating people the same may actually lead to treating them unequally lies in the provision of facilities for disabled people. If it were assumed, for instance, that access to buildings should be the same for everybody then that could well lead to an assumption that stairs were fine for all and the result would be discrimination against wheelchair users. Of course it sounds ridiculous, but the fact remains that the equality (or giving people equal treatment) lies around the access to buildings. If all people are to be given equality of access then there will need to be arrangements for people in wheelchairs. Exactly the same principles apply for example in the access people have to information. So to treat people equally in this regard might require that information is provided in several languages—it is in the access to information that people should be treated equally, but this will not mean providing exactly the same thing.

Another way of viewing equality revolves around the idea of a level playing field or in Ashcroft's (1996) terms getting people to the same starting point. Another term for this would be '*positive action*' where disadvantaged groups are given the necessary resources to ensure equal access to a particular service. An example would be training courses run by the police to enable people to meet the entry requirements to the police service. Such an approach is not without difficulty. Some people will argue that diverting resources to such initiatives is inherently unfair and actually disadvantages others, particularly if there is not open access to such training. In addition, the focus tends to be on the individual as the 'problem' rather than the structures and processes that disadvantage them in the first place.

A third way of viewing equality is as an interactive process that involves changes generated from both the individual and the institution. In this model, the individual would take responsibility for their own actions in relation to ensuring equality and fairness but this is supported at organizational level by challenging assumptions and processes. For example an individual police officer might actively seek to identify the specific needs of someone they were working with and to try to identify how the system would look from their perspective. The role of the police service would be to respond at the level of policy and processes to provide a framework to ensure that those needs were being met.

1.5 **National Occupational Standards for the Criminal Justice Sector**

National Occupational Standards (NOS) have become increasingly prominent in both the public and private sector in recent years. National Occupational Standards are developed and maintained by the Sector Skills Council (SSC) for the particular area. Policing activity is covered by Skills for Justice, the SSC for the justice sector. According to the Skills for Justice website:

> sector skills councils (SSCs) are independent, UK-wide organisations licensed by the Secretary of State for Education and Skills, in consultation with Ministers in Scotland, Wales and Northern Ireland, to tackle the skills and productivity needs of their sector throughout the UK. Sector skills councils actively involve employers in their work to:
>
> • reduce skills gaps and shortages;
> • improve productivity, business and public service performance;
> • increase opportunities to boost the skills and productivity of everyone in the sector's workforce, including action on equal opportunities;
> • improve learning supply, including apprenticeships, higher education and national occupational standards.

In terms of policing diversity, the key issues from the above description seem to be the need to improve public service performance (in respect to responding to diversity better) and the relevance of NOS which offer some precision in terms of what police officers need to be able to do and what they need to know and understand.

One of the first things that an SSC will develop is a functional map of the sector. This is aimed at identifying all the functions that are involved in a particular sector. Overarching this will be a statement of key purpose. The (draft) key purpose for the justice sector is:

> To protect and support individuals and communities by reducing crime, the fear of crime and the impact of crime, addressing offending behaviour, maintaining law and order and dispensing justice fairly (<http://www.skillsforjustice.com>).

By answering the question 'what needs to happen to achieve the key purpose?' the functional map can be developed. Functional maps are usually laid out in very similar ways, and will be structured as follows:

• Key areas   Broad groups of functions
• Areas of competence   Smaller groups of related functions
• Functions   Specific activities carried out in the workplace

The core component of the NOS is the 'Unit'. Units can be gathered together in a particular sector to provide a profile of the performance requirements, knowledge, and understanding needed for a particular job role. Units stand alone (although they are in relationship with others) and they have a common structure in that they will contain the following:

- *Unit title*—A summary of what the unit is about and who it is aimed at.
- *Elements*—The elements of the unit will describe what a person actually needs to be able to do and will have clear performance criteria to show the standard expected within a particular activity.
- *Range*—The range of contexts in which the activity is to be carried out may also be described in the form of a 'range statement'.
- *Knowledge and understanding*—At unit level there will also be a statement of the knowledge and understanding that is needed to underpin the performance requirements of the unit.

Evidence requirements for a National Vocational Qualification (NVQ) or a Scottish Vocational Qualification (SVQ) may also be made explicit in the unit. The requirements for these vocational qualifications usually require that the individual consistently meets the performance criteria and that they have the necessary knowledge and understanding to underpin this.

The units each have a unique code identifier and those that are most applicable to the business of policing diversity are:

1A1   Use police actions in a fair and justified way
1A2   Communicate effectively with members of communities
1A4   Foster people's equality, diversity and rights
1A5   Promote people's equality, diversity and rights

Amongst other things, the purpose of this book is to consider the knowledge and understanding components of the units that have a direct bearing on policing diversity. Throughout the book references will be made to that underpinning knowledge in the wider context of related issues. For the full details of the units please visit the Skills for Justice website (<http://www.skillsforjustice.com/category.php?ID=86>) where you will be able to view the standards.

1.5.1 Critique of National Occupational Standards

Skills for Justice (2005) claim that: 'Today, national occupational standards are viewed by modern managers as an indispensable tool for managing a highly skilled workforce'. There is little doubt that they have become very influential in many employment sectors and that NOS have many uses that span far beyond merely articulating training requirements. Having said that, it would be unwise to assume that they are beyond any form of criticism. Some of the issues that need to be considered include:

- The need to have confidence that the standards are comprehensive in their scope; that they are clearly written and understood; and that the evidence requirements will effectively test an individual's performance in a particular unit.

- The knowledge and understanding component of a standard needs similarly to be comprehensive and have captured a reasonable and rational underpinning for the performance.

- Standards per se have no worth unless the people working in a particular sector are actually putting them into practice. Particularly where they are linked to vocational qualifications there needs to be confidence that the assessment of achievement in a particular standard is not merely a box-ticking exercise and that the individual is genuinely achieving the performance in both a sustained way and with the appropriate knowledge and understanding. This is particularly important in the field of diversity where the knowledge, understanding, and attitudes needed to perform effectively are often very complex and may defy attempts at reduction to simplistic statements. Rather like diversity and equality, policies that look fine on paper but have no worth unless they are implemented in practice, NOS should also be viewed as a point of departure rather than an end in themselves.

- A further issue surrounds that of the nature of teaching and learning. It is very important that people working in complex areas such as criminal justice not only have knowledge and understanding but that they also develop the intellectual skill of critical analysis, so that as a new situation confronts them they are able to apply existing understanding to new and different situations. Just knowing things is not enough—the ability to apply that knowledge is vital. There remains some doubt as to whether NOS of themselves will equip people with this ability to critically analyse situations.

REFLECT ON PRACTICE

Given the critique of National Occupational Standards above, reflect on the extent to which you believe them to be an end in themselves or merely a starting point in the pursuit of effective performance.

Given the caveats noted above, bear in mind that NOS are very important in the development and maintenance of police performance, and if you are a police officer or member of the wider 'police family' of your own performance. Judgements of police performance will be made against the standards and it is therefore very important that they are taken seriously, both in recognizing them and more importantly in their implementation.

1.6 Diversity and the Initial Police Learning and Development Programme

1.6.1 The National Police Learning Requirement for Race and Diversity Training

In the years up to 2005, a great deal of work has been done, sponsored by the Home Office, to establish what the learning requirement is to be an effective police officer. This has now been translated from a Learning Requirement into the Initial Police Learning and Development Programme (IPLDP). The responsibility for delivering the IPLDP has been passed from the Central Police Training and Development Authority (Centrex) to individual forces in England and Wales, and forces are now making arrangements to deliver their own programmes. Many forces are linking their programmes to NVQs; others are linking their training to foundation degrees with higher education institutions.

In 2005, a National Learning Requirement for Race and Diversity training was published as a separate document to supplement the main learning requirement for police officers. This is available from the Home Office website (<http://www.homeoffice.gov.uk/docs3/national_learning_require.pdf>).

EXERCISE

Study the introduction to the National Learning Requirement for Race and Diversity Training shown below and then consider the questions that follow.

Race and Diversity training is required in order to ensure that all staff and communities are valued and believe that they can contribute to society in terms of law and order and be treated in a manner which respects this. This Learning Requirement outlines the knowledge, understanding and skills required by all those working in the Police service so as to determine attitudes and behaviour in order to achieve this aim.

A strong and clear emphasis on personal responsibility is key to this Learning Requirement. The training to be designed develops an understanding of race and diversity as a core value that is embedded within the role and responsibility of every Police Officer, Police Staff member or Police volunteer.

This Requirement therefore has influence beyond the formal training process and, although compliance is mandatory, the principles must be embedded within everyday service delivery.

This Requirement sets down clear guidance about the design, delivery, assessment and evaluation of race and diversity training. As such it provides a framework through which progress in relation to Race and Diversity training will be monitored".

(Source: Home Office (2005a) National Learning Requirement:
Race and Diversity Training:1)

> - What do you think the introduction is saying about the aim of race and diversity training?
> - What is implicit in the phrase 'race and diversity'?
> - To what extent can an organization exercise control over an individual's attitudes?
> - What does the introduction have to say about personal responsibility?
> - How and in what ways can progress be monitored against the design, delivery, assessment, and evaluation of training?

One of the key drivers for the national learning requirement on race and diversity has been the report published by Her Majesty's Inspectorate of Constabulary (2003) 'Diversity Matters'. Given its importance for understanding the wider issues of diversity facing the police service, we will examine this report in more detail in Chapter 6. For the time being it is worth noting and commenting on some of the key issues that the inspection uncovered and which are noted in the National Learning Requirement (Home Office 2005a: 2).

'The overall strategy for training and development in this area lacks clarity, direction and unified commitment'

Many would agree that in response to the Stephen Lawrence Inquiry Report (Macpherson 1999), the police service made considerable efforts to introduce training in response to recommendations 48–51.

48. That there should be an immediate review and revision of racism awareness training within Police Services to ensure:
    a. that there exists a consistent strategy to deliver appropriate training within all Police Services, based upon the value of our cultural diversity;
    b. that training courses are designed and delivered in order to develop the full understanding that good community relations are essential to good policing and that a racist officer is an incompetent officer.
49. That all police officers, including CID and civilian staff, should be trained in racism awareness and valuing cultural diversity.
50. That police training and practical experience in the field of racism awareness and valuing cultural diversity should regularly be conducted at local level. And that it should be recognized that local minority ethnic communities should be involved in such training and experience.
51. That consideration be given by Police Services to promoting joint training with members of other organisations or professions otherwise than on police premises.

However, the delivery of such training varied greatly in its quality and scope, and by the time HMIC published its inspection report in 2003 by no means all members of the police 'family' had received such training.

'The learning requirement is not clearly articulated and it is unclear what outcomes are to be achieved. . .'

Much of the training that was delivered was unclear about its overall purpose. In some respects this was justifiable in that at the time there were no NOS and the related statement of knowledge and understanding requirement on which to base the training programmes. In addition the use of the word 'awareness' in relation to the training is also problematic. Awareness means different things to different people. The focus in these recommendations is very much on the design and outcomes of the training rather than the learning. This is not, of course, surprising since the report was not taking a particularly educational point of view. In addition it is not at all clear what is meant by 'awareness', or how someone can be 'trained' to value cultural diversity. There seems to be an implicit assumption that it is possible to do something to someone in training that will change people in terms of their value system. The recommendations seek to make sure that all police officers including CID are 'aware of racism and the value of cultural diversity'. Whilst it is hard to argue with the sentiments expressed (although some do), it is the case that the focus on the outcomes, 'be aware of', 'understand what is expected of' fall somewhat short of being explicit in what they mean in terms of learning.

'The various staff appraisal systems do not explicitly link with, nor discernibly support, the training being delivered'

Staff appraisal, as we shall see elsewhere in the book, has prior to recent times been one of the weak links in managing the performance of the police. For too long staff appraisal lacked the weight and influence that it should have had to justify the effort put into it. It was also arguable that the right things were not being appraised and that those doing the assessing were not consistent in their judgements. Again it could be argued that this was in part, at least as far as the criteria for assessment were concerned, a result of the lack of appropriate occupational standards to use as a yardstick. In terms of policing diversity, it has become essential that at least part of the judgement of an individual's performance should relate to their ability to deliver a service to the public that confirm to the higher aspirations around diversity.

'Ineffective or inadequate supervision/line management undermines any message that is contained within training'

In Chapter 4, which deals with the development of equality and diversity issues over the years, we will see that a constant critical theme has been the ability of first line managers effectively to manage the equality and diversity performance of their staff.

'Race and diversity content is not, as suggested, fully integrated into all aspects of police training and development'

Based on the assumption that all of policing is essentially about policing diversity, there is a generalized view that all aspects of police training and development should consider and respond to the implications for diversity. There have been many attempts to articulate what is meant by terms such as (above) 'fully integrated', 'mainstreamed', 'embedded', 'golden thread', and so on. All of these have the same general thrust of meaning that equality and diversity should be a common feature of all thinking about policing in its wider sense. The problem comes when trying to do something about it. This is in part because it can lead to a notion of 'tokenism', where there is merely a nod to diversity and it is not really addressed in any meaningful way. An additional problem is that where equality and diversity is reckoned to be 'mainstreamed' or a 'golden thread' it is all too easy for it to be lost altogether. Very often such approaches will be left to the discretion of individual trainers and the extent to which equality and diversity are dealt with will depend on the trainers' own attitudes, skill, and understanding. *The Secret Policeman* documentary (see page 25 below) seemed to provide evidence that in the hands of an unskilled or unknowledgeable trainer, the diversity theme can at best be lost and at worst be damaging to the learning of the student.

'The processes of selection, assessment, management and support for trainers delivering race and diversity content are not totally satisfactory'

In a piece of research that I conducted in relation to the skills and attributes needed by trainers in the field of equality and diversity (Clements 2000), it was found that they could be grouped together as shown in Table 1.2 below:

Table 1.2 Skills and attributes of diversity trainers

Skills	Attributes
Intervention	Resilience ('take it on the chin')
Facilitation	Belief in what you are doing
Conflict management	Mental agility
Ask tough questions	Deep understanding of issues
Flexible	Positive outlook
Manage group dynamics	Recognize own limits
Knowledge of law	Been through the process
Manage resistance strategies	Sincerity
Knowledge of policy issues	Sensitive to people's needs and concerns
Knowledge of own prejudice	Non-neutral in facilitation
	'Walk the talk'/'Own the ethos'
	Motivation in the subject
	Well trained in the subject

HMIC (2003) found that only 44 per cent of forces had published policies for selecting, training, and supporting their trainers. A glance at this table reveals that trainers who are involved in delivering equality and diversity need a considerable level of skill and accompanying attributes that may well go beyond those generally assumed to be needed. Of course if all training is to have diversity integrated into it then there has to be an assumption that the trainers will have the additional skills and attributes that delivery of diversity demands. As the HMIC (2003: 103) noted:

> If the mainstreamed approach is to work, there is a clear case for all trainers to be capable of integrating race and diversity issues within their delivery, either through designed objectives or in response to input by a learner attending training.

Later in the book we will explore the debate around whether the best way to deal with this is to have specialist trainers or to expect all trainers to be able to effectively integrate diversity into their training.

'There is insufficient community involvement in all aspects of the training cycle'

This aspect of diversity training was picked up by the HMIC (2003: 36) who noted: 'the (police) Service as a whole cannot afford to ignore the added value that strong links with communities provide to all aspects of the training cycle, not just delivery'. One very positive outcome of thinking about race and diversity over the past few years has been the increased recognition that communities matter and that in a liberal democracy where policing can only be conducted by consent, it is vital that the communities that comprise society are involved. Some police forces have done less well than others in this regard, and whilst there have been some attempts to involve members of communities in training delivery, they have not been sufficiently involved in the design and subsequent evaluation of training. Taking both these issues, it seems to make sense logically that if members of communities are to be involved in delivery then they also need to be involved in the design of what is delivered and have a right to be involved in the evaluation of its effectiveness. Having considered some of the drivers for the National Learning Requirement for Race and Diversity Training we now turn briefly to the requirement itself.

The core of the training requirement has two strands. The first strand relates to generic training based on the needs of the police service in relation to the six areas of race (which is the primary focus and would include issues around gypsies and travellers, and asylum seekers), gender, disability, age, sexual orientation, and religion and beliefs. The second strand is one of contextualized training. Essentially this means making the links with the local context in which an officer will work. The UK is made up of many different communities and the pattern of these communities differs widely between forces. The needs of an officer in terms of his or her ability to deliver the policing service may differ widely in a large metropolitan area from those of an officer working in a more rural context. Both strands need to take account of the NOS and the Integrated Competency Framework.

The National Learning Requirement is also based on a framework. This has three integrated elements Home Office 2005a (p 5):

- The strands in relation to the police service
- The strands in relation to one another
- A delivery framework with a focus on role and rank

You will find it helpful to download the National Learning Requirement document and study it in its entirety (<http://www.homeoffice.gov.uk/docs3/national_learning_require.pdf>).

For the purposes of this chapter we will focus on the aims of the generic programme of study which is intended to be completed by all new entrants to the police service and should be followed by the building of a portfolio and assessment both in the training environment and in the workplace context through a system of Performance Development Review.

The aims and outcomes of the generic programme (drawn from the National Learning Requirement, p 13) are as follows:

Aims

- To provide generic training which raises awareness of the individual's responsibilities for inclusive behaviour as a member of the community.
- To develop the participant's understanding of the diverse make-up of the community of twenty-first century Britain with specific reference to race (primary focus), gender, disability, age, sexual orientation, religion, and beliefs.
- To provide the participant with the skills, knowledge, attitude, and behaviours to enable them to adopt inclusive practice within the workplace and when dealing with the customer.

Outcomes

On completion of the programme of training the participant should:

- Be able to define diversity and distinguish this from equal opportunities.
- Understand and demonstrate inclusive behaviours within the workplace.
- Be able to articulate one's own identity and acknowledge the similarities/differences to that of the communities which we police.
- Be aware of the types of discrimination faced by members of minority groups and demonstrate the use of appropriate skills to challenge such behaviour.
- Demonstrate an appreciation of cross-cultural communication practices.
- Understand national legislation and local policies which promote equality within the work environment.
- Be able to construct a needs analysis and plan for continuing professional development in relation to race and diversity issues.
- Have an understanding and appreciation of the social geography and different cultures of the community being policed.
- To understand the problems faced by vulnerable people and to be able to demonstrate ability to identify and implement appropriate solutions.
- Demonstrate an appreciation of the relevance of the above and its application to the workplace.

1.6.2 Critique of the aim and outcomes of the generic programme

One of the key questions that needs to be asked in critiquing the aims and outcomes of this programme is 'does it provide clarity about what a police officer need to be able to do, know and understand in relation to the business of policing diversity?' Two features of the aims need to be treated with some caution. The first, already noted above, is the problematic nature of what people may or may not mean by the term awareness. So raising awareness of individual responsibility may not go far enough. Most people are 'aware' that it is wrong to drive over the speed limit but this does not necessarily mean that they will keep to it. So I might be aware of my responsibilities in relation to inclusive behaviour, but still be prepared to take risks, for example with my language when

I feel it may be safe to do so. The second feature that may present a problem is the assumption that I can be 'provided' with the appropriate attitudes for inclusive behaviour in the workplace and with the person receiving the policing delivery. There remains a big question as to the extent to which attitudes fall within the remit of training at all. Certainly it could be strongly argued that although they may be influenced by training they cannot be 'provided' in the sense that seems to be in the aim of the generic programme. We will explore later the whole question of the relationship between attitudes and behaviour.

1.7 Chapter Summary

In this introduction we have outlined in more general terms a number of the key issues that are relevant to thinking about the notion of policing diversity.

The concept of diversity

We noted that whilst there is still no coherent theoretical framework for diversity, it is not adequate to think of diversity merely in terms of the 'way in which people are different' or ' the avoidance of monoculture'. Diversity is much more than that. Many commentators will delimit diversity in terms of differences between people that are likely to lead to prejudice or discrimination (such as social class and educational background). Very often these differences go beyond what is defined in legislation as areas that may lead to prejudice and discrimination. That said, in order to keep our thinking about diversity in manageable bounds, we noted that the police service defined areas of race, age, disability, gender, sexual orientation, and faith and belief will be those on which the subsequent discussion in this book will focus.

The difference between diversity and equal opportunities

Equal opportunities and diversity are not the same concepts although they do have common grounding. Equal opportunities have traditionally been associated with matters to do with employment and its associated legislative requirements. Diversity on the other hand has a much broader perspective and relates to the way we understand the differences between people in society at large and how we respond to the issues that are raised. The point was made that if society is properly embracing diversity and in doing so is working towards the elimination of prejudice and discrimination on a wider front, then the notion of equal opportunities would start to become redundant because as diversity is mainstreamed, then the need to legislate for unfairness would become less. However, British society has a long way to go before such an aspiration is achieved.

The nature of equality

Treating people equally is not merely treating them the same. A fundamental aspect of diversity is that people have different needs in society for a variety of reasons. They may have different educational needs, different language needs, different physical needs, and so on, and for this reason if they are to be treated *fairly* then it is important that their individual needs are taken into account and where possible met. We also looked at two other perspectives on equality. The first is the 'level playing field' where conditions are put in place to ensure that people are not hamstrung by disadvantage right from the outset. The second perspective is where individuals seek to deliver equal treatment but this is supported by an organizational level concern to have the necessary frameworks in place to deliver such equal treatment.

National Occupational Standards for professionals in criminal justice

There are now National Occupational Standards and an Integrated Competency Framework that define the business of policing in the UK. In this chapter we briefly outlined the nature of NOS and also provided a brief critique of them. Notwithstanding the fact that there are some caveats that need to be borne in mind when thinking about standards, they have an important role to play in the development of policing generally through the individual development of police officers. All units within NOS have a knowledge and understanding component in recognition that skills do not exist in a vacuum and that a person meeting a particular standard will only be able to do so if they have the appropriate knowledge and understanding on which to base their actions.

The National Police Learning Requirement for Race and Diversity Training

The last section of the chapter gave consideration to the learning requirement for race and diversity training in the British Police Service. We noted that the learning requirement is an important way forward in determining what knowledge and understanding is necessary for a police officer effectively to deliver a service to a diverse population. We paid particular attention to and commented on the findings of the HMIC report 'Diversity Matters' which provided a set of drivers for the development of the learning requirement.

In Chapter 2 we turn to some of the key concepts that are implicit in understanding diversity.

Key Concepts in Relation to Diversity and Fairness

2.1 **Chapter Outline**

In this chapter some of the main sociological and psychological concepts in relation to diversity and fairness will be introduced. There are a number exercises and opportunities to reflect on the practice of policing in relation to the particular concept under discussion. The following areas will be covered:

- Relevant knowledge and understanding from the National Occupational Standards (NOS)
- Introduction to the concepts
- Prejudice and discrimination
- Stereotyping and labelling
- Attitudes, values, and beliefs
- Institutional racism and discrimination
- Police culture.

2.2 **National Occupational Standards Relevant to this Chapter**

There is a strong link in this chapter with Unit 1A1 of the NOS (<http://www.skillsforjustice.net/nos/index.htm>). This unit is titled 'Use Police Actions in a Fair and Justified Way'. The main thrust of the unit is the proportionate and fair use of the range of police powers both statutory and non-statutory. This would include powers such as in relation to stop and search, arrest, searching persons and property, detention, and the use of powers of entry. The knowledge and understating requirement of this unit includes such factors as:

Legal and organizational requirements

The individual's right to equal and fair treatment before the law, regardless of race/ethnicity, religion/faith, sexual orientation, social status, poverty, physical disability, age, gender/sex, property, language, learning disability and mental health, family status, employment status, heritage, political belief, or association with any other minority group (e.g. asylum seekers, travellers).

Applying principles of reasonable suspicion or belief

How to exercise police powers and actions fairly and without bias.

Using police actions proportionately

How to direct police actions in a non-arbitrary and fair way.

Using police actions fairly

The fair and unbiased use of police actions.

The need for reliable and objective information and observation.

The need to consider how others, who may be observing your actions, may react.

A review of the examples above which are all knowledge and understanding components drawn from Unit 1A1 demonstrates the close link with the issues we will be covering in this chapter. For example if you look again at the legal and organizational requirement to know and understand the individual's right to equal and fair treatment before the law, regardless of the diverse factors that come into play (such as race/ethnicity, religion/faith, sexual orientation, and so on) it will become apparent that this can only be achieved if the individual police officer has a well developed sense of the potential for prejudice, discrimination, and stereotyping. More importantly perhaps, it also assumes that the individual officer not only has that well developed sense, but also has responded to the potential in a positive way. As we work through these issues, keep referring back to the knowledge and understanding requirements and try to make the links with your own feelings about the issues. Before moving on, complete the exercise below.

REFLECT ON PRACTICE

Think about the aspects of diversity mentioned in Unit 1A1:

race/ethnicity, religion/faith, sexual orientation, social status, poverty, physical disability, age, gender/sex, property, language, learning disability and mental health, family status, employment status, heritage, political belief, or association with any other minority group (e.g. asylum seekers, travellers)

If you were asked to prove that your actions were fair and unbiased in relation to ALL of the groups mentioned: What evidence would you give?

2.3 **Introduction to the Concepts**

In Chapter 1 we opened up a possible theoretical framework for diversity. Such a theoretical framework has implicitly a number of concepts that are essential to understanding the social and psychological processes through which unfairness and discrimination may manifest themselves in criminal justice generally and in policing in particular. As part of the framework we examined the way in which we need to view policing from the inside out and from the outside in. In other words, issues of diversity and fairness have a bearing both on the way colleagues in a criminal justice organization (police, prisons, probation, and so on) interact with each other, and, importantly, how they deliver their service to members of the public at large.

In the sections that follow we will firstly look at two concepts that are absolutely crucial to an understanding of policing diversity, namely prejudice and discrimination. Closely related to these are the concepts of stereotyping and labelling, the processes where characteristics assumed to be typical of a particular group are overlaid onto all the members of that group. Elsewhere, we will look at how a striking example of this has manifested itself since the bombings in London on 7 July 2005 where many innocent members of the Islamic community in Britain have been wrongly stereotyped as fundamentalist Islamists. Staying with personal responses to diversity, we will examine the nature and strength of attitudes values and beliefs. Finally, we will look at the notion of institutional racism and discrimination. Whilst institutional racism was not a new idea, it gained a great deal of currency in the aftermath of the Stephen Lawrence Inquiry Report which was published in 1999. It remains an important concept not only for the police but for all other institutions in the UK. Much of the training conducted since 2000 within the criminal justice sector has been predicated on the general duty to promote good race relations (Race Relations (Amendment) Act 2000) and is concerned with addressing individual prejudice and individual and institutionalized discrimination. The chapter concludes with a consideration of culture, from an inside-out and outside-in perspective. We will consider the notion of culture in the context of thinking about diversity and also what various commentators have said about the nature of so-called police culture.

2.4 **Prejudice and Discrimination**

When discussing issues relating to the policing of diverse communities, the notions of 'institutional' prejudice and discrimination have largely dominated the agenda in recent times. Understandably, the Stephen Lawrence Inquiry (McPherson 1999) has served to place these concepts at the forefront of debate. However, this emphasis on the institutional level of debate has taken place in something of a theoretical vacuum with regard to the social and psychological origins of prejudice as a concept. Certainly the Stephen Lawrence Inquiry has provided us with a working definition of institutional racism that has been accepted by the government and the police, but this definition is not placed in the wider contexts of prejudice and discrimination and thus individuals are required, by necessity, to turn to other sources to 'fill the gaps' in order fully to understand these concepts. So we need to examine the nature and origins of prejudice and discrimination through a review of existing social and psychological literature.

2.4.1 Defining prejudice and discrimination

The first requirement is to provide appropriate definitions of 'prejudice' and 'discrimination', and to distinguish between the two. The terms 'prejudice' and 'discrimination' are often used interchangeably, but it is important to be clear about the difference between them.

EXERCISE

- How do you understand the meaning of prejudice and discrimination?
- What do you see to be the key differences between the concepts?

In terms of a discussion of how the concepts fit into the broader context of policing diversity, prejudice can be described as a type of *attitude* towards members of a social group, whilst discrimination can be described as a *behaviour* or an *action* arising from that attitude and directed towards members of a social group. In other words discrimination is essentially 'prejudice in action' (Baron and Byrne, 1994).

As a separate entity, discrimination can take many forms. Its expression is often restrained by, for example, laws and social pressures but where such forces are absent or weak, prejudicial attitudes may be expressed in overt forms. The nature of these expressions is discussed in more detail below (see Allport's Scale of Prejudice (Figure 2.1 below)) but it is important to note that even the subtlest forms of discrimination, whether direct or indirect, can have serious consequences for its victims. It can result in differential treatment or exclusion from services and provisions, and may extend further to include forms of aggression and violence.

Case Study

The Secret Policeman was an 'undercover' documentary made by BBC reporter Mark Daly. (Aired on Tuesday 21 October 2003 at 21:00)

Read through the following extract from the programme and consider how this illustrates the notions of prejudice and discrimination:

PC: 'Police are racist mate, police are racist. They are, they fucking are.'

Daly: 'If you were walking down the road, and you see ****, (bleep) what are you immediately thinking?'

PC: 'Stopping him.'

Daly: 'Why?'

PC: 'Searching him, cos he's black, cos he's Asian. . . . because most Asians carry knives. And I'd fucking search him . . . plus he's a fucking, he's a Paki I'm searching him. Its fucking proactive policing yeah innit? He's a Paki

> and I'm stopping him—cause I'm fucking English (LAUGHTER). At the
> end of the day mate, we look after our own, you know that don't ya?'

Given that we now have a widely accepted (or at least widely used) definition of 'institutional' prejudice and discrimination one might reasonably assume that an equally acceptable definition of prejudice as a concept has long been in existence. This, however, is not the case. Instead of one universal definition there are in fact numerous definitions of prejudice, all of which are subtly different but essentially allude to the same thing.

The word 'prejudice' is derived from the Latin noun *praejudicium*, meaning *precedent*, and in the English language the term came to mean a premature or hasty judgement. More recently the term has also acquired its emotive sense of favourableness or unfavourableness now associated with such a judgement (Allport 1954). According to one early definition, prejudice is a 'pattern of hostility in interpersonal relations which is directed against an entire group, or against its individual members; it fulfils a specific irrational function for its bearer' (Ackerman and Jahoda 1950: 4).

However, Gordon Allport, arguably the most prominent of all researchers and writers on this subject, disagreed with the assertion that prejudice always holds some form of irrational function for the bearer. Instead Allport argued that prejudice often has a 'functional significance', but nevertheless is often simply a matter of blind conformity with some prevailing common ideology (and therefore has no functional significance whatsoever for the bearer). As such he defines prejudice as:

> An antipathy based upon a faulty and inflexible generalisation. It may be felt
> or expressed. It may be directed toward a group as a whole, or toward an indi-
> vidual because he is a member of that group. The net effect of prejudice, thus
> defined, is to place the object of prejudice at some disadvantage not merited
> by his own conduct. (Allport 1954: 9)

Under such a definition, prejudgements become prejudices only if they are not reversible when the holder is exposed to new knowledge or evidence relating to the object of his or her erroneous judgement. According to Allport a prejudice is actively resistant to all evidence that would unseat it. Therefore, the difference between ordinary prejudgements and prejudice is that one can discuss and rectify a prejudgement without emotional resistance.

However, Brown (1995) takes issue with both of the above definitions. He argues that by referring to an 'inflexible generalization' or to an 'irrational function' these writers are making unwise suppositions. Whilst at the time their definitions may have been wholly accurate given the existing level of knowledge, Brown suggests that to think of prejudice as being impervious to change or as having no rational function for its bearer is to fail to appreciate the variety and complexity of the forms prejudice can take, and its tendency to be unstable in its nature and to change under certain circumstances. Thus, to take account of these issues, Brown (1995: 8) defines prejudice as 'the holding of derogatory social attitudes or cognitive beliefs, the expression of negative affect, or the display of hostile or discriminatory behaviour towards members of a group on account of their membership of that group.'

Similarly, and more simply, Baron and Byrne (1994: 218) define prejudice as 'an attitude (usually negative) toward the members of some group, based solely on their membership in that group.' Here the definition implies that a prejudiced individual evaluates members of a particular social group in a specific manner simply because they belong to that social group, and thus the individual traits or behaviours of the target hold little significance for the prejudiced person. Baron and Byrne suggest that attitudes such as prejudice often function as schemas (cognitive frameworks for organizing, interpreting, and recalling information). They argue that prejudiced people process information about the object of their prejudice differently from other groups to which they hold no prejudicial views.

As such, information consistent with their prejudices tends to receive more attention, is cognitively rehearsed and reinforced more frequently, and tends to be remembered more accurately than other information. Therefore, in the absence of strong contradictory evidence, prejudice becomes a 'cognitive loop' that grows stronger and more deep-seated over time. Consequently, prejudice as an attitude can then move beyond a simple evaluation of a group to include negative feelings and emotions and stereotyping on the part of the bearer. This can in turn lead to negative actions or behaviours (ie discrimination) directed towards the objects of prejudice, although it is important to note that prejudicial attitudes do not always transform into discriminatory behaviour.

2.4.2 Gordon Allport's *'The Nature of Prejudice'*

Unsurprisingly there are numerous competing perspectives that seek to identify and explain the origins of prejudice and discrimination. Arguably the most significant early contribution was that of Gordon Allport in his seminal work, *The Nature of Prejudice* (1954). Although competing ideas have since been advocated, Brown (1995) acknowledges that Allport's work has come to be regarded as the departure point for all modern research into aspects of prejudice. Furthermore, Brown states that so significant was Allport's contribution that his theorizing has provided the basis for programmes designed to improve race-relations in American schools for the past fifty years or so. Allport's work is encyclopaedic in its nature but it is entirely appropriate for us to open with a brief overview of some of Allport's thoughts regarding the origin of prejudice before moving on to examining some more modern perspectives.

According to Allport (1954) prejudice is a normal and rational (that is to say, predictable) human behaviour by virtue of our need to organize all the cognitive data our brain receives through the formation of generalizations, concepts, and categories whose content represents an oversimplification of our world and experiences therein. This process is essential to our daily living and the forming of generalizations, categories, and concepts based on experience and probability helps us to guide our daily activities and to make sense of the world around us.

For example, as Allport suggests, if we see heavy clouds in the sky we may prejudge that there is a high probability based on past experience that rain will fall and we adjust our behaviour accordingly (for example, by wearing a raincoat and taking an umbrella with us). Similarly, for the most part, it is also easier for us to over-generalize about a subject or issue (for example 'all students are lazy'), or to quickly make an assumption that enables us to make life easier (for example, if we see a car being driven erratically it is easier for us to prejudge that the driver is drunk than it is to actually take the trouble to find out for certain).

Allport also suggests that we form certain concepts that have not only a 'meaning', but also provide a 'feeling'. Take, for example, the concept of a 'Londoner'. The vast majority of us will know what a 'Londoner' is, but our individual concept of a 'Londoner' may stir an accompanying personal feeling that we may harbour towards 'Londoners' in general even though it is unlikely that we will have met every single one. In this sense our over-simplification of the world leads us to one of Allport's more significant points; that the formation of our generalizations is just as likely to lead to irrational generalizations, concepts, and categories as it is to rational ones.

Similarly, Allport suggests that in order to further simplify their lives human beings naturally homogenize, often for no other reason than convenience, which in turn creates separateness amongst groups. According to Allport, humans tend to relate to other humans with similar presuppositions for the purpose of comfort, ease, and congeniality. However, it is this separateness, coupled with our need to form generalizations and categories, which lays the foundations for psychological elaboration and the development of prejudice. Allport argues that people who stay separate have fewer channels of communication, are likely to exaggerate and misunderstand the differences between groups, and develop genuine and imaginary conflicts of interests. It is this, according to Allport, that contributes largely to the formation of 'in-groups' and 'out-groups' and therefore to the *potential* formation and development of in-group loyalty and out-group rejection and the subsequent *potential* expression of prejudice and discriminatory behaviour towards a particular out-group.

Although this is a much-simplified account of the foundations of prejudice as defined by Allport, it is from this basis, he argues, that people develop their prejudicial nature, both positive and negative. Allport believes, however, that any negative attitude tends somehow to express itself in action although the degree of action will vary greatly from person to person. To illustrate this Allport (1954: 14) provides a five-point scale to distinguish different degrees of negative action:

Figure 2.1 Allport's Scale of Prejudice

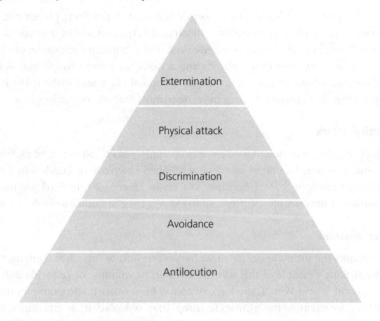

Extermination

Physical attack

Discrimination

Avoidance

Antilocution

Antilocution

The discussion of prejudices, usually with like-minded friends. Antilocution frequently occurs in the form of humour. Very often people will make the excuse 'I was only joking' when trying to justify humour about another group. At another level, the expression of prejudice in language is more dangerous and damaging such as that expressed in the case study material above. Antilocution will always involve 'bad-mouthing' in some way and in fact is the first stage of a scale of prejudice which involves discrimination. The importance of antilocution as a function of prejudice cannot be overstated and in many ways puts into perspective some of the frequently sterile debates about political correctness in language which often seek to underplay the significance of the words people use.

Avoidance

A more intense prejudice leads the bearer to avoid members of the disliked group, although he or she does not inflict direct harm upon the disliked group. Having said that, avoidance by those who have a duty to provide a public service may well have at the very least a significant indirect impact on a particular group. In terms of policing service delivery, the avoidance by individual police officers of particular groups will have a negative impact on the quality of service provided. Furthermore, inside the police service, where colleagues are avoided through prejudicial attitudes towards a particular social group, the effect will be damaging marginalization and ostracization.

Discrimination

Here the prejudiced individual makes detrimental distinctions played out in action. Again, such discrimination is illustrated in the material in the case study above. If we refer back to the knowledge and understanding component of Unit 1A1—'how to exercise police powers and actions fairly and without bias'—we can see that where police actions are NOT applied fairly and without the bias that springs from prejudice, then overt discrimination will be taking place.

Physical attack

Under conditions of heightened emotion prejudice may lead to acts of violence or semi-violence. The racist murders of Stephen Lawrence in London in 1993 and more recently that of Anthony Walker in Liverpool July 2005 are tragic examples of how people are prepared to express their prejudice in violent acts.

Extermination

This marks the ultimate degree of violent expression of prejudice. Perhaps the most striking example of this was the German programme of genocide during the Second World War. There have of course been other tragic examples since the War, for example the 'ethnic cleansing' that took place in Bosnia during the 1992–95 War, or the gas attack on the Kurdish population in Halabja, Iraq in March 1998.

Allport is at pains to point out that most people never go beyond the anti-locution stage, and those who do will not necessarily move progressively up the scale. However, the scale does serve to call attention to the huge range of activities that may occur as a direct result of prejudiced attitudes and beliefs. From this position Allport goes on to discuss his views of how individuals may develop such prejudiced attitudes and the impact they can have on target groups.

REFLECT ON PRACTICE

For each of Allport's categories below, try to identify an actual example of how this form of prejudice might manifest itself in practice.

- Antilocution
- Avoidance
- Discrimination
- Physical attack

While remaining inspirational and hugely significant, Allport's work is now somewhat dated. We now examine some more recent theorizing, much of it a direct result of Allport's original ideas, particularly those concerning 'in' and 'out' groups. What follows is a simplified overview of some of the key theories put forward to explain the origins of prejudice.

2.4.3 **Realistic conflict theory**

Arguably the oldest theory of prejudice, realistic conflict theory proposes that prejudice stems from competition between social groups for valued commodities or opportunities (Bobo 1983). The theory states that as the competition for scarce economic resources intensifies, members of competing social groups will come to view each other in increasingly negative terms that, if permitted to foster, will develop into emotion-laden prejudice (White 1977). The evidence for this process is strong, and is most notably applicable in the explanation of the widespread lynchings of ethnic minority Americans in the south of the country during a period of particularly harsh economic conditions endured in the fifty years or so prior to the research of Hovland and Sears (1940). Nevertheless, more recent research has supported the link between economic decline, the development of prejudice and subsequent hostility, and violence. Interestingly, however, these research studies tend to suggest that prejudice is only inevitable when group interests are threatened, and that when an individual's interests are similarly challenged the development of prejudice is far less certain.

2.4.4 **Social categorization**

This group of theories essentially supports and replicates the ideas of Allport outlined above. As such they require little further elaboration beyond simply adding that the formation of 'in-groups' is, as Tajfel (1982) suggests, a result of the need for individuals to enhance their self-esteem by identifying themselves with specific social groups. This action inevitably leads the people involved to view their social group as somehow superior to other, competing social groups and, since all groups form and develop in the same way, prejudice can arise out of the resulting clash of social perceptions.

2.4.5 **Social learning**

According to Baron and Byrne (1994), social learning theories suggest that attitudes such as prejudice are learned in childhood through contact with older and influential figures who reward children (with, for example, love and praise) for adopting their views. Indeed, Brown (1995) suggests that children as young as three years of age are aware of two of the major social categories, namely gender and ethnicity, and that from that age children can readily identify with some categories rather than others, and can demonstrate clear attitudinal and behavioural preferences among these categories. Similarly, Baron and Byrne explain, children also adopt and conform to the social norms of the group to which they belong, resulting in the development and expression of prejudicial attitudes towards others. However, Brown (1995) argues that using a child's 'passive absorption' of existing prejudices in society as an explanation of the development of prejudice is too simplistic. He suggests that other factors relating to a child's social and cognitive development may in fact hold the key to a more comprehensive understanding of the origins of prejudice (for an explanation of these, see Brown 1995: 119–160).

2.5 **Stereotyping and Labelling**

Brown (1995: 82) states that:

> To stereotype someone is to attribute to that person some characteristics which are seen to be shared by all or most of his or her fellow group members. A stereotype is, in other words, an inference drawn from the assignment of a person to a particular category ... [stereotypes] are embedded in the culture in which we are raised and live, and they are conveyed and reproduced in all the usual socio-cultural ways—through socialisation in the family and at school, through repeated exposure to images in books, television and newspapers.

Furthermore, Allport (1954) and Brown (1995) both suggest an additional explanation for the origin of stereotypes that they term the 'grain of truth' theory. Here, stereotypes derive from some aspect of social reality, regardless of how tenuous that link to reality might be. For example, if a lecturer has a class that he or she deems to be particularly lazy that view may be attributed by the lecturer to his or her other classes, and perhaps to the student population as a whole. Allport (1954: 191) defines a stereotype as:

> An exaggerated belief associated with a category. Its function is to justify (rationalise) our conduct in relation to that category. The stereotype acts both as a justificatory device for categorical acceptance or rejection of a group, and as a screening or selective device to maintain simplicity in perception and in thinking.

The second half of the last sentence of Allport's definition clearly indicates that stereotypes act as schemas (cognitive frameworks, see above) which Baron and Byrne (1994) suggest exert a strong effect on the ways in which we process social information. Essentially, they argue, stereotypes lead the bearer to pay attention to specific types of social information consistent with their prejudice, and to actively refute information that is inconsistent with their beliefs. Thus, stereotypes lead to biased processing of social information that in turn leads to a situation whereby stereotypes become self-confirming and this in turn ensures continued prejudiced attitudes.

Closely related to this cognitive aspect of stereotyping is the notion of 'illusory correlations' (Baron and Byrne 1994). These consist of perceived relationships between different variables where no such relationship exist. In other words, illusory correlations occur where relatively rare events draw our attention and are remembered more readily than common events. For example, if we take the former Home Secretary, Jack Straw's comments of a few years ago that 'Scousers are always up to something' (BBC News 1999) it is possible that an illusory correlation suggesting a strong link between people from Liverpool and criminal activity will emerge. Whilst it is true that a proportion of Liverpudlians are involved in crime, the illusory correlation may lead people to assume that the relationship between Liverpudlians and criminal activity is actually higher than it is. Furthermore, people may draw the conclusion that Liverpudlians commit crime simply because they are from Liverpool, and not because of other social and criminogenic factors. As Baron and Byrne suggest, individuals pay just enough attention to sources of information to form an erroneous perception of the social world.

EXERCISE

What stereotypes have you come across in relation to the following groups working in criminal justice and groups in society in general? Make a note of the key features of the stereotype and then consider what the foundation of that stereotype may be.

- Police officer
- Prison officer
- Lawyers
- Christians
- Muslims
- Jews
- Black people
- Asian people
- Gypsies/travellers
- Gay men

It is important to note that people do and will stereotype and label others. Some police officers may well argue with some justification that stereotyping is a necessary part of the job not least because it gives a better chance of being prepared for the unexpected, and may form part of a personal risk assessment when dealing with a suspect.

REFLECT ON PRACTICE

- When and in what circumstances have you needed to stereotype someone as part of a risk assessment?

The problem, of course, is where a stereotype is so strong that it effectively blinds the individual to other possibilities. The way must always be left open to challenge initial judgements.

2.6 **Institutional Racism and Discrimination**

On 24 February 1999, the Macpherson Report on the investigation of the racist murder of Stephen Lawrence was published. In the report, criticisms were levelled at the actions of the Metropolitan Police throughout their investigation of the murder. One criticism, which still remains at the forefront of the race and policing debate, is that institutional racism played a major role in the failed investigation. In the report, institutional racism is defined as:

> ... consisting of the collective failure of an organisation to provide an appropriate and professional service to people because of their colour, culture or ethnic origin. It can be seen or detected in processes, attitudes and behaviour which amount to discrimination through unwitting prejudice, ignorance, thoughtlessness and racist stereotyping which disadvantage minority ethnic people. (Macpherson 1999: 6.34)

Until Macpherson's interpretation of 'institutional racism', the term had failed to receive an acceptable standard definition particularly amongst those mostly at the receiving end of such allegation: the police. Prior to the report, the ambiguous nature of the term was obvious in the variety of meanings attached to it. There was a lack of consensus, which can be said to mirror the long-standing contradictory arguments surrounding the existence of racism at the institutional level. Ambiguities laid in both the definition of 'institutional' and the interpretations of actions that constituted racism.

More often than not, the norm in the pre-Macpherson era was to individualize the source and existence of racism. For example, it was common for police to blame individual officers—invariably deemed 'bad apples'—for damaging the organization's reputation through racist behaviour. This individualization tactic was not only confined to policing but could also deployed in other institutional settings. As the Commission for Racial Equality (1985: 2) stated:

> For too long racism has been thought of in individual psychological terms, reducible to the actions of prejudiced individuals. The concept of institutional racism draws attention to the structural workings of institutions, which exclude ethnic minority people regardless of individual attitudes.

However, accusations of institutional racism were rejected at the highest levels. In his report, following the 1981 Brixton Disorders, Lord Scarman (1982: 2.22) stated:

> It was alleged by some of those who made representations to me that Britain is an institutionally racist society. If by that is meant that it is a society which knowingly, as a matter of policy, discriminates against ethnic minority people, I reject the allegation. If, however, the suggestion being made is that practices may be adopted by public bodies as well as private individuals which are unwittingly discriminatory against ethnic minority people then this is an allegation which deserves serious consideration, and where proved, swift remedy.

In his definition, Scarman referred to institutional racism in its overt and intentional forms whether shown in practices and/or policies. On the basis of this understanding, he denied the existence of institutional racism. Significantly, however, Scarman still made reference to 'unwitting discrimination' as relevant to how we interpret the disadvantageous effects institutional and individual practices may have on ethnic minority people and on other visible minority groups.

Another attempt to explore the issue of institutionalized racism in the police has drawn upon the cultural context of policing. Located within occupational norms and values are prejudices into which individual police recruits are socialized, regardless of what prejudices they held prior to joining the police. Whatever form such prejudices take, they serve to maintain the functioning of an occupational culture governing relations between the police and the public. A similar argument is applied to the notion of police 'canteen culture' where adherents to group norms may thrive on expressions of prejudice including the use of racist language.

One issue which arises concerns the impact of prejudice on behaviour. A study of Metropolitan Police officers undertaken during the 1980s found no evidence that prejudicial-attitudes were 'acted out' in the form of discriminatory practices on the streets (Smith and Gray 1983). On the other hand, police culture is, according to Reiner (1992: 111), centrally guided by 'a sense of mission' to protect society from those who threaten it by committing crimes and engaging in unconventional activities deemed harmful to the fabric of society. To pursue this mission, police culture identifies strongly with the notion of territorial control for the purpose of waging defence against disorder. The claim to an area, Holdaway (1983: 3) argues, 'imposes a unity on the myriad tasks which constitute police work'. Streets in which police officers patrol form their territories over which they have rights to suspect, stop and search, and arrest people in them. This concept of territorial control in police culture extends to an assumption of control over people, and each of these guiding principles of police work is an influence on police officers' relationship with social groups with whom they come into contact. The police have their own categories of 'problem' and 'non-problem' groups, and those categories they perceive as posing a threat to police culture are disdained, many of them being defined as mere 'police property' (Reiner 2000: 93–94). Such categorization is, inevitably, affected by considerations of class, ethnicity, race, and gender.

Despite the various ways in which police racism has been alleged or denied, Macpherson's allegations against the Metropolitan Police and his definition of the term 'institutional racism' were to open a new forum for further debates whilst providing us with a valuable opportunity to reflect on its meaning. Previously, to analyse the meaning of institutional racism, concepts such as 'direct' and 'indirect' racism or 'conscious' and 'unconscious' racism were employed. Institutional racism has been related to policies and operational modes of an institution that are directly or indirectly discriminatory. It is direct in the sense that racism is *overtly* and *deliberately* embedded in an institution's policies and mode of practice whether or not the person who enforces the policies is a racist. This means that a racist or non-racist police officer can implement institutional racism. Indirect institutional racism is covert, and occurs when institutional policies and practices, which *supposedly* apply to everyone, have racist consequences that are disadvantageous to particular racial groups. For example, police crime control policies and practices that target inner city localities and the unemployed, irrespective of race or ethnicity, can have more detrimental effects on ethnic minority people because of their high concentration in the inner city and their higher unemployment rate.

Macpherson's definition draws attention to the structural framework within which the police operate. Institutional racism is identified with the collective, racially-based, discriminatory practices of the police as an institution, and not perceived as a problem of racist attitudes on the part of individual officers. It was a definition that was acceptable to the then Metropolitan Police Commissioner, Sir Paul Condon, who agreed that such a form of racism existed in his force.

However, an important point to note is that the definition characterizes discrimination in its unintentional form—as clearly shown in the use of the word 'unwitting'. 'Unwitting' was crucial to Scarman's understanding of institutional racism and eighteen years later the word 'unwitting' was to be a central component of Macpherson's definition of institutional racism. Does this mean that institutional racism cannot be witting or intentional or conscious? Despite what seems to be a widespread acceptance of the definition, an outstanding question to be answered is whether indirect racism can be intentional even though it appears not to be? Thus the word 'unwitting', as used by Macpherson, raises critical questions.

To claim that racial discrimination is a product of unintentional 'prejudice' and 'racist stereotyping' seemingly presents the perpetrators as ones who have no control over their conceptions of others. Even if racist stereotypes are collectively internalized through the process of socialization, is it not possible that we can be aware of how they can lead to discrimination? Is it not also possible that to allow or not to allow prejudices and racist stereotypes to affect our actions can be a conscious decision?

REFLECT ON PRACTICE

Take the opportunity to reflect on the way institutional racism or discrimination may manifest itself in your own area of professional practice.

Use the questions below to help your reflective thinking.

- What manifestations of institutional racism or discrimination of other kinds can you identify from within your organization? Try to think of specific examples.
- What outcomes result from this in terms of internal and external relationships?

- What is your organization doing to reduce the incidence of institutionalized discrimination?
- How is your own practice influenced by the need to eliminate institutionalized discrimination?

2.7 **Attitudes, Values, and Beliefs**

It is important in responding effectively to diversity, to recognize what attitudes, values, and beliefs are generally understood to be, and also to gain a sense of how they relate to the way we handle issues of diversity generally. Everyone has attitudes, values, and beliefs to a greater or lesser extent, and self-reflection on them is a very important dimension to the self-knowledge that goes with effectively responding to issues of diversity.

2.7.1 **Attitudes**

There have been many attempts to define attitudes. A good working definition of the components of an attitude is provided by Reber and Reber (2001):

- Cognitive (a consciously held belief or opinion);
- Affective (the emotional, mood, or feeling dimension to an attitude);
- Evaluative (the way of determining whether the attitude is a positive or negative orientation towards something);
- Conative (an ordered arrangement of elements (such as stereotypes) which is likely to lead to a particular behaviour).

Taking a slightly different perspective, Clark and Miller (1970 cited in Clements and Jones 2002: 59) describe an attitude as:

> A disposition acquired through previous experience, to react to certain things, people or events in positive ways. Attitudes represent a tendency to approach or avoid that which maintains or threatens the things one values. Like the values from which they are often derived, attitudes have an effect upon and are consistently related to beliefs and behaviour.

Attitudes can be detected at an individual level, in small groups, communities, and even whole populations of people. Such attitudes held in common can contribute to group culture.

As hypothetical constructs, attitudes are in themselves not directly observable, but we are able to describe them as they become manifest in speech, writing, non-verbal communication, and physical behaviour. Given their importance in relation to issues of diversity, a key question is the extent to which attitudes are fixed or can be changed.

EXERCISE

Think about your own attitudes towards the following:

- Black people
- Asian people
- Gay and lesbian people
- Gypsies and travellers
- Old people
- People who are HIV positive

Thinking about your strongest negative attitude in relation to either one of the above or another group you may have though of—what would it take for you to change that attitude?

Attitudes can and do change over time and this can often be detected in generational shifts and responses to significant events in the life of a particular society. Look at Figure 2.2 below which tries to capture just one representation of how societal attitudes in the UK may have changed over time.

Consider:

(1) The extent to which your own attitudes may have changed in the areas shown.

Figure 2.2 Changing attitudes

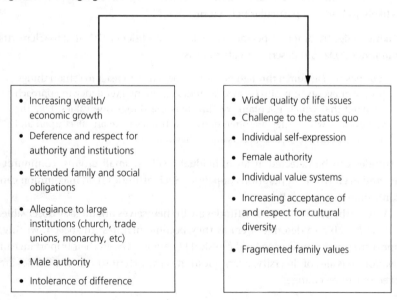

- Increasing wealth/ economic growth
- Deference and respect for authority and institutions
- Extended family and social obligations
- Allegiance to large institutions (church, trade unions, monarchy, etc)
- Male authority
- Intolerance of difference

- Wider quality of life issues
- Challenge to the status quo
- Individual self-expression
- Female authority
- Individual value systems
- Increasing acceptance of and respect for cultural diversity
- Fragmented family values

(2) The extent to which you believe the attitudes of others with whom you work may have changed.

Whereas the attitudes that may be regarded as generational in changing over time, attitudinal change in small groups is a different concept. A useful way of (Clements and Jones 2002) seeing approaches this type of change can be expressed in terms of:

- The power/coercive approach
- The empirical/rational approach
- The normative/re-educative approach

The power/coercive approach is predicated on an assumption that changing behaviours or adopting new ones is likely to lead eventually to attitudinal change. Such an approach owes more than a little to behaviourist/behaviour modification. The process is likely to comprise four distinct stages. In the first stage, specific measurable behaviours are expressed in terms of the desired outcomes, for example non-discrimination in the use of legal powers. Such behaviour will be modelled, typically by a trainer, and then the individual will be required to continuously repeat the desired behaviour until it is assumed to be embedded. The final stage will be one of feedback to the individual about perceived changes. There are obvious weaknesses in such an approach. You will have realized by now that diversity and the key concepts that underpin it are not easily reducible to simple behavioural traits. There is nothing to say that because a person behaves in a certain way that that behaviour is necessarily underpinned by appropriate attitudes.

The empirical/rational approach takes the view that much discrimination and prejudice arises from simple ignorance, in the sense that the person does not know enough about another culture, for example, and therefore can have those prejudices challenged by the acquisition of knowledge. Examples of attempts to change attitudes by appealing to rational logic would include anti-smoking campaigns and drink-drive campaigns. A further example of why this approach on its own is not very effective in changing attitudes would be the genetically modified (GM) foods and fox-hunting debates that raged in 2003. In such cases each side attempted to change the attitudes of the other by information campaigns designed to convince that fox-hunting is not cruel or that GM is safe and vice versa. It is apparent from the outcomes of both debates that information alone does not have a great impact on changing attitudes. This leads us to consider an aspect of human experience that goes deeper even than attitudes, namely values and beliefs. We shall briefly visit these in the next sub-section.

The normative/re-educative approach is probably the most effective method of achieving attitude change. Such approaches would encourage people to expose their attitudes, values, and beliefs and offer these to the peer group for review. Feedback would be given in a supportive and (critically) non-judgemental learning environment. Individuals are encouraged to confront their attitudes and consider what changes they may need to make for themselves. There is a strong link here with the ethical principle of responsibility which is outlined above.

2.7.2 **Beliefs**

A belief represents the knowledge or information that we hold about the world as we see it. Fishbein and Ajzen (1975) argue that beliefs link an object of the belief to an attribute of some kind. For example a belief about justice may be linked to the attribute of goodness. For a belief to manifest as an attitude, there will be a dimension or ingredient of value, which has to do with what, for example, an individual senses is good, worthwhile, bad, or worthless. Whereas attitudes and values are usually formed over a period of time, beliefs may be formed over much shorter periods. Another way of seeing beliefs is that they are the result of both a cognitive and emotional process where an individual will respond to a proposition, statements, or other kind of information. Given that beliefs may be formed from a combination of emotional and cognitive response, it is not uncommon for beliefs to be formed on incomplete knowledge, whereby the holder is unable to demonstrate the full information to show the veracity of the belief. This can be amply demonstrated in the way people hold beliefs in relation to aspects of diversity. Very often the beliefs that certain people hold in relation to say, black people, women, or gay people will be held by focusing on certain features (often negative) but will rarely be the complete picture.

2.7.3 **Values**

There is a strong link between attitudes, values, and beliefs, but although the words are often used interchangeably, they are not identical in meaning (Gross 1996). Most adults will hold thousands of beliefs, hundreds of attitudes but only dozens of values (Rokeach 1968). Put simply, a value is an enduring belief that a specific mode of behaviour or an end state of existence is personally or socially more desirable than the converse mode of behaviour or end state of existence. For example, in relation to responding to diversity in criminal justice, a personal or social state of *fairness* might be valued against the converse state of unfairness.

Attempts have been made to classify values. Allport (et al 1951) developed a scale of values to illustrate their relative relationship to an individual's way of seeing the world. In these terms values can be classified as:

- Theoretical (problem solving, knowing how things work)
- Aesthetic (the arts, theatre, music)
- Political (political systems and power structures)
- Economic (orientations towards financial issues)
- Social (general concern for the welfare of and interrelation with others)
- Religious (concern with moral issues, life after death and so on).

> **EXERCISE**
>
> Think about your own values in relation to the classification shown above.
>
> • What values that you hold can you identify in relation to each?
>
> It is not uncommon for people's personal values to be in conflict with values that society may have enshrined in law and policy. Try to identify some values that people may hold personally but which conflict with wider societal values.

2.8 **Culture**

An examination of police culture, or perhaps more correctly police cultures, is central to an understanding of policing diversity. Recent research has shown that there needs to be an acknowledgement that there are in fact many cultures in policing. This can be at force level with differences say between large metropolitan police services and those that are smaller and more rural in nature. Different cultures can also exist at police station level, with one squad, unit, or shift operating in a quite different cultural framework to another even in the same building.

What seems to be certain is that culture can have a major role in determining the way police service delivery operates. By its nature, police culture can interfere with attempts by management or government to improve the quality of policing, and can, at its worst, mean that policing is applied unfairly and in a discriminatory fashion. To understand what culture in an organizational setting is we can turn to the literature on organizational culture generally. In doing so we need to make the links with how culture impacts on the notion of policing diversity.

2.8.1 **Organizational culture generally**

Schein (1984: 3) proposes a definition of organizational culture as:

> The pattern of basic assumptions that a given group has invented, discovered, or developed in learning to cope with its problems of external adaptation and internal integration, and that have worked well enough to be considered valid, and, therefore, to be taught to new members as the correct way to perceive, think, and feel in relation to those problems.

Culture, in this definition, can then be assumed to be potentially problematic in terms of achieving organizational change. The orientation implicit in the expression 'we have always done it this way, so why change things' is often a function of the power of organizational culture. Another feature of this definition that has implications for policing is the power of organizational culture to influence new entrants to an organization. The pressure to conform to norms that a recruit to the police service may feel can be enormous.

REFLECT ON PRACTICE

Think about your own experience of joining the police or another organization.

- What kind of pressure to conform did you experience?
- If that pressure ran counter to your own attitudes, values and beliefs—what strategies were you able to adopt to resist it?

The exercise of discretion is a key feature of the role of a police officer, that is the ability to exercise (within the constraints of the law) choice about action. A feature of organizational culture is that it will tend to thrive more where an organization allows high levels of discretion in the working practices of its staff and where the attitudes and actions of staff have low levels of external scrutiny. Where discretion is high and scrutiny low, informal 'working cultures' will tend to develop more forcefully and be more difficult to detect and challenge. Organizational culture can be reflected in ideas about the 'right' way to do things, underlying assumptions about the 'best way' to operate, or in 'tricks of the trade'—ways of getting 'around' problems or obstacles, often learnt 'on the job' and passed on by longer serving staff, rather than (or in despite of) formal or official training. Over the years a recurring theme of police training has been that whilst attempts have been made in initial training to help recruits learn the correct way of doing things, the subsequent informal training on the job has tended to take a more pragmatic orientation. The danger represented by this is exacerbated when the informal learning is done in the context of a negative culture.

2.8.2 Police culture specifically

The study of police culture really began in the 1960s and 1970s with research that provided a wealth of information through observation and analysis that was later to be used to formulate theories of police culture. The supposed 'characteristics' or 'dimensions' of police culture have tended to remain static since the early days of police research and are significantly, almost without exception, negative.

EXERCISE

- How would you define the idea of police culture?
- Make two lists: one of the positive aspects of police culture and one of the negative.

The sociological study of police culture, which goes back many decades, has a tendency to be critical of that culture which is seen essentially as a negative force which causes problems with the delivery of policing. Some general points about the nature of police culture are:

- Culture is informal and represents the reality of what actually does happen.
- Culture is at the root of the worst problems in policing.
- Culture has the power to undermine and subvert what police managers, police authorities, or even government, wish to happen.

The characteristics of police cultures have been identified over the years mainly through observational and qualitative research. Those that have a direct impact on the issues relating to policing diversity can be summarized as follows:

- A sense of mission—there is a 'job to be done' and the police are the 'thin blue line' between order and chaos (Waddington 1999a, 1999b; Reiner 1992). Despite recent attempts by government to increase the number of police officers, the ratio of police to population remains relatively low. The high demand for police resources brought about by the terrorist attacks on London in July 2005 have brought into sharp focus the idea of a 'thin blue line'.
- Pragmatism—(Reiner 1992). Whilst Reiner was primarily writing about a tendency to cut corners to achieve results, recent government imperatives on the achievement of policing targets have reinforced the need for pragmatism.
- Autonomy—we're on our own on this one and no one should try to interfere with us doing what we need to do (Goldsmith 1990). The autonomous aspect of police culture has received a number of challenges in recent years. For example the Crime and Disorder Act 1998 places a duty on local authorities and the police, with other key agencies and the community, to work together at district level to develop and implement strategies for reducing crime and disorder in the area.
- Conservatism—a tendency to be on the 'right' politically and 'illiberal' over such matters as civil rights and the rights of suspects, defendants, and those convicted (Waddington 1999a, 1999b; Skolnick 1966).
- Conformity and conventionalism—a tendency to accept the authority of those in power but not to accept as legitimate any challenges to that authority (Frewin and Tuffin 1998): a tendency to be unsympathetic to those with non-conventional lifestyles and moralities (Scripture 1997).
- Prejudice, intolerance, and stereotyping—a tendency to 'group' and stereotype sections of the community with negative or hostile labels; a lack of understanding of an empathy with 'outsider' or 'alien' groups (Drummond 1976; Chan 1997).
- Cynicism—a cynical attitude about the world, about change, about others' motives, about 'do-gooders', etc (De Lint 1998; Waddington 1999a, 1999b; Reiner 1992).

- Machismo—sexist/masculine attitudes inside and outside the police organ-ization, 'horseplay' and harassment at work, contempt for 'deviant' sexualit-ies (Waddington 1999a; Reiner 1992; Fielding 1994).

A review of the dimensions of police culture shown above reveals that they are essentially negative, and therefore problematic for the delivery of fair, high quality, policing. But to what extent is this a true picture? It could be argued, given the recency of 'undercover' documentary research such as in *The Secret Policeman* (see the case study above) that little has changed. There are, however, a number of other factors that need to be taken into account.

Firstly, we need to take account of changes within police culture over time. Different patterns of police recruitment and internal human resource develop-ment may very well be rendering some at least of these attributes as more fea-tures of the past than features of the present. Secondly, we should question whether these qualities are peculiar to the police profession or whether they are exhibited elsewhere, particularly within working class culture. Research con-ducted around other social groups has found that the police are often not as authoritarian, racist, or aggressive when compared to others. As far back as the early 1980s a study by the Policy Studies Institute found that racist language from the police did not necessarily manifest itself in racist discrimination with-in their working environment (Smith and Gray 1983).

2.9 Chapter Summary

In this chapter we outlined a number of the main concepts that underpin an understanding of diversity.

Relevant knowledge and understanding from the National Occupational Standards

We noted that there is a strong link between the ideas in this chapter and the requirements of Unit 1A1 of the National Occupational Standards "Use Police Actions in a Fair and Justified Way". It will only be possible to achieve this if the individual has an understanding of the mechanisms that under-pin the notion of policing diversity.

Prejudice and discrimination

These two concepts lie at the very heart of non-discriminatory practice and are pre-requisites for anyone engaged in anti-discriminatory practice. Whilst prejudice and discrimination are often used interchangeably, they do have a qualitative difference, where the former is essentially an atti-tude and the latter is the expression of that attitude in behaviour. We noted, drawing on the work of Gordon Allport, that the manifestation of prejudice can be described in terms of a scale that ranges from antilocution to extermination. We briefly reviewed other theoretical explanations of prejudice namely social conflict theory, social categorization, and social learning.

Stereotyping and labelling

Stereotyping and labelling were introduced as primarily psychological ways of making sense of the world generally and in particular the people we meet and deal with. We noted that stereotyping is a process that police officers may have to use to make an assessment of the risk of a particular situation, but the danger in this comes when a particular stereotype is so strong that the individual is not able to challenge it and therefore may be forced into making a wrong judgement.

Attitudes, values, and beliefs

We all have attitudes values and beliefs to a greater or lesser extent. Most of us hold thousands of beliefs, and hundreds of attitudes, but we may only have dozens of true values. Attitudes may have the following components: cognitive (a consciously held belief or opinion); affective (the emotional, mood, or feeling dimension to an attitude); evaluative (the way of determining whether the attitude is a positive or negative orientation towards something); conative (an ordered arrangement of elements (such as stereotypes) which is likely to lead to a particular behaviour). We saw that a belief represents the knowledge or information that we hold about the world as we see it. Very often, beliefs may be made up of incomplete knowledge and will be linked to a particular attribute of the object of the belief. Values are different to attitudes and beliefs. We often have fewer of them and they may be much stronger and more deeply ingrained in the way we see the world. Attempts have been made to classify the areas in which we hold values. One framework we looked at classified values as:

- Theoretical
- Aesthetic
- Political
- Economic
- Social
- Religious

Institutional racism and discrimination

We surveyed the issues surrounding the notion of institutional racism that came out of the Stephen Lawrence Inquiry Report in 1999. We noted that the definition of institutional racism challenged the previous tactic of alleging that problems of racism in policing were essentially caused by 'rotten apples in the barrel' and not by any systemic failure of the service. We considered the notion of 'unwitting' and the extent to which actors in the larger institutional framework are or are not in control of the actions associated with played out prejudice.

Police culture

The chapter concluded with a consideration of the nature of organizational culture generally and also the specific nature of police culture. Most commentators on police organizational culture frame their analysis in essentially negative terms. We looked at the way in which culture and in this case police culture has the potential to be informal and represent the reality of what actually happens in policing, is at the root of the worst problems in policing and how police culture has the power to undermine and subvert what police managers, police authorities, or even government, may wish to happen.

Diversity—The Business, Ethical, and Legal Case

3.1 **Chapter Outline**

There have been in recent years some cynical views expressed that diversity is merely an industry that has developed in response to changing social and political thinking. Such a view is dangerous, because it has the effect of marginalizing the issues as if they are of no importance. One of the things that police officers, indeed anyone in society who is concerned for fairness and equity, need to carefully consider is *why* we should be so concerned about diversity. This concern needs to be at two levels, the first is why organizations should be concerned and the second is why individuals should be concerned, particularly those who are in positions of authority or have power over others such as the police. So in this chapter we will explore the key question 'what is the case for responding to a diverse society'? We will need to try and answer this question from three perspectives. The first is to consider what we might term the 'business case'. The second is to answer it from an ethical perspective. The third is to consider the question from a legal perspective. In this chapter then, we will cover the following ground:

- The business case for diversity including:
  — The idea of best value.
  — What is meant by 'business case'.
  — Business benefits.
- The ethical case for responding to diversity including:
  — What we mean by taking an ethical perspective.
  — Some of the key components of an ethically based response to diversity.
  — The relevance of human rights to the ethical argument.
- The legal case for responding to diversity. This will not be a detailed exposition of the law (which is available in other text books in this series), but a higher-level discussion of the way in which legislation has been put forward to ensure that people receive fair treatment.

3.2 **The Business Case for Responding to Diversity**

In opening up the discussion in this chapter we really need to consider to what extent can policing be regarded as a 'business' at all? There was a time not all that long ago when the notion of making a business case for anything in the police service, particularly in terms of service delivery, was almost unknown. It was assumed, for example, that for any particular criminal case to be investigated, whatever resources were needed would be provided. It was not long before such an approach was seen to be unworkable given the increase and change in crime and demands on police time and effort. For example crimes such as theft and robbery of mobile phones and computer equipment did not even exist twenty years ago. Terrorist activity, although of great impact, was largely limited to domestic issues whereas now it is global, and the nature of the threat has changed considerably and now includes the possibility of chemical, biological, radiological, and even nuclear attack. The police, along with other public sector organizations, have been forced to make choices about how limited resources should be deployed. But the question was not just about making choices regarding the deployment of scarce resources, it was also about being accountable for the choices that were made and justifying how the resources were being used to best effect.

Running parallel to an increasing government agenda to ensure that all the public services, police and others (for example, the National Health Service) provided value for money, and worked towards 'best value', was the need to argue the case for why resources were put where they were. The police service of course is not required to make a monetary profit, but it has become increasingly accountable for how money is spent, how resources are allocated, and more importantly the way in which best value for those resources can be achieved. In the next section we briefly discuss what the idea of best value entails.

3.3 **Best Value**

We should note at the outset that best value is not just about getting the most for the minimum outlay (although that is bound up in it), it is also about the quality of the service that is delivered. This takes us immediately to the issue of providing a service to a diverse society. The best service delivery (and by implication the best value) will be achieved when the police service delivers a quality of service that takes account of the needs of a diverse society.

The Local Government Act of 1999 placed a duty on all police authorities to ensure that policing was delivered to a high standard, and that savings be made wherever possible. Establishing whether best value is being achieved is usually done in the form of 'best value reviews'. At its most basic level a best value review will need to consider five areas which can be identified as four Cs plus 'sustainability':

- *Challenge*—why and how each service is being provided or whether it should be provided at all. In terms of diversity within the policing function, best value type thinking has had a major impact in recent years. The introduction of Police Community Support Officers (PCSOs) would be a good example of how what may have been considered to be solely a function of the regular police service has now been extended to being delivered by a quite different group.
- *Consult*—with local taxpayers, service users, and the business community, particularly about performance targets. Consultation with communities and the end user of policing services lies at the heart of a positive response to policing a diverse society. We will deal with the bigger issue of consultation in Chapter 5. For the time being, however, it is worth noting that for police to

be able to deliver a high quality of service, and therefore achieve best value, it will be necessary not only to consult widely but to listen and be seen to be listening to the results of that consultation. In terms of performance targets, evidence consistently shows that public perceptions of what would constitute a high performing police service are very often at odds with centrally imposed performance targets.

- *Compare*—the performance of services across a variety of indicators with other authorities and relevant outside organizations. In terms of comparing the performance of police forces against each other, there is a wealth of information available. Comparative performance of different police services in relation to race equality and diversity is very often captured by the various thematic inspections conducted by Her Majesty's Inspectorate of Constabulary.
- *Compete*—seek to embrace fair competition as a means of securing efficient and effective services. This might not at first glance appear to have much relevance to police but there are a number of ways in which it actually does have a direct and significant impact on the best value that a police service achieves. Some years ago policing was seen as a monopoly where few other agencies were involved. The situation is very different in the twenty-first century. Many policing type functions are now carried out by other agencies, including investigation (for example HM Revenue & Customs), there has also been a rapid expansion of so called 'private policing' where for example shopping centres employ their own staff to carry out a security function. Again many internal functions are now 'contracted out' such as maintenance, catering, training, and so on. So police services have a responsibility to ensure that where services are contracted out they are competitive. In addition, the police need to be aware that where they are not providing best value there are many functions of policing that do not require the individual to hold a warrant granting them powers of arrest.
- *Sustainability*—issues should be addressed, by assessing the potential impact of a service on the environment and the extent to which there is potential for sustainable improvement.

Best value therefore is a duty placed on the police service which seeks to ensure value for money and a high quality of service. This leads us to consider the notion of 'business case' and the way in which a proper response to diversity can be expressed in sound business terms.

3.4 **The Meaning of 'Business Case'**

In this section we will start by attempting to define in general terms what constitutes a business case. We will then take a brief look at the way in which this has been translated into thinking about the business case for responding to diversity.

3.4.1 **Business case defined**

A business case is a statement that addresses, usually in high-level terms, the (business) need that it seeks to meet. It will need to include:

- The reasons for the activity;
- The expected business benefits;
- The options considered including the reasons for rejecting the recommend-ation of each option (there will usually be an option to do nothing with an associated discussion of why this is not desirable);
- A statement of the expected costs of the activity;
- The associated risks of the activity.

At some stage in the future there will need to be a review to ensure that the business case is still valid and that the original need identified is being met.

The definition above relates primarily to specific projects that an organization might undertake within its business. But the business case for responding to diversity includes the core principles. In other words there will be a number of 'business' benefits to the police in engaging with diversity. There are options in relation to this and there is of course the option to do nothing, although such an option is usually countered at the very least by the moral, ethical, or legal imperative.

There is a sense in which some people might be repelled by the very notion that there could be a business case for responding to diversity. It could be argued, for example, that the diversity of human beings is solely a matter of their human rights, particularly their right to be treated with dignity and respect and to not be the victims of discrimination on any grounds that may be irrel-evant. That said, there has been an increasing tendency in both the public and private sectors to articulate the business case for diversity. This has partly been a response to the resistance that some organizations have displayed in responding adequately to the diverse needs of their workforces and partly a genuine affirm-ation that responding adequately to diversity has tangible business benefits and that organizations engaging properly with the challenges of a diverse workforce actually gain a competitive edge.

EXERCISE

- How do you respond to the notion of a business case for diversity?
- Do you think it is important or do you think there are more pressing reasons why the police service should respond to diversity?

3.4.2 **Diversity and the police—the business case**

Her Majesty's Inspectorate of Constabulary (2003: 15) recognized both the business moral and ethical case for diversity.

> Recognising the value of increasing the scope of consultation and cooperation with all sections of the community, however diverse can further enhance the business case. Such activity assists in the gathering of vital intelligence, securing witnesses and isolating criminality. Furthermore, helping staff to achieve their full potential can mean the realisation of intrinsic motivation, drive and commitment and demonstrate that employment within the police service is a worthwhile and valued career, accessible to and safe for anybody.

It is important to note from what the HMIC says that the case for diversity has two strands. The first is the benefits to be accrued from engaging effectively with communities in terms of intelligence gathering, securing witnesses, and isolating criminality. These are of course vital functions in effective policing and even more so where policing relies on public cooperation and consensus. Isolating criminality has become even more important in the light of extremist terrorism where the individuals who perpetrated the attacks on the London transport system on 7 July 2005 had been previously largely invisible to police.

One note of caution needs to be sounded in articulating the benefits of engaging effectively with diverse communities in order to gather intelligence and so on. This is the way in which various communities may view such a strategy with justifiable cynicism if there are perceptions that the police are only doing this in order to achieve an operational policing aim and not because they genuinely want to engage with the communities and listen to their needs and aspirations.

The HMIC report goes on to articulate the consequences of not engaging fully with diversity (the equivalent of the option of doing nothing in the business case definition above). In summary the risks are identified as:

- Serious public disorder
- An imbalance of workforce representation
- Litigation
- Adverse publicity
- Low levels of confidence in the police service.

REFLECT ON PRACTICE

Look at the list of consequences of not engaging fully with diversity given by the HMIC.

- What examples from your own experience can you think of that illustrate the points made?

In terms of the imbalance of workforce representation, this has continued to be a challenge to the police service although considerable efforts have been made (particularly after the Stephen Lawrence Inquiry Report) to increase the representation of minority groups in police numbers. As reported by the Commission for Racial Equality (2005a) the police service was set targets for the recruitment of officers from minority ethnic backgrounds to increase representation as follows:

1999—2%
2002—3%
2004—4%
2009—7%

The figure for 2009 represents parity with the available working population and is adjusted for individual forces to take account of local populations. So for example the figure for the Metropolitan Police in London is much higher. By 2003 the overall figure reached was 2.9 per cent (ie the target for 2002 had not been reached).

There are many reasons why the target figures may not have been reached and there is ongoing research into why people from minority groups do not feel attracted to join the police service. There is in much of the research literature a strong theme that there is a strong cultural disincentive to join an organization which is still perceived as untrustworthy and culturally unwelcoming to people from diverse backgrounds. *The Secret Policeman* documentary mentioned in Chapter 1 is just one example of this. In 2005, the Commission for Racial Equality (CRE) published the report of its investigation into the Police Service in England and Wales. Sir David Calvert Smith, who led the investigation for the CRE, in presenting the report said:

> There is no doubt that the Police Service has made significant progress in the area of race equality in recent years. However, there is still a long way to go before we have a service where every officer treats the public and their colleagues with fairness and respect, regardless of their ethnic origin.
>
> Willingness to change at the top is not translating into action lower down, particularly in middle-management where you find the ice in the heart of the Police Service. For example, managers are not properly supported or fully trained on how to handle race grievances, so relatively minor issues are often unnecessarily escalated. (<http://www.cre.gov.uk>)

Given such comments it is not surprising that the targets for recruitment are not being reached.

Representation alone is not the sole answer, however. There are examples of other police forces (such as the Los Angeles Police Department in the United States) where there is a much higher proportion of minority groups in the workforce, but which are still beset by incidents of discrimination and unfair treatment. Increased representation needs to be supported and nourished with an appropriate organizational culture where people can safely feel that they belong and are valued. Schneider (2001:1) in constructing a case for diversity in business terms notes:

> While representation is still seen as part of the issue, diversity is primarily about creating a working culture that seeks, respects, values and harnesses difference. This includes visible differences such as sex, ethnicity and some disabilities, but also others that are not necessarily evident immediately.

3.4.3 The Government's case for diversity

The stated aim of the Home Office, the government department with responsibility for the police, is 'building a safe, just and tolerant society' with the aim to make a difference in the real world, helping build a society in which people are safer from crime, and there is equality and fairness for all. The case for diversity has also been outlined in a number of documents relating to the Government Modernization Agenda. In its far-reaching proposals to modernize government, the 1999 White Paper set out its strategic intention in relation to diversity:

> We must accelerate progress on diversity if this country is to get the public services it needs for the new millennium. The public service must be a part of, not apart from the society is serves. (HM Government 1999)

Another paper on reforming the civil service developed this theme further:

> We need a civil service that is genuinely diverse. Only a truly diverse service will be capable of delivering the services, which our diverse society is entitled to expect. To be really effective the service must make fullest use of its people, give them the chance to play their part, develop and progress to the maximum of their potential. (HM Government 1999)

Organizations in the public sector, including the police, and the private sector as well need to recognize that there are huge benefits to be gained from a workforce that is representative of the diversity in society provided that the diverse workforce is well managed and supported. These include those that are shown in Table 3.1 below—but there are many others—see how many other benefits you can identify.

Table 3.1 The benefits to organizations of a diverse and well-managed workforce

Motivated staff	Greater pool of talent
Greater pool of ideas	Avoidance of monoculture
Understanding of 'customers' needs'	Increased productivity
Reputation of the organization	Reduced sickness and stress
Respect for the organization	Low level of grievance
Trust in the organization	Better morale

3.5 **The Ethical Case for Responding to Diversity**

3.5.1 **Introduction**

We noted above that some people will argue that a moral and ethical argument for diversity takes primacy over any business benefits that may accrue. In short, responding to diversity is an imperative because it is the right and good thing to do. People have a right to be treated fairly and with dignity and respect not because there is some business benefit to be gained from it but because they have a fundamental and absolute human right. The way individuals treat others will largely be grounded in their attitudes, values, and beliefs about fairness and justice. We can illustrate this with an exercise which draws on an example from policing.

EXERCISE

With very limited exceptions, when a person is arrested they must be cautioned in the following terms 'You do not have to say anything. But it may harm your defence if you do not mention when questioned something which you later rely on in court. Anything you do say may be given in evidence.'

- If you are a police officer you will be very familiar with these words. But now consider *why* and *how* the caution may be given.
- Make a note of as many ideas as you can.

What did you come up with? Here are some ideas that occur to me (some of them drawing on my experience as a police officer):

- People are cautioned because the law says they must be;
- People are cautioned so that the officer can say they were when asked in court;
- People are cautioned only if other people are looking;
- People are cautioned because the officer has been trained to do so;
- People are cautioned and it is done in such a way that they have no possibility of knowing or understanding what was said to them;
- People are cautioned because the officer believes that the suspect has the right in law to be cautioned and he or she will make sure that the suspect understands what is being said to him/her.

Which of these approaches to cautioning represents an ethical approach to policing? The first and last reasons are aligned to ethical policing with the last one being the most closely aligned. The point is that an ethical approach is not one that is merely complying with some law or directive, it is one that is grounded in a belief in the rights of the suspect. If we now transfer this to responding to diversity, there are close parallels. We can choose to respond to diversity either from the standpoint of belief and commitment to the rights of others and genuine respect for their difference, or we can water this down to a mere question of compliance with organizational expectations. But of the two, which is the more ethical? Again this can be illustrated with an example from my own experience.

I was once at a briefing session at my force headquarters. One of the speakers who I would describe as a 'jack the lad' type character gave a twenty-minute presentation that was laced with sexist and racist innuendo. A number of us in the audience were feeling very uncomfortable about this but others in the audience clearly found it very amusing. At the conclusion, the senior officer who was in charge of the briefing stood up and thanked the speaker and then sensing the mood of some of in the audience said: 'In these days of political correctness I ought to distance myself from some of the things we have just heard—I hope none of you were offended'. It seems to me that a number of things were revealed in what the senior officer said. Firstly, there was no sense that he was personally committed to challenging what was wrong in what we had heard. Secondly, he was revealing that his attitude as a senior officer to such behaviour was not to deal with it and put the person right but merely to give a nod to force policy. Thirdly, he was wrong in hoping that none of us were offended; we were. Paying lip service to diversity does not demonstrate commitment and belief in the issues, it merely reveals that the individual is not taking an ethical approach. This leads us now to look in a little more detail at what we mean by the ethical case for diversity.

3.5.2 The nature of ethics

Ethics is a complex area of philosophy and it is well beyond the scope of this book to delve too deeply into the issues. That said, a good deal has been said and written about the notion of ethical policing, and the ethical approach to diversity, and since ethics is so closely bound up with the idea of values and beliefs it is important to have some idea of the issues involved. Broadly speaking, ethics is to do with the values we hold, the way we live, and how we make the decisions we make about the things that we do. With some exceptions, most adults have a well-developed sense of what is right and what is wrong. This sense of what is right and wrong will lead us to make decisions but very often those decisions are made in the context of different ethical frameworks. Living in a post-Christian secular society such as Britain, ethical frameworks have become much more diverse and in many ways less clearly defined. Ethical standpoints are usually situational, relative, or absolute. What do we mean by this?

Situational ethics

Situational ethics refer to where ethical decisions are made according to the circumstances. A recent example of this would be the debate that has been going on in relation to the use of torture, the question being 'is it ever right to torture someone?' Before we continue—consider that question yourself.

EXERCISE

- Can you conceive of circumstances when it might be right to torture someone?

You may well have approached this by thinking that torture is never right. But if you thought more deeply, you might have started to conceive of circumstances when it might be necessary to torture someone for the greater good. The most current example of this is the 'ticking bomb' scenario where it is argued that if a suspect can be proved to know the location of a bomb he has planted and there is imminent risk of the bomb detonating, with the probable loss of many lives, then it would be right to torture him to gain information about the location of the device. Now this raises a whole host of other questions but it does serve to illustrate the point that there may be situations that will determine how an ethical decision might be made.

Relative ethics

Relative ethics refer to circumstances where there is a relationship between decisions that will be made that may or may not be in conflict with each other. For example difficult decisions about experimenting on animals may be made in relation to the greater ethical good of achieving an outcome that will help human beings. The one decision is made relative to the other.

Absolute framework

Absolute frameworks for ethical decisions are often easier to hold, but in fact are much less prevalent than might have been the case in the last century. People who hold absolute approaches to ethical problems often fail to recognize the complexity that problems hold.

EXERCISE

Consider the proposition that it is absolutely wrong to kill another human being.

- What are the implications of this absolute ethical standpoint?

Whilst it may be attractive to hold such a view for its simplicity, unfortunately life and the decisions we have to make are not that simple. Would it be wrong for example for a police firearms officer to kill another person in a case of justifiable self-defence? We have to make such judgements all the time in relation to many ethical issues. For example, we may make judgements about abortion, euthanasia, or capital punishment or indeed punishment of criminals generally.

It will not come as a surprise that people view these issues very differently. The same principles apply to the moral judgements we make around race and diversity. Some aspects of discrimination are easy to condemn; others may be less so. Ethics has to do with the frameworks we use to come to those judgements, they help us to decide and determine the principles by which such decisions are made.

3.5.3 Ethics in the context of policing diversity

Having briefly discussed the nature of ethics we can now turn to the way in which these ideas may be applied to the context of policing. Four of the classical ethical frameworks that have developed over time are those of virtue, care, duty, and utility. Drawing on these ideas, Neyroud and Beckley (2001: 47–48) offer eight principles for ethical policing. Neyroud and Beckley offered these principles for policing in general, but we can now apply them to the issue of the way police officers might respond to diversity. As you read through them, consider how they may relate to your own professional experience and whether they adequately capture how and why a given individual (or you) might respond to the diversity of others with fairness and non-discrimination.

1 Respect for personal autonomy

In other words a respect for the fact that people have a right to be who they are. This would include respecting their rights as citizen and treating each person with dignity and respect. This principle goes to the heart of the problem of the way in which police culture has a tendency to 'normalize' people into it. Right from the start of an officer's career, there are enormous pressures on an individual to conform to the prevailing culture. You may have experienced this yourself. Sometimes the antipathy felt by certain groups within the police is of an extreme and damaging kind. This is illustrated by remarks made by Vic Codling national co-ordinator of the Gay Police Association (Police Professional, 30 June 2005) who said 'what we have got in some forces is members of staff having their property vandalised, having rubbish—condoms, lubricating jelly, that sort of thing—left in their lockers or pigeon holes because they are simply *suspected* of being gay'.

2 Beneficence

Simply means active goodness or kindness. Again, the nature of policing and the cultural framework in which it operates sometimes makes this principle all but invisible. Thankfully there are numerous examples of police officers overtly acting with beneficence—so many that they rarely feature in the news. Examples of where an officer has failed to show active kindness of goodness are those that generally come to attention and do great damage to the officer and the reputation of the police service in general. The issue of beneficence is largely grounded in how the particular officer views the business of policing. An officer who believes that policing is a supportive, service delivery function is more likely to be disposed to beneficence than one who views policing as the coercive application of power. Beneficence or the lack of it has the potential to either do great good in relation to minority groups or great damage.

3 Non-malfeasance

In other words the absence of wrongdoing. When taken with 2 above this means, for example, in the case of people working in the police service, helping people without harming others. As we have noted above there are numerous examples of wrongdoing and the impact of these instances far outweigh the impact of good practice. Malfeasance manifests itself in many forms, from racial and sexist banter through to overt discrimination against colleagues and the public. In the aftermath of *The Secret Policeman* documentary (see Chapter 1) one senior officer involved with recruit training rightly suggested that the time had come for police officers not to merely exhibit the absence of wrongdoing but to proactively demonstrate their support for the values of the police service by identifying themselves with pro-active anti-discrimination and overtly supporting their colleagues from minority backgrounds.

4 Justice

Neyroud and Beckley (2001: 48) argue that for police officers this means ensuring that policing is a 'public good, delivered according to need, with a high value on human rights and legality'. There are many impactions in this principle for the policing of a diverse society. For example, policing according to need will require members of the service to establish what the need is. This will mean a sincere commitment to the idea of consulting and engaging with communities (see Chapter 5 below) with a high value being placed on listening and responding to the needs of the various diverse communities served. As we will see in the next section of this chapter, there is also a need to place a high value on the law, not only that which relates to the exercise of power, such as powers of stop, search and arrest, but also the law which seeks to prohibit discrimination and unfair treatment.

5 Responsibility

People have personal responsibility for their actions and need to be able to justify why they do what they do. From all that we have said so far about an ethical response to diversity, it should be apparent that personal responsibility is an important factor in the response. We have seen, for example, that people make decisions about their lives, their behaviour, and the way they see the world based on their own ethical frameworks. This is a personal not organizational responsibility. This does seem to be particularly important for policing. Officers out on patrol have a high degree of autonomy in terms of what they do. More often than not although operating in a highly regulated arena with rules about how their power should be exercised, the decisions they make are based on discretion. Such decisions can either be made with integrity or not. People are personally responsible for the values they hold and conflict arises when those values are at odds with the values of the organization.

6 Care

There is a natural human response of care towards each other. This is also connected with the notion of 'interdependence', a concept that is fundamental to many aspects of criminal justice. There is a strong tradition of care towards colleagues in the police service. When an officer needs 'urgent assistance' all his or her colleagues will be willing to instantly drop what they are doing and go in support of the officer in need of help. There are frequent references to the police as a 'family' with all the implications that description has for the ways in which families show care and support for their members. But for it to operate in an ethical way, care needs to be unconditional and not determined by the extent to which a particular member of the police is considered to fit into the 'in-group'.

7 Honesty

Honesty is not simply confined to honesty in dealing with others but also in the veracity of one's own self-reflection in relation to the issues. The first point is of course important in that the police need to be honest and straightforward in their dealings with members of the public. This will include such things as being scrupulously honest in the grounds for suspicion and being honest with communities when things go wrong. The second point is about being honest in one's own self-reflection. In Chapter 8 we will look at how we go about learning the issues that surround diversity. A key feature of this learning process is the ability to be honest both with others and with oneself. It is difficult, if not impossible, to address aspects of our own behaviour if we are not aware of the attitudes, values, and beliefs that underpin them. So we need to be honest in self-reflection, this will include honesty about the prejudices we hold as well as honesty about our own performance.

8 Stewardship

This relates to the notion of careful stewardship of powers over others in society. Stewardship of power involves the careful use of that power and the use of discretion. Most professionals involved in the criminal justice process have power to a greater or lesser extent over others, and have a responsibility in relation to the careful use of this power in a way that is not fair and not discriminatory. The power to deprive someone of their liberty, or to search their person or home must only be used in the legal context in which it was framed. Any abuse of that power will inevitably result in the breakdown of trust and confidence in those on whom it is exercised. Where communities feel beleaguered already because of discrimination in society generally, they will feel an even greater sense of grievance when they are, or perceive they are, being unfairly treated by the police.

EXERCISE

Having read through the principles of ethical policing outlined above, think about your own response to them.

- Do you think they are comprehensive?
- To what extent do you follow the principles within your own ethical framework?

3.5.4 The HMIC case for an ethical approach to diversity

The HMIC in the report 'Diversity Matters' (2003: 14) outlined the ethical context of diversity. The key points made in the report may be summarized as follows:

- Policing is a people business—of people by people.
- Communities are diverse as are the people within those communities;
- Handling race and diversity internally as well as externally is vital to police performance.
- Policing has a unique aspect in terms of the levels of power involved. This in turn generates the case for mainstreaming diversity into all of the policing functions, especially leadership, performance management, and fundamentally, service delivery, and the training provided in relation to each.
- Service delivery is not simply about crime resolution. It is also about engaging with communities.
- An ethical approach to race and diversity would see an appropriate set of standards and emphasis being applied to any situation, irrespective of the diverse issue involved.

The principles outlined above would also seem to be relevant to any aspect of criminal justice where at each stage, the practitioner is in a power relationship with members of communities. Whilst what an organization does impacts on people's lives, the interface is more often than not at the level of the individual.

3.6 The Legal Case for Responding to Diversity

3.6.1 Introduction

I was once a participant in a particularly difficult training course on equal opportunities and police service delivery. It was difficult because many of the participants were resistant to any notion that they should challenge their own thinking and behaviour in relation to treating people fairly. The trainer was clearly becoming quite frustrated with the group and in the end said: 'well you must—because it's the law'. This type of situation is not uncommon in training where people either cannot or will not see the need to challenge the way attitudes, values, and beliefs impact on the way service is delivered. It was unfortunate that the trainer was forced into the position of having to be prescriptive with the group, but she was actually making a very important point. In a liberal democracy, all members of society including the police are subject to the law and we have no option but to obey the law and comply with its requirements. There is a certain irony when police officers seem quite happy to enforce the law against others but are much more ambivalent about the laws they feel are important in relation to themselves. The fact is that there is a great deal of legislation that exists to try and ensure that people are not discriminated against and receive fair treatment.

It is perhaps a sad reflection on society and some of its institutions, including the police, that so much legislation has had to be passed. It was the Stephen Lawrence Inquiry for example, that led directly to the Race Relations (Amendment) Act 2000 which placed duties on public authorities to do far more in relation to the elimination of discrimination that had previously been the case.

In this final section of the chapter we will take a brief look at some of the ways in which the problem of discrimination in society has been tackled in legislation. This is not intended to be a detailed account of all the law that exists in relation to the pursuit of fairness. There are many other resources at your disposal written by experts that deal in detail with the meaning and application of the legislation. Rather we will take a high level view of some of the key features, both to establish the legislative context and to provide leads into areas that you may wish to research further.

3.6.2 Human rights

The idea of human rights gives us the point of departure for thinking about the law which enshrines people's rights to be treated with dignity and equality. The European Convention on Human Rights contains the rights and freedoms that may be enjoyed by all citizens. Until 2000, if a person wished to take action under the Convention it was necessary to go to the European Court of Human Rights but in that year the relevant provisions of the Human Rights Act 1998 came into force. Table 3.2 below sets out the main rights and freedoms. The full text can be obtained from many sources on the web but you will find the following link useful: <http://www.europa.eu.int/index.htm>

Clearly many of these rights and freedoms are of direct concern to the police service and the way the police exercise their powers will have a direct bearing on the rights and freedoms of individuals. Note in particular Article 14 which allows for the enjoyment of the rights and freedoms without discrimination.

The full text of the Human Rights Act 1998 can be found at <http://www.pfc.org.uk/legal/hra98.htm>

Table 3.2 European Convention on Human Rights—Key Articles

Article	Summary
2	Right to life protected by law
3	No torture, inhuman or degrading treatment or punishment
4	No slavery, servitude or forced labour
5	Liberty and security of the person apart from lawful arrest and detention
6	Fair and public hearing of charges within a reasonable time
7	No retrospective guilt for an act which was not a crime at the time it was committed
8	Right to respect for private life, home and correspondence
9	Freedom of thought, conscience, and religion
10	Freedom of expression (limited only by duties and responsibilities)
11	Freedom of peaceful assembly
12	Right to marry and found a family
14	Rights and freedoms in the convention to be enjoyed without discrimination on any ground such as sex, race, colour, language, religion, political or other opinion, national or social origin, association with a national minority, prosperity, birth or other status

3.6.3 The Race Relations (Amendment) Act 2000

The full text of the Act is available at <http://www.opsi.gov.uk/acts/acts2000/>

This piece of legislation was direct result of the Stephen Lawrence Inquiry. It was intended to have a number of effects in terms of extending the protection of people from discrimination on grounds of race, notably the following:

- The outlawing of race discrimination (direct, indirect, and victimization) in public authority functions (including the police), which had not been covered by the Race Relations Act of 1976.
- A widening of the definition of 'public authority'.
- Placing a general duty on specified public authorities (including the police) to promote race equality.
- The imposition of specific duties on some public bodies.
- Making Chief Police Officers vicariously liable for acts of discrimination carried out by officers under their direction and control.

Of particular interest to our discussion of policing a diverse society is s 71(1) of the 1976 Act, as substituted by the 2000 Act:

71.—(1) Every body or other person specified in Schedule 1A or of a description falling within that Schedule shall, in carrying out its functions, have due regard to the need—

(a) to eliminate unlawful racial discrimination; and

(b) to promote equality of opportunity and good relations between persons of different racial groups.

This made quite explicit the duty to eliminate unlawful racial discrimination in relation to the functions of the particular public authority in question and what was very new was the general duty imposed to promote equality of opportunity and good relations between persons of different racial groups. It was not left at this point, however, because the Act goes on to require that certain public bodies (including the police) should publish a race equality scheme setting out how they intended to deliver on this requirement.

EXERCISE

If you are not familiar with the Race Equality Scheme for your organization track it down and read it. It is worth considering how easy it was to find. All Race Equality Schemes should be easily accessible.

Table 3.3 Gives a flavour of what might be included in a typical race equality scheme for a police force. In this case it is the Thames Valley Police Scheme for 2005–08 (<http://www.thamesvalley.police.uk/news_info/diversity/pdf/res.pdf>).

The mere existence of a race equality scheme is of course no guarantee that appropriate action is taking place. In its investigation into the police service in England and Wales in 2005 the Commission for Racial Equality was critical of the implementation of many such schemes. In the second section of the report the commission concluded:

2.74 As will be clear to readers of this report, there is sometimes a gap between what forces and authorities claim to be doing to meet the race equality duty and what they are actually doing, as indicated by the answers to questions and our visits. Of particular concern is the lack of comprehensive ethnic monitoring in accordance with the employment monitoring duty, as well as systematic procedures to address both monitoring and impact assessment requirements across the service.

2.75 If producing a compliant race equality scheme is the first step towards compliance with the overarching general duty to promote race equality, the implementation of all the arrangements within the scheme must be the next. We have found that some police forces and authorities are taking steps towards this implementation, but others are very far behind. Even those that are making progress need to continue to develop this work.

Table 3.3 Contents of the Thames Valley Police Race Equality Scheme 2005–08

1   Foreword by the Chief Constable
2   Summary
3   The Background
4   The Thames Valley Perspective—Our structures, processes, monitoring and reviewing
5   What is the General Duty?
6   What are the Specific Duties?

POLICY & SERVICE DELIVERY—SPECIFIC DUTIES:

7   How we will assess which functions and policies are relevant to the General Duty
8   How we will assess and consult on the likely impact of proposed policies before they are adopted
9   How we will monitor for any adverse impact of existing policies
10 How we will publish the results of assessments, consultation and monitoring
11 How we will ensure that the public have access to information and to services
12 How we will train staff to carry out their duties

EMPLOYMENT—SPECIFIC DUTIES:

13 How we will ethnically monitor staff in post and applicants for jobs, promotion and training
14 How we will ethnically monitor and analyse grievances, disciplinary action, performance appraisal, training and dismissals and other reasons for leaving
15 How we will publish annually the results of the ethnic monitoring
16 How we will deal with complaints
17 How we will consult on this document
18 Your chance to contribute and comment
19 Contacts

ANNEX

A   Our Race Equality Scheme Action Plan 2005–2008
B   List of policies and functions screened for relevance
C   Race Equality Impact Assessment Guide
D   Ethnic Monitoring

3.6.4 Legislation in relation to discrimination/diversity

There has been a great deal of legislation relating to discrimination and more broadly the response to diversity in recent years. Table 3.4 below charts some of the major legislation that exists to deal with discrimination both in the workplace, in service delivery, and the extension of offences within the criminal law as well as the requirement to consult.

A review of the various pieces of legislation above illustrates the way in which the Government has, over the years, addressed an increasingly wide range of issues relating to the diversity in society and the need to ensure that all citizens enjoy similar freedom from harassment and discrimination. In October

Table 3.4 Key Legislation Impacting on Diversity

Year	Act/Regulation	Effect
1970	Equal Pay Act	Equal pay for men and women
1974	Rehabilitation of Offenders Act	Promotes fairness for ex-offenders
1975	Sex Discrimination Act (as amended)	Outlaws discrimination on grounds of sex
1976	Race Relations Act (as amended)	Outlaws direct and indirect discrimination and victimization on grounds of race
1983	Equal Pay (Amendment) Act	Changes to the 1970 Act
1986	Public Order Act	Includes types of behaviour that would stir up racial hatred
1994	Criminal Justice and Public Order Act	Racially aggravated offences
1994	Police and Magistrates' Courts Act	Police Authority Consultation
1995	Disability Discrimination Act	Outlaws discrimination against people with a disability
1996	Police Act (ss 8 and 96)	Requirement to consult
1998	Human Rights Act	Incorporates European Convention on Human Rights into domestic law
1998	Crime and Disorder Act	Local Authorities and Chief Officers jointly to formulate crime and disorder strategies
1999	Sex Discrimination (Gender Reassignment) Regulations	Extends the rights under the Sex Discrimination Act to individuals undertaking gender reassignment
1999	Local Government Act	Consultation in relation to best value
2000	Race Relations (Amendment) Act	Amends the 1976 Race Relations Act
2003	Employment Equality (Religious Belief) Regulations	Extension of employment rights and prohibition on discrimination under other legislation to religious belief
2003	Employment Equality (Sexual Orientation) Regulations	Extension of employment rights and prohibition on discrimination under other legislation to sexual orientation
2004	Civil Partnership Act	Allows for civil partnerships between same sex couples

2006 further legislation will be in place to deal with discrimination in relation to age discrimination in the workplace. Whilst much of the legislation deals with issues of freedom from discrimination in employment, the requirement for public authorities, including the police, to consult with the communities they serve is now in place. There are a number of points that we can note in relation to the need for all this legislation.

- The very fact that so much legislation has been needed illustrates the extent of the problem that is being addressed. If responding effectively to the diversity of society was a straightforward issue that people and organizations naturally engaged with then it could be argued that there would be no need to legislate so widely.
- In recent times, particularly since 9/11 and 7/7, there has been a growing debate about the way legislation and proposed legislation has impacted on the human right of freedom of thought and expression. In January 2006, the Government was defeated in its original proposals to introduce an offence of incitement to religious hatred, similar to the Public Order Act 1986 offence of incitement to racial hatred. The proposals were meant to protect religious groups such as Muslims who would not be included as racial groups (such as Jews and Sikhs). The outcome was a watered down version of the original Bill (see Chapter 7 on Hard Issues for a discussion of the effect on freedom of expression).
- The extent of the legislation now means that there is very little scope for an individual or an organization to fail to respond adequately to issues of diversity if they are to remain within the law. That said, time will tell whether the legislation will achieve its purpose. For example, the existence of the Race Relations and Sex Discrimination Acts for over a quarter of a century have not eliminated all discrimination against women and people from racial groups, so there would still seem to be much work to do.

3.7 Chapter Summary

In this chapter we have surveyed the case for responding effectively to diversity in terms of the business, ethical, and legal case.

- We noted that the business case is rooted in the idea of best value in the sense that best value is an imperative for the police and other organizations and that best value for a public service is only likely to be achieved if it is responding effectively to diversity.
- We attempted to define what a business case is and related that to the idea of a business case for diversity in terms of policing. We noted that it is particularly important that a business case for diversity is anchored in a genuine desire to serve communities well and not just to see them

as a source, for example of intelligence for operational policing (although that would be a beneficial outcome).

- The ethical case for responding to diversity is grounded in the notion of doing the right thing. We took a brief look at the nature of ethical frameworks and related this to the notion of policing a diverse society. Ethical policing will involve such things as respect for personal autonomy, beneficence, non-malfeasance, justice, responsibility, care, honesty, and stewardship and all of these will have a direct relationship to the way that a diverse society is policed.
- The chapter concluded with a general introduction to the legal framework that provides for individuals, organizations, and society at large to operate in an environment that is free from discrimination. We noted that the legislation is now extensive, but that alone will be insufficient and that people and organizations still have much to do to ensure that citizens can enjoy their lives free from the fear of discrimination.

4

Diversity Developments

4.1 **Chapter Outline**

Issues of race and diversity in relation to policing have been the subjects of increasing interest and focus in the past twenty-five years. The report by Lord Scarman into the riots that occurred in Brixton in London in 1981 was, at the time, regarded as a watershed in terms of the way the police should be responding to the needs and issues of local communities. Since then there have been numerous inquiries, inspections, and reports into how the police have responded to equal opportunities and diversity issues. In this chapter, we will chart a route through some of those reports and developments to try and establish from a critical perspective some of the key issues that have emerged and which police in the twenty-first century need to be responding to in a positive way. The ground we will cover includes the following:

- Diversities in policing
- Police associations
- The Scarman Report
- The Stephen Lawrence Inquiry Report
- A Home Office Study of the impact of the Stephen Lawrence Inquiry
- Her Majesty's Inspectorate of Constabulary thematic inspections
- Other Reports:
  - The Morris Report
  - Commission for Racial Equality investigation into the Police Service of England and Wales
- The role of the Independent Police Complaints Commission
- The proposed Commission for Equality and Human Rights

Space in this chapter allows for only a brief discussion of each of the developments, and it is not possible to do proper justice to each of them so where relevant, key websites are given as the starting point for your further research.

4.2 **Diversities in Policing**

In the same way as we talk about the diversity that exists in society, an increasing focus of attention has been the range of diversities in policing. Throughout this book the word 'police' and 'policing' are used and this usually conjures up an image of uniformed and detective police officers who are members of one of the police forces in the UK. But there is diversity in policing too, particularly in terms of those who carry out the function. For example in a report submitted to the Metropolitan Police Authority (MPA 2003), the Commissioner of the Metropolitan Police outlined what now constitutes the 'extended police family'. The report noted that the policing function has been supported for a number of years by the Special Constabulary, the Traffic Warden Service, and the Volunteer Cadet Corps. This has, in recent times, been supplemented by

Police Community Support Officers and (in London) Volunteers in Policing. The report also makes reference to other functions such as case managers and detention staff as well as the use of private security company wardens. Additionally elsewhere in the book we have noted that the investigation function of police as well as roads policing is no longer the sole preserve of the mainstream police force.

4.2.1 Implications for diversity

This extension to the police family has a number of implications. In terms of benefits there is evidence to show that greater proportions of people from black and minority ethnic groups can be brought into the policing function than are able to be recruited into the regular police service. There are benefits to be accrued from the greater transparency that is achieved by larger numbers of people being involved in policing who are able to view policing issues from an insider's perspective. People involved in the policing function who are drawn from a greater variety of community backgrounds are also able to act as ambassadors for the police and the policing function within their own communities. The Security Industries Association, which is the regulatory body for private security, also recognizes the role it has to play in the wider police family. One of the Association's aims is 'strengthening the extended police family by encouraging and supporting further engagement of the private security industry' (SIA 2005).

Websites for further research

<http://www.the-sia.org.uk>
<http://www.mpa.gov.uk/committees/mpa/2003/030925/13.htm>

4.3 Police Associations

A significant diversity development in the last decade or so has been the establishment of a number of associations of people with a common interest. There had for many years already been associations of people in the police with religious affiliations such as the Christian Police Association and the Catholic Guild, but there had been no formal associations of other minority groups within the police. There are now many such groups comprising police staff (not just police officers) who have joined together both for mutual support and to provide a forum to bring pressure to change to bear, not least in the area of countering police culture and identity. The following three examples give a flavour of what these groups do but there are others, such as the Jewish Police Association and the Muslim Police Association.

4.3.1 **National Black Police Association**

The National Black Police Association (NBPA) was formed in 1999 and now represents and provides a coordinating forum for over forty local Black Police Associations. It is important to note that 'black' in the terms of the NBPA does not refer to the colour of a person's skin. Rather it seeks to draw on the experiences of people from black African, black Caribbean, and Asian origin in opposition to racism. At the time of the establishment of the first Black Police Associations there was, in some quarters, ambivalence in supporting them from both senior officers and others at lower levels. For example, according to Rowe (2004: 58)

> Although the leadership of the BPA has maintained that it is not a rival organisation to the long established Police Federation which is effectively the trade union for officers below the rank of superintendent, anecdotal evidence suggests that the Federation was sceptical about the BPA and felt that the new organisation would be divisive and that, in any event, it (the Federation) was representative of all officers.

Mission statement

> The National Black Police Association seeks to improve the working environment of Black staff by protecting the rights of those employed within the Police Service and to enhance racial harmony and the quality of service to the Black community of the United Kingdom. Thereby assisting the Police Service in delivering a fair and equitable service to all sections of the community. (NBPA 2006).

The mission statement of the NBPA reflects one of the original intentions of the formation of the first Black Police Association in London, namely to improve the working environment of black officers working in the police family to encourage and facilitate their recruitment, selection, and retention with an associated aim of improving police service delivery to minority ethnic groups in society.

Work of the NBPA

Black Police Associations in general, and the NBPA in particular, now engage in a wide variety of work in support of the strategic aims. The NBPA's website outlines all of the objectives, a selection of which are given below.

- Provide a support network;
- Influencing the direction of policies nationally in line with equality issues and anti-discrimination policies in the Police Service and Wider Criminal Justice Systems;
- Representing the views of all representative members of the Constituted Black Police Association (herein known as BPA's) who are affiliated to the NBPA;

- Influencing the direction of policies nationally in line with equality issues and anti-discrimination policies in the Police Service and Wider Criminal Justice Systems;
- Advising and consulting on matters of racism, nationally;
- Working towards improving the relationship between the Police and the minority community of the United Kingdom;
- Working towards improving the recruitment, retention and progression of staff members within the Police Service;
- Assisting the Police Service in the development of new and existing policies, where necessary.

It is clear from these objectives that the NBPA takes both an 'outside-in' and 'inside-out' view of its work. The objective to support and encourage black people in the police service is linked to concern to make a difference to the experience of those who are on the receiving end of police delivery. The NPBA and the BPAs it represents have been a considerable force for good in the police service and initial fears of some people and groups about divisiveness have proved to be unfounded.

4.3.2 **British Association of Women in Policing**

The British Association of Women in Policing (BAWP) has existed for longer than the NBPA having been formed in 1987. According to Home Office Statistical Bulletin (Home Office 2005e) at 31 March 2005, 30,162 of the 142,795 police officers in England and Wales were female. This figure represented 21 per cent of the strength compared to 20 per cent in the previous year. However only 10 per cent of the officers of chief inspector and above were women (although this was an increase of 2 per cent on the previous year) and 24 per cent of constables were female. The BAWP, whose president is a female chief constable, seeks to represent the needs and aspirations of female police officers and in similar vein to the NBPA works closely with other representative bodies such as the Police Federation, the Superintendents Association, and other associations representing the interests of minority groups.

Aims of the BAWP

- To raise the awareness and understanding of issues affecting women within the Police Service.
- To facilitate and contribute to discussions on issues of concern to all officers—providing wherever possible the female perspective.
- To develop a network of professional and social contacts between officers nationally and internationally.
- To facilitate the sharing of information on issues affecting the Service, and women in particular.
- To contribute to the continuous professional development of all members.

The first aim, shown above, seeks to address the issues that women experience in the police service. Writing some time ago, Walklate (1996) identified a number of these issues that even in 2006 are still manifest. Firstly, although the raw figures of females in the police have improved from say the position in 1981 where only 8.6 per cent of police officers were female, there is still under-representation both in terms of overall numbers and the proportion of women in the higher ranks. Secondly, stereotypical views of 'women's' work persist and lead to under-representation in some specialist roles and almost complete absence from others. Thirdly, the association of certain roles in policing with what women are good at (dealing with children, domestic violence, and so on) rest on assumptions that may be false.

4.3.3 Gay Police Association

Gay men and women in the police service continue to face prejudice and discrimination. The first association to be formed was in 1990 under the title the Lesbian and Gay Police Association (LAGPA). This was subsequently renamed the Gay Police Association (GPA). The GPA exists to support and represent the interests of gay police service employees. The work of the association includes the development of policy, involvement in the investigation of homophobic hate crime, victim care, and family and community liaison.

Objectives of the GPA

The key objectives of the GPA are:

- To support gay Police Officers and Staff throughout the UK;
- To promote equal opportunities within the police service;
- To educate the police service and central government on all issues connected with sexual orientation and policing.

A notable achievement of the GPA has been its work in supporting gay police officers, many of whom have felt unable to be 'who they are' in the face of a police culture that accepted anti-gay prejudice and discrimination as the norm. The GPA website contains a number of links to news items which track both the progress of issues in relation to developments as well as examples of continuing prejudice and discrimination. At the more strategic level the GPA works with all the mainstream organizations such as the Home Office, HMIC, IPCC, and ACPO in an advisory capacity on the development of policy and practice for the police service.

4.4 The Scarman Report 1981

4.4.1 Context of the report

On the night of 10 April 1981, according to press reports, two police officers in Brixton, South London, were attempting to give first aid to a young black man who had been stabbed. A crowd gathered and became hostile and the confrontation quickly escalated into a riot involving hundreds of mainly young people. During the disturbances over 300 people were injured, 83 premises and 23 vehicles were damaged—the costs at the time were estimated to be in the region of £7.5 million. Many members of the local community had felt aggrieved by a police operation known as 'Operation Swamp 81' that had been using the (now infamous) 'sus' laws to stop and search people in the area. According to Newburn (2003) nearly 950 stops had been made under 'sus' and this had led to 118 arrests. In excess of 50 per cent of the people stopped were black and of the charges made one was for robbery, one was for attempted burglary, and twenty were for theft or attempted theft.

4.4.2 Findings and recommendations

Lord Scarman was appointed by the Government to conduct an inquiry into the disorders and the events surrounding them. The subsequent report (Scarman 1982) was widely regarded as a watershed in thinking about police community relations. Newburn (2003) provides a commentary on the findings and recommendations of the inquiry which addressed such issues as:

- Recruitment of people from minority ethnic communities to the police;
- Arrangements for statutory consultation;
- The introduction of lay visitors to monitor police behaviour at police stations, particularly in relation to custody;
- Independent review of complaints against the police;
- Tightened regulations for dealing with discriminatory behaviour by police officers.

It is important to note that Scarman explicitly rejected the notion of institutional racism as an explanation for what had happened in the public disorders. As Newburn (2003: 89) notes in quoting Scarman:

> [if] the suggestion being made is that practices adopted by public bodies as well as private individuals are unwittingly discriminatory against black people, then this is an allegation which deserves serious consideration.

The idea of 'unwitting' was to be further developed in the Stephen Lawrence Inquiry many years later. Indeed as Rowe (2004: 11) points out 'much of the language, and conceptualisation with which the Scarman and Macpherson reports discuss racism in the police are broadly the same'.

4.5 The Stephen Lawrence Inquiry Report

Without doubt, one of the most significant developments in diversity and the police response to it has been the Stephen Lawrence Inquiry (Macpherson 1999). It is hard to underestimate the impact that the findings of the inquiry had both for the police and other public bodies. The report led directly to a number of changes in policing and also to changes in the law, including the Race Relations (Amendment) Act 2000, and the establishment of the Independent Police Complaints Commission. Marlow and Loveday (2000: 1), writing a year after the report was published, noted that 'It is the impact of Macpherson's definition of "institutional racism" that is the key issue in the Report's legacy'.

4.5.1 Context of the report

On 22 April 1993, a young black man, Stephen Lawrence, was stabbed to death in a racist attack in Eltham, South London. The tragic events surrounding the murder, which probably lasted no more than fifteen to twenty seconds, have reverberated for years afterwards.

> Stephen Lawrence's murder was simply and solely and unequivocally motivated by racism. It was the deepest tragedy for his family. It was an affront to society, and especially to the local Black community in Greenwich. Nobody has been convicted of this awful crime. That is also an affront both to the Lawrence family and the community at large. (Macpherson 1999: 2).

As a result of pressure from the family of Stephen Lawrence the then Home Secretary, Rt. Hon. Jack Straw MP, established a public inquiry in July 1997 led by Sir William Macpherson. The terms of reference for the inquiry were 'to inquire into the matters arising from the death of Stephen Lawrence on 22nd April 1993 to date, in order particularly to identify the lessons to be learned from the investigation and prosecution of racially motivated crime' (p 6).

4.5.2 Selected findings and recommendations

The findings of the inquiry were hard-hitting and direct. In the conclusion and summary the report notes:

There is no doubt that there were fundamental errors. The investigation was marred by a combination of professional incompetence, institutional racism and a failure of leadership by senior officers.

As the report comments, it is difficult to provide a summary of the findings and the summary below is even briefer. It is recommended that you read the full report, which can be obtained from the web address given at the end.

First aid

There were strong criticisms of the ability of the police to give effective first aid to Stephen Lawrence who although he had gross injuries was given only cursory first aid treatment.

Initial response

There was a lack of direction and organization in the first few hours after the murder. 'Lack of imagination and properly co-ordinated action and planning which might have led to the discovery and arrest of suspects was conspicuous by its absence' (p 317).

Family liaison and victim support

Family liaison failed and was not corrected by senior officers. There was a lack of information given to the family and Stephen's parents were treated with insensitivity and a lack of sympathy.

Racism

'At its most stark the case against the police was that racism infected the Metropolitan Police Service and that the catalogue of errors could only be accounted for by something more than incompetence' (p 321). It was suggested in submissions to the inquiry that if the colour of the victim and attackers had been reversed, then the police would have acted very differently. The inquiry concluded that there was strong evidence of unwitting racism. This included:

- Insensitive and racist stereotypical behaviour at the scene;
- Patronizing and thoughtless approaches by officers at the hospital;
- Ignoring and racist stereotyping of a (black) witness who should also have been treated as a victim;
- Failure by some officers to accept that this was a racist murder;
- Using inappropriate and offensive language.

Community concerns

The report noted that there was a serious problem with trust in the police and the criminal justice system as a whole. Many people from minority groups perceive themselves to be discriminated against by an unfair system.

'Just as justice needs be seen to be done, so fairness needs to be seen to be demonstrated' (p 323). The concern for trust led to the first of seventy recommendations—namely 'That a ministerial priority be established for all police services: "To increase trust and confidence in policing amongst minority ethnic communities" ' (p 327).

Website to download a copy of the Stephen Lawrence Inquiry

<http://www.archive.official-documents.co.uk/>

4.5.3 The Impact of the Stephen Lawrence Inquiry

In October 2005, the Home Office published a study (Foster, Newburn, and Souhami, 2005) that assessed the impact of the Stephen Lawrence Inquiry. As we have seen above, the inquiry promoted large-scale reforms of many aspects of policing and the purpose of the study was to assess the impact that these reforms had achieved and to identify further areas of concern. The research found that there had been significant improvements in:

- The recording, monitoring, and responses to hate crime;
- The organization, structure, and management of murder investigation;
- Liaison with families of victims of murder;
- Consultation with local communities; and
- The general excision of racist language from the police service.

These improvements are qualified however. For example, although the use of racist language has largely disappeared from the culture of the police service, many black and minority ethnic officers felt that this was cosmetic and masked little change in underlying attitudes. This was partly illustrated buy the tolerance (still) of sexist and homophobic language and behaviour that the research team found to be widespread. The change in the use of racist language appeared to be linked to a perception of greater scrutiny and the possibility of disciplinary action. The improvements noted above were not uniformly apparent in all the sites that were researched, and there seemed to be greater attention paid to improvements that were easily identifiable.

Institutional racism

A significant difficulty seemed to be the response of forces to the idea of institutional racism (one of the key findings of the Macpherson Inquiry). The concept is still not widely understood and still generates anger amongst police officers who perceive it as unfair. The report notes that institutional racism is 'the single most powerful message' arising from the report. Some still regard the term racism within the definition as referring to the racism of individuals rather than the collective of the institution. This is exacerbated by a similar false impression of the concept promulgated by the media both at the time of the inquiry and subsequently.

The impact of the inquiry

Interestingly the research found that just under three quarters of the officers surveyed (72 per cent) felt that the Stephen Lawrence Inquiry had had a positive impact on policing. However, the increased scrutiny of what the police do has led to police officers feeling under greater pressure and particularly so in the case of the exercise of stop and search powers where there was an increased sense of the risk of being accused of racism when stopping and searching people from minority ethnic communities. To quote directly from the report:

> These anxieties suggested that the Lawrence Inquiry had alerted officers to the possibility that their behaviour might be perceived and, crucially, successfully defined in a way that was at odds with their own intention and perception. (p x).

Relationships with minority communities

The report also found that:

> there have been significant improvements in the structures for consulting with local communities, and in understanding the need to consider community impact more broadly. In all research sites, local citizens felt the police had made such advances in the way they consulted with communities that they were now equal or better than other agencies (p xii).

One aspect of this improvement has been the development of the use of independent advisory groups (IAGs) both on a regular basis and in response to specific needs. The research did reveal, however, a theme which we will discuss later in the book namely that the purpose of consultation often lacks clarity and may be characterized by a police led agenda rather than allowing community led advice to set the agenda based on locally perceived needs and concerns.

Local service delivery

The research found that all forces had implemented community race relations (CRR) training. It was interesting that the majority of those who had undergone such training found it worthwhile and that there was a greater awareness of differences in cultural protocols. Having said that, the report found that one negative impact on local service delivery was that officers failed to recognize the way policing is perceived by differing communities and this, it is argued, goes to the heart of 'the central notion of institutional racism' (p xiii). An aspect of this is that operational tactics which disproportionately affect members of minority communities and in particular those that focus on youth are likely to be a barrier to the building of trust between the police and those groups.

The points noted above are just a flavour of what is contained in the report and it is suggested that you visit the website shown below where you can download the complete report for further study.

Key website for further research

<http://www.homeoffice.gov.uk/rds/policingdc.html>

4.6 **Reports by the HMIC**

4.6.1 **Winning the Race: Policing Plural Communities (1996–97)**

This report by HMIC, published in October 1997 built on and extended the work that had been done in a previous report 'Developing Diversity in the Police Service' (HMIC 1995), which focused essentially on equal opportunities in relation to policing. 'Winning the Race: Policing Plural Communities' had three key areas of examination as its terms of reference:

(1) How far is community and race relations work within the service integrated into mainstream policing?
(2) How is ethnic monitoring and other statistical data being analysed and used within the service to evaluate and monitor community and race relations?
(3) What formal and informal links exist between forces and different sections of their various local communities and what use is made of these? (HMIC 1996–97: 17)

Despite the first words in the title, the inspection had a broader remit than just race and in fact dealt with a number of issues, notably the concern over police handling of homophobic hate crime. A number of concerns that had been expressed by community representatives were highlighted: the selection given below covers the ones that had a direct bearing on the issues of policing a diverse society:

- Community beat officers (CBOs) are valued by communities and yet forces often failed to recognize this 'value'. Too often CBOs are 'withdrawn' for routine force demands, and there is a perceived lack of continuity in the role;
- Disproportionate stop/searches of visible ethnic minorities;
- A lack of informal mechanisms for consultation and two-way communication;
- A lack of faith in the police complaints system;
- Inadequate understanding and training of police officers in racial and homophobic incidents as well as community and race relations;
- The quality of police leadership and first line management interventions;
- Ineffective monitoring and analysis of data.

Bearing in mind that this report was published before the Stephen Lawrence Inquiry that reported in 1999—a glance at these concern reveals that the police service at the time was not adequately engaging with the reality of policing a diverse society. The police service needed to recognize more fully that in a liberal democratic framework, where successful policing could only be secured with the consent of the people, then the police would need to work harder to secure the support of the communities they served. The HMIC proposed:

> as communities become more plural, gaining their trust will require both improvements in the quality of service they receive and the adoption—as a core element of all policing activity—of a community focused strategy which *recognises diversity* and is underpinned by well articulated policies. (HMIC 1996–97: 8)

A number of examples of good practice were noted in the report. There were several instances noted of attempts to provide relevant training for staff in such areas as equality of service delivery and enhancing service delivery to a multi-cultural society. In addition, good practice was noted in the efforts of some forces to develop multi-agency relationships.

Twenty recommendations were made, and it is beyond the scope of this section to review all of them. The first recommendation however stands as one, which, it could be argued, subsumes the others:

> Forces should publicly re-affirm their commitment to investing in good community and race relations as a core function of policing, this being reflected in the production of sound policies and strategies. (HMIC 1996–97: 57)

We have seen elsewhere that good community relations, and a healthy approach to diversity are never to be regarded as a 'bolt-on' to the business of policing but are core to it. Policing by its very nature in British society is policing diversity and the commitment of police forces to this concept will be reflected both at the strategic and policy level of how that policing is conducted.

4.6.2 **Winning the Race: Revisited (1998–99)**

'Winning the Race: Revisited' was an attempt by the HMIC to chart the progress of forces against the recommendations that had been made in the original report two years earlier. The HMIC seemed to express coded frustration in noting:

> the conclusion of findings indicates that progress has been less than satisfactory with many of the recommendations (of the 1997 report) largely 'sidelined' and few forces placing the issue high on the agenda. (HMIC 1999a: 7)

One of the key recommendations of the original report had been that forces should invest in their commitment to community and race relations (CRR) as a core function of policing and that this should be reflected in policy and strategy. In 'Winning the Race: Revisited' it was reported that two years after the recommendation was made, only sixteen forces had a CRR strategy or its equivalent in place, and ten forces claimed to have a strategy under development. Put another way just about half of the forces in England and Wales appeared to have taken the issue of community and race relations seriously enough to develop force strategy around it. In terms of leadership on CRR issues, it was noted that these were not dealt with at strategic level in the same way as other issues. Interestingly, the report noted that, 'the integration into mainstream policing has been most effective in forces that have brought the responsibility under a chief officer' (HMIC 1999a: 39). The report offered a fairly detailed analysis of service delivery; community consultation issues, racial and homophobic incidents and attacks, and noted that progress on some of these issues was less than satisfactory.

4.6.3 Winning the Race: Embracing Diversity (2000)

This was the third in the series of reports by the HMIC that sought to not only inspect but to challenge the police service in its commitment to community and race relations. All forty-three forces in England and Wales were inspected and it was noted that the publication of the Stephen Lawrence Inquiry report was providing a 'catalyst for change' (HMIC 2000: vii). The aim of the inspection was to benchmark all forces against the recommendations that had been made in the preceding thematic inspections. Some of the themes that emerged are given below.

Consultation

The HMIC was encouraged to find that there was a renewed commitment to consultation with communities, particularly those whose voices had previously not been heard. It also pointed out that consultation is vital both for the credibility of force strategy and policy but also in communicating the limits that may exist on what the public say they want from the police.

Community intelligence

Community intelligence needs to a part of the 'information conduit'. The effective gathering of community intelligence will provide a more accurate picture of the quality of life (in terms of crime and policing) that communities experience.

Serving the community

The HMIC noted that the definition of a racist incident was by now widely known in the police service, but that there was still resistance in some quarters to acknowledge and respond to the underlying rationale for the definition. It was the responsibility of leadership in the police to 'penetrate the residual resistance of the cynical' (HMIC 2000: 4) to ensure that racist incidents were universally well dealt with. Comment was also made on the need to balance secrecy in relation to operations with the need to be seen to be open and transparent with the communities served.

Reflecting the community

Policing by consent requires that the police service is representative of the people it serves:

> The effort and initiative to improve the recruitment profile is not matched by equivalent energy and creativity in addressing progression and retention. These three strands are implicitly intertwined and cannot be unravelled without the definite possibility of overall failure. (HMIC 2000: 5)

Website for further research

<http://inspectorates.homeoffice.gov.uk/hmic/>

4.7 **Other Reports**

There have been numerous reports published in the last ten years each of which contribute to what we might broadly call developments in diversity and policing a diverse society. The following sub-sections will briefly introduce two of these to give a flavour. As noted above, the brevity of these summaries will not do justice to the reports but will, I hope, stimulate your interest in reading them.

4.7.1 **The Morris Inquiry**

On 14 December 2004, a report was published of an inquiry that had been led by Sir William Morris. The inquiry had been commissioned by the Metropolitan Police Authority with the following terms of reference:

> To inquire into the conduct by the Metropolitan Police Service of the following matters in relation to police officers and police staff:
>
> - Policies, procedures and practices for and resolution of complaints and allegations against individuals and grievances by individuals;
> - Policies, procedures and practices for and resolution of Employment Tribunal claims, in particular those claims involving allegations of race or other discrimination against the MPS; and
> - Policies, procedures and practices for and resolution of workplace conflicts falling short of allegations or grievances. (Morris Inquiry 2004)

The report is of interest to a student of policing diversity because, although it was ostensibly looking at the internal workings of standards in the Metropolitan Police it had a good deal to say about the experience of officers from minority ethnic backgrounds. In the words of the report 'we have heard much about the approach of the MPS to "diversity". Indeed it dominated the evidence we received' (para 1.20). The report concluded that there was no common understanding of diversity in the MPS and that it (diversity) 'at worst [remains] a source of fear and anxiety and at best, a process of ticking boxes'. It further noted that the efforts to promote diversity in the MPS might have triggered a backlash that was beginning to become evident and that such a situation would be 'catastrophic'. One of the key findings was that there was disproportionality in the way that black and minority ethnic officers were treated in the management of their conduct. The issue of lack of confidence among managers in the MPS in dealing with issues of difference was also noted.

Website for the inquiry report

<http://www.morrisinquiry.gov.uk>

4.7.2 The Commission for Racial Equality

In March 2005, the Commission for Racial Equality (CRE) published its final report into the police service in England and Wales. The investigation was instituted under the CRE's power (Race Relations Act 1976, s 48) to investigate and focused on three areas of the police service in England and Wales:

* The recruitment, training, and management of police officers;
* Monitoring of these areas by the police service and police inspectorates; and
* How police authorities and forces are meeting the statutory general duty to promote race equality, and related specific duties to publish a scheme and carry out employment monitoring.

The introduction to the report outlines a number of key messages.

Race equality duty

The final report followed on from an interim report in which a number of forces had been identified as not complying with their duties under the Race Relations (Amendment) Act 2000 in terms of monitoring and assessing performance and in meeting other aspects of their duties. The process of complying with the legislation will in the view of the CRE have the effect of helping the police service to establish its anti-racist ethos and will also protect it from being driven by unwelcome events (such as *The Secret Policeman* documentary).

Standards, recruitment, and training

In these areas the good work of the service in developing the National Occupational Standards and Integrated Competency Framework was noted, but the CRE warned that these would need to be 'carefully scrutinized' for the effects on racial equality. The same applied to the way that officers are screened before recruitment. The content and delivery of training programmes were not seen to be of a uniformly good standard, and some officers were unable to see the value and relevance of the training to their day-to-day work. Training should not be seen as a stand-alone addition to other training merely to achieve a certain level of political correctness.

Management of behaviour

As was found in the Morris Report above, some managers were identified as being unable adequately to deal with the management of behaviour where the problem involved or was perceived to involve the issue of race. White officers felt that they were treated unfairly when complaints were made against them, and when black officers were the complainants, they all to often saw their complaints being escalated to the extent that they then became the subject of victimization. The police service needs to address the issue of the way that behaviour is managed to ensure that all officers feel that the system is fair. It is important too that addressing poor behaviour is not just seen as an issue of racist language but that the deeper issues of racist motivation are tackled.

Website for further research

<http://www.cre.gov.uk>

4.8 **The Independent Police Complaints Commission**

The Independent Police Complaints Commission (IPCC) came into being on 1 April 2004 and replaced the former Police Complaints Authority. Although as a non-departmental public body it receives its funding from the Home Office, the Commission is entirely independent of the police, interest groups, and political interference in its decision-making processes. The main role of the IPCC is to investigate complaints against the police in line with the duties imposed under the Police Reform Act 2002. A chair, deputy chair, and fifteen commissioners, each of whom takes responsibility for a number of police forces, oversee the IPCC.

4.8.1 **Investigations**

The IPCC has an investigation role in relation to certain complaints against the police. It will make an independent investigation of serious incidents and serious allegations involving the police. Serious incidents include those that involve death or serious injury. Serious allegations will include allegations of serious or organized corruption in the police, allegations against senior officers, allegations that involve racism, and allegations that relate to perverting the course of justice. In other cases, the IPCC will supervise the internal investigation of less serious complaints within police forces. A recent high profile example of the work of the IPCC is the independent investigation they conducted into the shooting of Jean Charles De Menezes at Stockwell tube station in July 2005. Such high profile events do put the Commission under the spotlight of media attention and it is vital that it is both truly independent and seen to be so in order to maintain public confidence in its work. When the Commission was set up, it was necessary to bring into its strength a number of former police officers, and officers on secondment (mainly detectives). This was primarily because it was felt that at the time it would not be possible to get the necessary investigatory experience from elsewhere. In order to try and head off the obvious implication that it could not be truly independent given its use of police officers, strict rules of conduct for all members of the IPCC were laid down. Nonetheless the true independence of the Commission does rely on the integrity of those working for it and time will tell whether the use of police investigators will undermine confidence.

4.8.2 Guardianship role

In addition to its investigatory role, the IPCC has a responsibility for guardianship of the police complaints system. This means that the organization is responsible for:

- Monitoring, review, and inspection of Police Force Complaints systems;
- Promoting confidence in the complaints system as a whole;
- Ensuring the accessibility of the complaints system;
- Drawing and promoting the lessons of the IPCC's role.

As would be expected, the IPCC in pursuit of its guardianship role has taken steps to evaluate the confidence of the public in the police complaints system. A report published in February 2006 (IPCC 2006) aimed to measure confidence in the complaints system, people's willingness to complain and their general awareness of the IPCC and its work. Approximately 4,000 people were surveyed in addition to a large sample of people from minority ethnic backgrounds. In terms of willingness to complain, 77 per cent of respondents said that they would definitely or probably complain if they were really annoyed with a police officer. Previous negative experiences of police would adversely affect a person's willingness to complain. Interestingly a third of respondents believed that complaining would not make a difference, a third thought that they would not be taken seriously, and a third did not know how to make a complaint. White people said that they would be willing to make a complaint at a police station, but there was a significant difference between these and people from black and Asian backgrounds who said that they would be more likely to complain to another body such as a Race Equality Council or to a solicitor or legal advice centre. Overall the survey found that the majority of people would be willing to complain, and that they believed the system to be independent of the police, but that significant numbers of people from minority ethnic groups were sceptical about the system and would not be inclined to use it. The report acknowledged that there was no room for complacency in making sure that people of all groups and backgrounds have confidence in the complaints system.

4.8.3 IPCC and diversity

We have seen in the above sub-section that the diversity of society becomes a theme in the confidence of people in the police complaints system. The ability to complain about treatment by the police is one of the 'pillars' of police accountability (IPCC 2006: vii). Whilst reasonable levels of confidence are reported for the majority white population, it is important that all groups enjoy the same levels of confidence in that they are willing to make a complaint, know how to do it, and can be sure that they will be treated seriously when they do complain. The IPCC has taken a number of steps to ensure that it is adequately responding to the needs of a diverse society. This has included efforts to raise awareness of the IPCC and its work by communicating in a number of formats, the publication of a race equality scheme, and more recently in response to concerns from the Muslim community to ensure that all complaints arising out of arrests under the prevention of terrorism legislation are referred to the IPCC for them to determine the level of scrutiny required to ensure that people feel they are being dealt with fairly and justly.

Key website for further research

<http://www.ipcc.gov.uk>

4.9 The Commission for Equality and Human Rights

The Commission for Racial Equality, the Equal Opportunities Commission, and the Disability Rights Commission, all have responsibility for equality and fairness in their own particular area of interest. In a White Paper published in May 2004, the Government proposed the setting up of a new single body to replace these. The main motivation for this seems to be that fairness and equality is not a minority concern and that separate bodies which oversee the rights of certain groups are actually exclusive rather than inclusive of all in society. In a written statement to the House of Commons on 30 October 2003, the Secretary of State for Trade and Industry, Patricia Hewitt, outlined the key priorities for the new Commission which will be called the Commission for Equality and Human Rights.

- Promoting equality and diversity in the round, fostering understanding of their importance in underpinning a prosperous and cohesive society; promoting a culture of respect for human rights and acceptance of the responsibilities that go with them.
- Giving full attention to the specific needs of individual groups who receive legislative protection against discrimination, ensuring the availability of relevant skills and expertise.
- Improving support for individuals through better and more accessible provision of services, particularly advice and information.
- Working in partnership with business and public sector organisations, meeting the requirement expressed strongly by business and others for a single, accessible source of advice and guidance covering the breadth of legislative obligations as well as advice and support on good practice.
- Mainstreaming equality and human rights in the public sector and public service delivery. Key tools will be the promotion and enforcement of the Race Relations Amendment Act statutory duty on public bodies to promote equality of opportunity, the planned disability duty, awareness of the duties under the Human Rights Act and working to encourage good practice in equality and human rights generally.
- Developing partnerships with a range of bodies at regional and local level, including statutory, voluntary and business organisations, to deliver local, accessible information and advice to individuals, public sector bodies and businesses.
- Bringing a strategic, modern approach to enforcement of equality legislation supported by up to date enforcement tools.
- Promoting community cohesion through providing support to local initiatives to promote dialogue and understanding between different communities and groups, where relevant drawing upon the balance between rights and responsibilities contained in the Human Rights Act.

I have quoted these priorities in full because they illustrate the scope of the new Commission and give an indication of some of the problems that have been evident with three separate bodies. We have already noted the importance of the need to be inclusive in thinking about diversity and fairness which should be for all and not just specific groups. Elsewhere we have noted also that responding to diversity is complex and the existence of three bodies has served to increase that complexity. People and organizations do not have a single point of reference when they are trying to develop their strategy, policy, and practice in relation to diversity and it is argued that a single Commission will go a long way to solving this. Clearly there will be a concern that the needs of specific groups could easily be lost with a single Commission taking a broader view, but this concern has been taken account of in the White Paper proposals. The formation of an Equality and Human Rights Commission is a significant development in the response to diversity and will undoubtedly have a considerable impact on the diversity agenda and the police response to it.

Key website for further research

<http://www.dti.gov.uk>

4.10 **Chapter Summary**

In this chapter we have taken a brief tour of some of the issues that may be regarded as diversity developments in the last few years and some of the reports that have influenced them.

- Our point of departure was to consider the idea of 'diversities in policing'. There is now a large extended family of people involved in policing and that is not restricted to the work of police services themselves. The very idea of what policing is needs to be thought of in broad terms. One of the benefits of such arrangements for policing is that a far greater number of people involved will inevitably result in a greater representation of society in the policing function.
- We noted that there are, in the police, a number of associations of people from different backgrounds and lifestyles who have formed together to offer mutual support, education, training, and involvement in the development of police policy. We considered the way in which the National Black Police Association, the British Association of Women in Policing, and the Gay Police Association have provided examples of the benefits not only to their members, but also to the betterment of the delivery of the policing service.
- The Scarman Report was highly influential in its day in raising awareness and making recommendations in relation to police community relations. Arrangements for lay visitors to police stations and statutory consultation with communities are both legacies of the Scarman Report. Having said that, some commentators have noted that had Scarman been fully implemented and acted upon then there may not have been a need for a Stephen Lawrence Inquiry at all and policing would have matured to the extent that its own house had been put in order. This turned out not to be the case.
- The Stephen Lawrence Inquiry Report was published in 1999 and contained seventy recommendations for improvements in policy and practice. The report was highly critical of individual incompetence and management failings and identified institutional racism as being at the core of the problems that interfered with a successful and sensitive investigation of the murder of Stephen Lawrence in 1993. We noted some of the findings of the report, in particular the failure of the investigation and the impact of racist stereotyping. In the years that have followed

the publication of the inquiry report, it is possible to chart considerable action in response to the need to increase trust and confidence among minority ethnic groups. The actual progress against that action is more difficult to assess and the evidence from reports that assess aspects of that progress is in places quite patchy.

- This led us briefly to consider a Home Office Study of the impact of the Stephen Lawrence Inquiry that was published in October 2005. This was a major piece of research work which sought to establish what progress had been made since Macpherson published in 1999. The report noted that there had been 'significant' improvements in a number of areas but in most cases these improvements needed to be qualified. For example, although the report found that racist language had been almost 'excised' from the police service there was no corresponding reduction in sexist or homophobic language. This could well demonstrate that such change in behaviour is not driven by a deep change in attitudes towards respect and fairness but by the fact that such language is high on the agenda together with the fear of discipline.

- Her Majesty's Inspectorate of Constabulary thematic inspections have made a considerable contribution to the development of thinking about diversity both in the police service and its response to it. A series of three inspections spanning 1996 to 2000 have all rehearsed similar themes in regard to police community relations and the way the service is responding to the diversity agenda. Leadership, commitment, training, and most importantly making sure that diversity is not seen as an added extra but is fundamental to policing were consistently addressed in the reports.

- The Morris Report and the Commission for Racial Equality's formal investigation into the police service in England and Wales were noted as being good illustrations of the public scrutiny under which the police service now operates. Although coming from different angles both noted that progress has been made but that there is still more to do. By way of illustration, a common theme to emerge was the still inadequate way that behaviour and complaints are managed in the service. Many managers still lack the confidence to deal with such issues effectively.

- The new Independent Police Complaints Commission was a further development we discussed in this chapter. We noted that the ability to complain about the police is one of the pillars of police accountability and that for this to be effective, people must have trust and confidence in the system, so that they will be willing and able to make a complaint and that they know the complaint will be taken seriously. Recent research by the IPCC suggests that there is still work to do to achieve this particularly in respect of minority groups in society.

- The proposed Commission for Equality and Human Rights was the last development mentioned. The Government has proposed in a White

Paper that a new Commission for Equality and Human Rights be set up to replace the existing arrangements. This, it is argued, will be a much more inclusive approach given that all citizens have the right to be treated equally and fairly. A concern that has been expressed about this proposal is that with a more generic body, the interests of some groups may not be properly represented.

Diversity and the Idea of Community

5.1 **Chapter Outline**

We hear a great deal about the idea of community and notions of community policing. In this chapter we explore some of these ideas and examine their implications for policing a diverse society. The ground we will cover includes:

- The idea of community, and how we might define it including the different perspectives on community that exist;
- Ideas of 'Britishness' and how the debate about multiculturalism has developed over recent years;
- An examination of what is meant by community policing;
- An exploration of ideas about community engagement, community cohesion, and community consultation and how these impact in policing;
- An overview of the role of Community Support Officers.

The chapter will conclude with a summary of the key points made and a brief discussion of the implications of the idea of community for policing a diverse society.

5.2 **What Does 'Community' Mean?**

Community is a word that is used by many people in many different ways. According to Smith (2001), it was not until 1915 that the first clear definition of community emerged and that related to a delineation of rural communities in terms of the trade and services that were based in villages. Our point of departure for this section, however, is to consider what the term means to you the reader.

EXERCISE

Write a definition of 'community'.

- What does the word mean to you?

It might be useful to compare your own definition with some of the definitions that can be found in literature. Bullock and Trombley (1999: 144) go as far as to say that the term is 'abused and ill-defined'. The term community, it is argued, refers to individuals who are 'bound together by a shared local environment rather than conscious interests or by links defined by a single characteristic such as class or ethnicity'. One way of seeing community is that it is a source of identity beyond family or close personal life but that the obligations and rewards of that community identity are more subtle than those that would for example be connected with national identity. We rarely for example, refer to the British community—the term is more sensitive than that. More properly, British society can be seen to be made up of a range of disparate communities. Johnston

(2000: 54) for example, argues that the 'singularity of community has given way to the plurality of communities'. These include:

- Moral communities (religious, ecological, gendered);
- Lifestyle communities (of taste and fashion);
- Communities of commitment (to personal and non-personal issues);
- Contractual communities (composed of subscribing consumers);
- Virtual communities (joined together in cyberspace).

Such communities, he argues, 'far from being homogenous are diverse, overlapping, pragmatic, temporary and frequently divided from one another'. The disparate nature of communities that can be identified has huge implications for the idea of community policing because very often there is an assumption that it is a singular approach. The question remains as to whether, given the range of communities a 'one size fits all' style of community policing will meet the needs of a range of communities.

It does seem therefore to be very important that we develop a clear idea about what community means. This becomes increasingly important in the police context given that so much is said about community based policing. If there is no clear idea about what it is, then the probability is that strategy and policy that is designed to meet the needs of the community will fall short of the mark.

A more usual and perhaps more helpful way of delineating communities is by reference to such factors as identity, purpose, belief, and geography. We will take a brief look at each of these in turn.

5.2.1 **Communities of identity**

This is perhaps the most common and strongest sense in which the idea of community is used. It refers to people who identify themselves as part of a group who share an important aspect of who they are as individuals, in other words people are able to identify with each other on the basis of some shared sense of identity. There are many examples of communities of identity.

EXERCISE

Make a list of all the 'communities of identity' that you can think of.

You will, I hope, have been able to identify many 'communities of identity'. You may have included for example, gay and lesbian men and women, the Asian community, the black community, single parents, or communities of people who identify themselves on the basis of their religion or faith. You may even have included police officers as a community of identity. Cohen (1985) argues that the idea of community of identity has two perspectives; the first is to delineate what a group has in common and the second is to identify what makes that group different from members of other possible groupings. So community of identity is not only about similarity it is also about difference. One criticism that is sometimes levelled against the very idea of diversity is that it too frequently identifies differences between people and pays too little attention to what binds then together. We will revisit this idea in the section on Britishness and multiculturalism below.

5.2.2 Communities of purpose

Where disparate groups of people have, or come together for a common purpose, they may be regarded as communities of purpose. Drawing on an example from university life we may refer to the 'scientific community' or the 'research community'. These represent large numbers of people who are bound not by factors such as class, gender, or ethnicity but by what they do in their professional life. Very often communities of purpose will be knowledge and practice based so that the development of knowledge and practice will depend on members of that community sharing with each other.

So-called learning communities provide another example of communities of purpose. Here the common ground for people is a shared commitment to learning. In developing the community its members will support each other, share information, and engage in debate. Such communities may be real or virtual. Increasingly, with the development of flexible learning pathways, virtual learning communities are emerging, making use of the facilities provided by information and communication technology (ICT). Again such a community will not have the features more typically associated with the idea of community, but will experience the cohesion brought about by their common purpose. So what has all this to do with the idea of community as it relates to policing a diverse society?

Firstly, it means that we need to broaden our concept of what community means and what the possibility of community offers. For example, with the increasing use of ICT, there is no reason why there could not be engagement with a virtual community of purpose, where for example the purpose was to improve policing in a particular area. Many people might, for example, feel more comfortable with engaging in discussion or putting forward their views in an environment that provided a non-threatening third party channel for them.

5.2.3 Geographic communities

It has been said that London is a collection of villages and that those villages have a geographic identity of their own. The sense of identity for some locations is often very variable in strength. For example many people will be proud of their identity as an 'East Ender', and they will want to take on and be identified with the various cultural artefacts that represent what it means to be from the East End. My own experience of living for many years in a geographic community in North West London was very different. There was almost no sense in which people specifically identified with the geographic location and very little sense of what might be called 'community spirit'. In fact, living in a road with over 200 houses, it was very common for people to have little or no knowledge of the people living in the immediate vicinity. Very often people would value 'keeping themselves to themselves' over all other aspects of possible community involvement. After thirty years of living in London, I moved to a very rural location in Wiltshire. Here my experience of geographic community has been very different. In a small village, people not only seem to know each other better but will make efforts to make people feel part of the local community. It is the geographic location that provides the sense of cohesion rather than many of the other factors outlined above. Far from wanting to keep themselves to themselves, people will want to be involved with each other. The village shop becomes the focus of the exchange of information, and it is actually quite difficult to be a private person. People will know your business and 'strangers' will be noticed in a way that is not possible in an urban environment. This does of course have some benefits in terms of crime prevention in that it becomes much easier to spot people who are in the village intent on criminal activity.

Lee and Newby writing as far back as 1983 noted that the mere fact that people live near to each other does not necessarily means that they will either have much to do with each other, or that they will necessarily feel part of a community. Rather it is the social networks that people develop that will give them community cohesion. These range from family and friends to work, church, mosque, synagogue, temple, and other focal points for a sense of inclusion and identity.

EXERCISE

Think about your own experience of geographic community.

- To what extent to you feel part of a 'local community'?
- What factors affect the extent to which you do or do not feel part of a local community?

5.3 **Britishness and the Debate About Multiculturalism**

There has been considerable debate in recent times about what it means to be British and this has been linked to a more generalized debate over the nature of multiculturalism and whether it is a good or bad thing for the future of a diverse society. There is a theoretical underpinning to the debate which relates to the topic that we need to briefly outline as it forms the backdrop to most discussion about the idea of Britishness and provides a way into thinking about multiculturalism. Three concepts are relevant: integration, assimilation, and separatism.

5.3.1 **Integration**

Integration is the term that most closely matches the idea of multiculturalism. It refers to the position where minority groups (usually minority ethnic groups) are integrated into the host society but are still able to maintain a unique identity. Thus cultural practices including for example modes of dress, religious and faith affiliations are able to thrive, but at the same time members of that community are able to enjoy equality and success in the host society.

5.3.2 **Assimilation**

Assimilation refers to the state of being where members of minority groups either choose to or are forced to assimilate into the host society. They would lose their unique cultural and religious identity and apart from obvious physical attributes such as colour become to all intents and purposes the same as members of the majority community.

5.3.3 **Separatism**

Separatism refers to the state of being where members of minority groups remain entirely separate and distinct from the majority group. All the cultural and religious artefacts associated with the minority group remain distinct. Ghettos would be a feature of separatism, as would education of children outside of the mainstream education system.

Clearly, there will be a considerable degree of overlap between these positions. For example, many groups would regard themselves as assimilated into British society but at the same time would retain some of their cultural uniqueness.

5.4 **Britishness and Multiculturalism**

There has been an ongoing debate about what 'Britishness' is and this to a large extent has been in the wider context of the idea of multiculturalism. It has relevance for our consideration of community and communities, because it goes to the heart of the way in which communities may be seen as part of or separate to the wider British national identity. In this section we will consider what Britishness means, the work of the Commission on the Future of Multi-ethnic Britain and the issues that have been raised in the debate about multiculturalism.

5.4.1 **Britishness**

In 2004, 141,000 people were granted citizenship of the UK. This represented a rise of 12 per cent on 2003. Responding to concern about the need for citizens to integrate into society more fully, the Government introduced in November 2005 a test for applicants for citizenship of the UK. The test quickly became characterized in the media as a test of 'Britishness'. Needless to say there was a great deal of discussion about the validity of such a test in terms of whether it really tested anything meaningful about what it means to be a citizen of the UK. Before we think about the types of things that are asked, do the exercise below and try to establish what Britishness means to you.

EXERCISE

Think about what 'Britishness' means to you.

• How would you define it?

It is likely that you have identified factors that might be broadly grouped such as values, culture, beliefs, traditions, institutions, and so on. The citizenship test on the other hand, asks questions such as:

• Where are Geordie, Cockney, and Scouse dialects spoken?
• What are MPs?
• Which of our four courts has a jury?
• What is the Church of England and who is its head?
• What phone numbers would you use in an emergency?

There is an issue as to whether this is a real test of what being a citizen of the UK is all about. In response to critical comment in the media the Home Office said it 'wanted to create a new, more meaningful way of becoming a citizen in an effort to help people integrate and share in British values and traditions'. Immigration minister Tony McNulty said: 'This is not a test of someone's ability to be British or a test of their Britishness'. (s BBC NEWS <http://news.bbc.co.uk/1/hi/uk_politics/4391710.stm> 1 November 2005).

There are a number of points that are pertinent to thinking about Britishness.

• The concept clearly means different things to different people and there is no single 'official' definition of what it means.
• A too stringent and restrictive conceptualization of Britishness might actually have the effect of excluding people rather than helping them become integrated.
• British society is in fact made up of a number of diverse identities all of which go together to make the richness and diversity that is modern Britain.
• The debate about Britishness illustrates the point that we have made elsewhere that very often diversity will focus on difference where in fact sometimes there is a need to focus on similarity. So in trying to determine what is 'British' we need to identify the factors that provide the social glue for difference, the things that actually bind people together and the things that make 141,000 people want to become citizens. These factors go far deeper than merely answering knowledge-based questions about accents or what telephone

numbers to use in an emergency. These deeper level factors are those that relate to commitment to liberal democracy, freedom of speech, human rights, a stake in economic success, freedom to practice religion, and a respect for the rule of law.

5.4.2 Identities in transition—the Parekh Report 2000

The Parekh Report (Runnymede Trust 2000) represented the output of the work of the Commission on the Future of Multi-Ethnic Britain. One section of the report directly addressed the issue of what it means to be British and forms a good point of departure for this discussion. The executive summary notes:

> All communities are changing and all are complex, with internal diversity and disagreements, linked to differences of gender, generation, religion and language and to different stances in relation to wider society ... no one community is or can be insulated from all others. Increasingly people have the capacity to manoeuvre between distinct areas of life and to be 'cross cultural navigators'. (Runnymede Trust 2000: xv)

The report goes on to ask and seeks to answer the question 'in this context does "Britishness" have a future?'

The Parekh Report argues that community and cultural identity are best seen as 'identities in transition'. This phrase refers to the way in which cultural and community identity is rarely fixed and is in fact a dynamic process. The rapid and continuing changes in all sorts of areas mean that communities adapt and respond. Whilst painting a fairly hopeful picture of the prospects for how communities in Britain have the potential for living together in harmony, the report notes a number of significant barriers that get in the way of such an aspiration such as:

- Britain continues to be disfigured by racism;
- Continuing phobias about cultural difference;
- Sustained cultural, economic, and social disadvantage;
- Institutional discrimination;
- A systematic failure of social justice;
- A failure of respect for difference. (Parekh 2000: 36)

The report provides evidence for the assertion in the bullet points above, but it is the last point that is of particular interest for our thinking about community. The thrust of the argument is that whilst cultural identities may be considered to be in transition, that is they are constantly changing and dynamic, assimilation is not the answer. People cannot be expected to give up their identity in order to belong. Racism and discrimination has continued, and assimilation has come to be seen, as 'an impossible price to pay—Black and Asianess are non-tradable. Cultural difference has come to matter more' (p 37). The way forward, it is argued, is not to see Britishness as a monoculture, but to see it as an identity that has the scope to include but not assimilate a wide variety of other cultural identities. But Parekh sees a so far insuperable barrier to this: 'Britishness . . . has systematic, largely unspoken racial connotations. Whiteness nowhere features as an exclusive condition of being British, but it is widely understood that . . . Britishness is racially coded' (p 38).

EXERCISE

- How do you react to the assertion that Britishness is 'racially coded'?

The argument is that whilst racism, oppression, and racial disadvantage is embedded in society together with opposition to cultural diversity, the idea of Britishness will always be flawed.

The debate about Britishness is complex, but in a speech made at the Manchester Council for Community Relations on 22 September 2005, Trevor Phillips, the chair of the Commission for Racial Equality, outlined his views of Britishness and set out three elements of what it means to be British that might be regarded as the glue which binds the arguments about Britishness together.

> First and foremost, our shared values: for example an attachment to democracy, freedom of speech, and equality, values which anyone who expects to live in Britain must respect and abide by, both notionally and in practice.
>
> Second, we share common traditions which, whatever we do at home, we all agree to respect and observe in our everyday encounters. Central to these I would say are our common language, our good manners, our care for children.
>
> Thirdly, we maintain diverse, individualistic, even eccentric lifestyles in our private lives. No-one tells us how to speak, how to dress, what we should eat or how we should worship. These are all individual choices, to be respected as long as they do not interfere with our fundamental values, or our long-cherished traditions. And unlike some other countries, we tend to embrace new additions to our lifestyle choices—whether it is new music, or new kinds of clothes. (Phillips 2005).

So simply put Britishness is about values, traditions, and freedom of choice. This leads us to move on to think about the notion of multiculturalism.

5.4.3 The debate about multiculturalism

Multiculturalism is a word that often features in discussions about diversity, but what does it mean, and is it even a helpful concept? At one level the word refers to the type of society that is multifaceted in its cultural make up. It is the opposite of monoculturalism. But is it a useful expression of how society should be? A number of commentators have challenged the idea on the basis that it no longer adequately expresses the realities that confront Britain in the twenty-first century. A notable contributor to the debate about multiculturalism has been

Trevor Phillips, the chair of the Commission for Racial Equality. In the speech referred to above (Phillips 2005), Phillips sets out his stall in relation to the idea of multiculturalism:

> ... there has to be a balance struck between an 'anything goes' multicultural-ism on the one hand, which leads to deeper division and inequality; and on the other, an intolerant, repressive uniformity. We need a kind of integration that binds us together without stifling us. We need to be a nation of many colours that combine to create a single rainbow.

Phillips is quite clear that assimilation is not the answer. But he goes on to say that one of the problems with multiculturalism is that there has been an over-emphasis on the 'multi' and insufficient focus on the common culture and the things that bind British society together (for example the values, traditions, and freedom of choice referred to above). 'Anything goes multiculturalism', it could be argued, springs from a far too simplistic understanding of what diversity is about. When we were discussing diversity in Chapter 1 we noted that a con-ception of diversity which simply refers to the differences between people is inappropriate because it does not recognize sensible or rational delimiters. For example it does not recognize differences delimited by law, neither does it recog-nize delimiters of cultural practice which may be at worst outside the law, and at best outside of British values and traditions. Phillips gives examples of these differences which are unhelpful in an understanding of multiculturalism and which have:

> allowed tolerance of diversity to harden into effective isolation of communit-ies in which some people think that separate values ought to apply. For example:
>
> - Evangelical African churches that see it as acceptable to traumatise a child, claiming they are ridding her of evil spirits.
> - Sikh activists who think that their feelings of offence caused by a play are more important than the principle of freedom of expression.
> - The almost casual acceptance that the majority of children in the African Caribbean community grow up without a father-figure, in spite of all the evidence that this causes immense damage both to them and to the com-munity as a whole.
> - And white communities so fixated by the belief that their every ill is caused by their Asian neighbours that they withdraw their children wholesale from local schools, and allow their children to make a sport of persecuting every local family that is not white.

These examples which Phillips puts forward are challenging and debatable, but nevertheless make the point strongly. For a further discussion of similar hard issues see Chapter 7.

5.5 **Community Policing**

5.5.1 **Community policing defined**

A useful definition of community policing is given by Wright (2002: 143) who says:

> community policing seems best understood as a range of specific techniques that the police and public use to work in partnership at a local level. Used in this sense, community policing is a micro-level concept. It is a concrete effort to promote community justice and social control by mobilising social resources within an identifiable group of people.

Implicit in a definition such as this is the idea that policing is not merely a function that is imposed on the fabric of society from outside, but is something that needs to be integrated into society and which harnesses the cooperation of members of that society. Where policing styles and approaches sit outside of the structures that make up the social fabric of society, they are far more likely to be characterized by instrumental social control and will tend to be reactive. An example of this, as we have seen elsewhere, was the way in which police reacted to the concerns about robbery in 1981 with an operation 'Swamp 1981'. Police became viewed as not a force working in collaboration with members of the local society but were characterized more as an occupying army. When Lord Scarman reported on the riots that ensued from this operation, he quite rightly focused on the fact that trust and cooperation had broken down and recommended that the police make attempts to re-engage with local communities to listen to their concerns and priorities.

5.5.2 **Elements of community policing**

Alderson (1998: 132) gave evidence to the Scarman Inquiry and in doing so outlined three elements that a notion of community policing should include:

- Community police consultative committees;
- Inter-agency cooperation and;
- Community police constables appointed to localities.

Bearing in mind that Alderson was writing in 1998, in the period before the Macpherson Inquiry, these elements of community policing he argued would make for a situation where there would be cooperative action for the prevention of crime and perhaps more importantly, the creation and reinforcement of trust in neighbourhoods. The three principles underlying community policing that Alderson suggests are, however, still very relevant namely the need for consultation (an issue that we will deal with in more detail below), the need to recognize that policing is not merely an activity done in isolation but one that needs to be done in cooperation with other agencies, and the need for police to be connected with and working in local communities. All of these themes have been picked up in subsequent thinking about community policing, for example the Stephen Lawrence Inquiry Report, the Crime and Disorder Act, and the Government's introduction of neighbourhood policing.

Johnston (2000: 47) notes that a way of seeing community policing is to describe it as 'maximal-proactive policing'. There has been increasing focus on community and problem oriented policing (POP) and the way that they have become increasingly influential as models of policing in the UK. There is an underlying assumption in community policing that conventional approaches are too reactive and that they fail to tackle the roots of crime and disorder to which officers are frequently deployed. Simply reacting to crime may in part 'keep the lid' on crime and disorder but will do little to contribute to the understanding of crime and crime patterns, is not necessarily intelligence driven and above all does not pay sufficient attention to the needs and concerns of local communities. Bennett (1994) identified a number of common themes or elements that might be considered as characterizing community policing such as:

- Community constables
- Community liaison officers
- Schools liaison schemes
- Youth programmes
- Police consultative committees
- Local crime prevention initiatives
- Neighbourhood watch schemes
- Decentralized command structures
- Commitment to foot patrol
- Police–public partnership arrangements
- An emphasis on non-crime problem solving.

REFLECT ON PRACTICE

Consider the list of elements of community policing above.

- Is the list comprehensive or do you have experience of community policing that falls outside these elements?
- How effective are the elements in achieving effective policing?
- How do the elements of community policing relate to the idea of policing a diverse society?
- Why is the idea of community policing not popular with some police officers?

5.5.3 Criticisms of community policing

The idea of community policing has not been without criticism. These are outlined below.

Firstly, Johnston (2000) notes that some radical writers fear that maximal proactive policing may have an invasive impact on local communities and see the emergence of a local 'police state'. Community policing, it is argued, can be viewed as a velvet glove surrounding the iron first of police power. Whilst this does represent a fairly extreme view, the actual practice of policing does give some support for the view. An example of this would be that in many police forces, community based officers may one day be undertaking their routine community based policing, and on the next they may be required for aid to police say a major demonstration where they could easily be deployed in full protective equipment and engaged in the policing of public disorder. In such situations the officers may experience confusion about their role, and find it quite difficult to return to a community based scenario in the aftermath of the public order/disorder situation. In whatever police force or service in the UK, where there is a community based approach to policing there will always be the underlying capability to move almost instantly to a coercive and reactive policing style. So it could be argued, albeit cynically, that the velvet glove of community policing actually masks the iron fist of police power.

Secondly, there is the issue surrounding whether community policing actually works. So far there has been an underlying assumption in what we have been saying about community policing that it is a good thing both for policing and for the public, but does it actually deliver what its proponents say it does? Reiner (1992) reviews the proliferation of community based policing initiatives in the USA and whilst it is acknowledge that some have been successful, the outcomes of others are far from certain. He notes (1992: 154) that the outcomes of similar schemes in the UK have been similarly patchy. Many in-house evaluations of community policing have been positive but those that have been conducted independently have led to the conclusion that 'nothing works'. Two of the chief difficulties have been the failure of the actual programme in terms of its implementation and the difficulty in linking such metrics as recorded crime or victimization rates to a particular policing initiative.

Thirdly, there are a number of other factors that may be seen as barriers to successful community policing:

- *Rank and file resistance to community policing programmes.* My own experience of policing tends to validate this point as a barrier to community policing. Resistance to engaging in community policing to a large extent depends on the perceptions that an individual has about what constitutes exciting work. If an officer's image of a police officer is one who engages in exciting, fast moving, even dangerous work then the idea of being a community officer is unlikely to appeal. A sense of mission, action cynicism, and pessimism (Reiner 1992) has been identified as characteristics of cop culture.
- *Management shortcomings.* Community policing is much more about the long game than about the achievement of short-term outcomes. On the one hand managers in the police are as susceptible to the aspects of cop culture and resistance noted above as anyone else. On the other hand community and neighbourhood policing initiatives may not deliver results in the short-term

105

that managers feel under pressure to deliver. The lack of visibility of success (or at least quick success) may be a strong motivator not to engage fully with community policing and put the resources into it that it needs.

- *Problems in establishing partnerships with communities.* We have already seen in this chapter that the idea of community is far from straightforward. Simply identifying the communities that make up a particular locality will be an ever-changing target. In addition there is the notion of 'hard to reach' groups—those that are either hard to identify or those that are resistant to dialogue with the police. Communities will be very variable in their willingness to engage in dialogue with police. This can be for a number of reasons. It may be that the experience of a particular community of the way it has been policed has been particularly negative. Trust and willingness to engage may take months and years to develop and can easily be broken down by negative experiences very often arising out of insensitive reactive policing. There is also the question of the extent to which community consultation can be effective; this will be dealt with in the section below.
- *Problems in working in partnership with other agencies.* There have been numerous imperatives for the police to work in partnership with other agencies and as we have seen this may be regarded as one of the key features of a community based approach to policing. The effectiveness of agencies working together can however be variable for a number of reasons. For example the commitment to inter-agency working can be patchy, there may be professional rivalries and jealousies, indeed the aims of the different agencies may be quite different and may reveal fractures in the process.

REFLECT ON PRACTICE

To what extent do you think the factors that may be barriers to community policing shown above are valid in your own experience?

5.6 Community Cohesion, Engagement, and Consultation

There are three further concepts that you will come across as you think and read about the idea of community, namely cohesion, engagement, and consultation. We will deal briefly with each of them in turn.

5.6.1 Community cohesion

Community cohesion is a term that has gained a lot of currency, particularly in government circles over recent years. It has strong links with the associated concepts of social inclusion and exclusion. In 2001, Britain saw a number of disturbances that resulted in the destruction of property and attacks on the police. These took place, amongst others, in the towns of Oldham and Burnley, and large numbers of people from a wide variety of cultural backgrounds were involved. The Home Secretary set up an inquiry team to try to establish the causes of the disturbances and to establish what action might be needed to bring about social cohesion amongst the communities involved. The report (Home Office 2002) of the inquiry team raised a number of issues, and importantly for our purposes here, discussed the notion of community cohesion. As with many concepts drawn from social inquiry there is not a universally agreed definition.

The Home Office Report draws on Forest and Kearns (2000) and identifies community cohesion as being made up of a series of domains. These domains are laid out in Table 5.1 below together with a description of what the domain refers to:

Table 5.1 The Domains of Social and Community Cohesion

Domain	Description
Common values and a civic culture	• Common aims and objectives • Common moral principles and codes of behaviour • Support for political institutions and participation in politics
Social order and social control	• Absence of general conflict and threats to the existing order • Absence of incivility • Effective informal social control • Tolerance, respect for differences, inter-group cooperation
Social solidarity and reductions in wealth disparities	• Harmonious economic and social development and common standards • Redistribution of public finances and opportunities • Equal access to social and welfare benefits • Ready acknowledgement of social obligations and willingness to assist others
Social networks and social capital	• High degree of social interaction within communities and families • Civic engagements and associational activity • Easy resolution of collective action problems
Place attachment and identity	• Strong attachment to place • Intertwining of personal and place identity

Source: Forest and Kearns in Home Office (2000)

We have already identified that there is no singularity about the idea of community. Implicit in the idea of community cohesion are the two related concepts of intra-community cohesion—that is the cohesion within a community, and inter-community cohesion, namely the way one community interacts with another. We saw in the section above how the idea of multiculturalism can in fact lead to segregation, and in these circumstances the idea of inter-community cohesion becomes all the more important.

5.6.2 Community engagement

Community engagement has a different focus to community consultation (which we will deal with under the next heading) although it is true to say that engagement by its very nature will include an element of consultation. Engaging with communities is about:

- Communication—making sure that channels of communication between police and the communities they serve are open.
- Consultation—which means that communities must not only have a say in how they are policed, but also that there is a demonstrable effect of that consultation.
- Participation—where members of a community have a direct involvement in the delivery of criminal justice (examples would be lay visitors, lay magistrates, membership of police authorities, and so on).
- Governance—where local people have a voice in the governance of policing (such as in lay advisory panels).

Chanan (2005) offers three definitions of community engagement:

> Joint working between agencies and the public to reduce crime and improve community safety ... people and community organisations working together with the police, local authorities and others to achieve a common goal.
>
> Community influence over the actions of agencies ... and holding them to account.
>
> Understanding of public/community needs ... to enable an organisation to interact with and understand community needs and reflect these in the delivery of services.

EXERCISE

Study each of the definitions given by Chanan above and try to draw out:

- The general principles of effective community engagement.
- Some of the issues that may need to be resolved for effective community engagement.

In terms of the principles that are revealed in the definitions there we find:

- Jointly working on problems (police, agencies, and the public);
- The achievement of common goals;
- Engagement as a mechanism for accountability;

- A joint understanding of the needs of communities;
- The reflection of a recognition of these needs in the delivery of policing services.

The issues that might need to be addressed for this to be effective however seem to lie in a number of assumptions:

- Assumptions about the notion of community and whether there is cohesiveness;
- Assumptions about the willingness of communities to become engaged;
- An assumption that the priorities for policing will be the same across different communities;
- An assumption that agencies will be willing to work effectively together and that the police themselves are willing to give over some of their power in deference to what communities say they want;
- Finally and perhaps most importantly, an assumption that the necessary communication channels are open to make all this happen.

In the foreword to the National Community Safety Plan (Home Office 2005b: 2), the Minister for Police, Hazel Blears, summed up the importance of community engagement for community safety:

> If we are to make our communities still safer, everyone—from the heart of national government, through regional and local partners, right through to neighbourhoods and the people who live in them—must play their part. We need to create a new relationship between public services and the communities they serve which will encourage accountability, trust, cooperation, and a mutual respect. And we need to work together to tackle extremism and racism in all its forms.

The White Paper 'Building Communities, Beating Crime: A Better Police Service for the 21st Century' (Home Office 2004a: 68) outlines what effective engagement with the community might look like for the police.

A police service which is engaging effectively with the community will:

- Have a detailed, neighbourhood level understanding of the demographics of the community it serves;
- Have a detailed—and regularly updated—picture of the interests, needs, priorities and preferences of every section of that community;
- Establish and facilitate an ongoing and consistent dialogue with all sections of the community by regularly discussing and sharing information about policing and community safety issues, and listening to and acting on feedback from the community;
- Understand how, and the extent to which, different sections of the community feel most comfortable in interacting with the police, and take this into account in tailoring their engagement strategies;

- Use a range of different, locally adapted means and strategies to facilitate ongoing dialogue and partnership working with all sections of the community;
- Allow its priorities and service delivery strategies to be influenced, changed and, where appropriate, driven by community concerns and priorities;
- Provide ongoing feedback to the community about how their input has impacted on local policing;
- Identify and maximize opportunities to deliver policing services in partnership with the community, both groups and individuals; and
- Understand that effective engagement with the community is core to the successful delivery of all police business, and not a 'bolt-on' or a specialism.

5.6.3 Community consultation

As we have seen above, community consultation is a core element of community engagement. There are a number of legislative requirements in relation to consultation that have been covered in Chapter 3. In this section we will explore some of the more general issues surrounding the idea of community consultation.

Elliott and Nicholls (1996) identify what may be regarded as seven aims of community consultation. Although there have been other imperatives to consult since this work was published the aims remain broadly the same. These are listed in Table 5.2 below which shows the three main stakeholders in consultation and how the aims relate to each of the stakeholders.

The HMIC Report 'Winning the Race: Embracing Diversity' (HMIC 2001) devotes a whole chapter to the idea of consulting with the community. Drawing on the Cabinet Office guidance on consultation, the report (p 23) notes the general benefits of consultation as:

- Helping plan services better to give users what they want and expect;
- Helping to prioritize your services and make better use of limited resources;
- Helping set performance standards relevant to the users' needs (and monitor them);
- Fosters a working relationship between your users and you, so they understand the problems facing you, and how they can help;
- Alerts you to problems quickly so you have a chance to put things right before they escalate;
- Symbolizes your commitment to be open and accountable;
- Puts service first.

REFLECT ON PRACTICE

- In your experience is the list of benefits of consultation cited by the HMIC complete?
- Would you add any to the list?

Table 5.2 The Aims of Community Consultation

	Authority aims	Police force aims	Public aims
1. Reaching a broad and representative sample of the population	✓	✓	
2. Identifying public priorities to influence annual policing plans		✓	
3. Identifying public priorities for immediate action and/or divisional plans		✓	
4. Providing the public with information on policing	✓	✓	
5. Developing partnerships with the public	✓	✓	
6. Obtaining rapid police action on public concerns			✓
7. Obtaining information from the police			✓

In terms of performance on community consultation processes, the HMIC found in 2000 that of the forty-three forces in England and Wales eleven were exhibiting good practice, twenty-eight were progressing satisfactorily, and four forces had scope for improvement. There can be little doubt that community consultation, although crucial to the success of involving communities and enhancing the quality of police service delivery, is by no means a straightforward process. Policing in a liberal democracy must harness the cooperation and collaboration of the people if it is to be effective. The success of policing by consent of the people will largely be determined by the success of the police and associated agencies in their consultation with the people to whom they deliver the service.

5.7 Police Community Support Officers

Community Support Officers (CSOs) were introduced to the police family as a result of the Police Reform Act 2002. By June 2005, there were 5,862 CSOs working in 43 police forces (Home Office 2005c). In 2004, the Government published a White Paper 'Building Communities, Beating Crime' which set out its proposals for a neighbourhood policing fund which amongst others things aims to provide 25,000 CSOs by 2008.

CSOs typically work as members of neighbourhood policing teams and complement the work of police officers. The primary role of CSOs is set out in the evaluation report.

> CSOs are police-authority employed staff who perform a high visibility, patrolling role intended to provide reassurance to their local communities and address specific local issues. CSOs typically work as part of neighbourhood policing teams. They complement the work of police officers by focusing predominantly on lower level crime, disorder and anti-social behaviour (ASB). CSOs also have a key role to play in freeing up police officer time—for example by undertaking some tasks which require police presence but not necessarily the skills and expertise of a fully sworn police officer. (Home Office 2004b: 1)

Over the years there have been consistent calls for 'more bobbies on the beat' and such calls have been features of numerous political party conferences. In fact the evidence for the effectiveness of visible patrol in terms of crime reduction is very mixed and it is by no means certain that increasing the amount of patrol does in fact reduce crime. That said, there does seem to be consistent evidence that visible patrol has an important part to play in terms of public reassurance. The evidence from the interim evaluation report seems to suggest that CSOs are in fact able to provide a consistent visible presence on the streets with over 70 per cent of their time being spent away from the police stations and with little time being spent on reactive policing.

The Home Office published emerging findings of the evaluation of the impact of CSOs in October 2005 in advance of the full evaluation report. The headline findings are given below.

- CSOs are providing a much-wanted service and they are valued by the police, the public and businesses for their visibility and their accessibility.
- CSOs have been used to tackle low level crime and anti social behaviour (ASB).
- The powers most often applied by CSOs are those requiring name and address of those behaving in an anti social manner and confiscating alcohol from under 18s.
- They spend much of their time dealing with youth disorder and alcohol related issues and this is appreciated by the local community.
- CSOs have succeeded in becoming a regular presence in the community and they have built relationships with members of the local community.
- CSOs are seen as more accessible than police officers by some members of the public who are reporting issues, including instances of ASB, and intelligence to them that they would not necessarily 'trouble' a police officer about.

- Some forces are using CSOs in specialist roles e.g. in schools or on transport.
- The diversity of CSOs, particularly in terms of ethnicity and age has been one of the successes of the implementation of this new role. (Home Office 2005d: 1)

REFLECT ON PRACTICE

- To what extent do the emerging findings from the evaluation study match your own experience of working with CSOs?

One key feature of the findings is that mentioned in the final bullet point above, and relates to the diversity in terms of gender and ethnicity represented in the numbers of CSOs. Drawing on the interim report again these figures can be seen clearly in Table 5.3 below.

Table 5.3 CSO and Police Officer Ethnicity and Gender

	All staff (fte)	Minority ethnic strength (% of total)	Female strength (% of total)
CSO strength as at 31 March 2004	3,418	17.0	39.0
Police standard direct recruits (March 03–March 04)	11,297	7.4	32.7
Police officer strength as at 31 March 2004	140,563	3.3	20.0

Source: Home Office (2004)

These figures seem to show that the role of CSO is consistently attracting a greater proportion of people from minority ethnic backgrounds and women than that represented by police officers generally. Whilst these numbers are helpful in making the extended police family more representative of society at large, there remains a need to fully understand why this is the case. Is it for example that the role of CSO is particularly attractive to these people, or is it that there is something about mainstream policing function that is putting them off from applying?

5.8 Chapter Summary

In this chapter we have explored the idea of community and how that relates to policing a diverse society.

- In the opening section we noted that 'community' is not a particularly helpful term in that it is better to refer to the disparate types of communities that exist in British society. People in Britain are bound together by communities which can be characterized by a sense of morality, lifestyle, commitment to issues, faith, sexuality, and with the internet we can even speak of virtual communities. Another way of grouping communities is to see them in terms of identity, purpose, and geography.

- We considered what is meant by the term 'Britishness' and how this relates to the idea of multiculturalism. Integration, assimilation, and separatism were identified as ways in which people may engage to a greater or lesser extent in mainstream society. Britishness means different things to different people and we explored the idea of how identities within society can be seen to be in transition. We considered a speech made by the chair of the Commission for Racial Equality where he (Trevor Phillips) argued that what we share in terms of being British really boils down to shared values, common traditions, and freedom of choice to be who we are. Multiculturalism is not always a helpful concept, particularly where it implies an 'anything goes' approach to cultural difference.

- We explored the idea of community policing and noted its importance in a liberal democracy. Community policing, whilst an aspirational ideal, is not without criticism and we noted that some commentators regard it as a velvet glove masking an iron fist, and that others have questioned the basis on which it is claimed that community policing actually works.

- We briefly introduced the ideas of community cohesion, engagement, and consultation and the significance these have for policing a diverse society.

- The chapter concluded with a brief survey of a recent innovation in the addition of community support officers to the 'police family' and the role they have to play in extending the police service's engagement with communities.

Responding to Diversity—Strategy, Policy, and Leadership

6.1 **Chapter Outline**

In this chapter we will be exploring responses to diversity from three broad perspectives—strategy, policy, and leadership. The first two are of course bound together by the last in the sense that any strategy and policy is likely at best to be ineffective and at worst fail if it is not supported by the appropriate level of leadership. Under each of the broad headings we will review a number of the key themes that they contain.

- In terms of strategy we will be looking at the nature of organizational strategy and how it is developed. This will be followed by a brief discussion of some of the influencing factors in the development of strategy, namely the drivers for strategy formulation, globalization, and the political agenda. The section will conclude by considering why some strategies fail and we will try to draw out some lessons for policing diversity.
- Policy relating to diversity has primarily been on two fronts. Firstly, there has been policy in relation to the internal workings of the police, and secondly, there has been considerable policy development in relation to operational policing. In this section then we will look at what policy is and how it is developed and will draw on some recent examples by way of illustration. These examples will include policy in relation to racial incidents, and hate crime.
- The third perspective will be a consideration of critical importance of leadership in relation to diversity. This discussion will include an exploration of some of the theory in relation to leadership and will be linked to the need for leadership in relation to the response to diversity. We will look at the potential characteristics of leaders in diversity.

6.2 **Organizational Strategy**

6.2.1 **The nature of strategy and its development**

Our point of departure for this section is to give some consideration to some of the words that are used in relation to the development of the general direction of an organization. As we saw in our discussion of the business case for diversity, most of the literature on the subject has a clear focus on the business community and it is often necessary to adapt thinking to suit the needs of public service organizations such as the police. That said, the words do matter, and whilst they are often used interchangeably they do tend to have specific meanings all of which contribute to the way organizations develop and seek to achieve their purpose. Table 6.1 below outlines some suggestions as to what the words in this area mean and gives some examples of how it might look in practice.

Table 6.1 Terminology relating to organizational direction

Mission	This is a statement of the overall and enduring purpose of an organization. A mission statement will normally be very short and to the point will be easily remembered by people both within and outwith the organization and may reflect, albeit in simple terms, organizational values. It will often be singular in nature.
Example	'Working towards safer communities'
Goals (Sometimes termed strategic goals)	Unlike the mission, goals may be plural and will usually be expressed in terms that represent an end state. It is this end state that will be expressed, although goals are not usually associated with metrics that enable clear and direct measurement.
Example	'Our goal (towards the mission) is to increase public reassurance by increasing visible patrol'
Objectives	Objectives are much more specific than goals. They will be plural and will address a specific goal. A common way of expressing objectives is bound up in the acronym SMARTER, which expresses the need for objectives to be Specific, Measurable, Achievable, Relevant (to the goal) and Time-limited in some way. The ER refers to Evaluated and Reframed if necessary. This recognizes the need to check the objectives against actual achievement and change them if it becomes apparent that they cannot be achieved.
Example	'By the end of 2006–07 we will increase visible patrolling of the city centre area by 25%'
	'During 2006–07 we will examine and review all functions within force headquarters with a view to releasing further officers for patrol duty'
	'During 2006–07 we will recruit a further fifty Police Community Support Officers'
Strategy	The strategy of the organization will essentially represent the plans that have been put in place to achieve the goals and objectives of the organization. It will also include statements of the decisions that have been made by the organization and its stakeholders in relation to the achievement of its purpose.
Example	Strategies will often be quite substantial documents as for example in the police. It is common practice in large organizations, such as most police forces, to break strategy down into manageable chunks, for example there will often be a specific diversity strategy, crime reduction strategy and so on. What glues them together will be the achievement of the goals set to achieve the mission.

The development of good strategy will depend on a number of factors, but two of these are of particular interest to our discussion—analysis and creativity.

Analysis

Organizations, both private and public sector, need to pay great attention to the analysis of the context in which they work. Many sophisticated models of analysis are available to assist in this process, but typically they will cover the examination of factors such as the political environment and political imperatives, the economic context, and in public sector terms the money that is available to provide the service. This part of the analysis will very often lead to hard decisions having to be made about what can be achieved with finite resources. This becomes particularly acute in public services such as health and policing where the core business relates directly to the quality of life of citizens. The prevailing social conditions will need to be taken into account. This is why strategic goals, although typically set for up to five years, have to be changed from time to time in order to accurately reflect the prevailing social conditions. Later in the book we will consider the impact of terrorism on the policing of a diverse society and this provides just one example of the changing social context. Other issues that will be factored into the analysis will include the changing technological environment, the legal framework, and environmental factors. Taking technology as our last example, this is a rapidly changing scene and analysis of capability of the police as well as the changing technological capability will form an important part of what is possible and what is necessary in setting strategic goals.

Creativity

Creativity is the second factor that comes into play in terms of the development of strategy. It is easier to think of this in terms of private enterprise where creativity in thinking has had an important role to play. There have been many such examples recently whether it be vacuum cleaners that do not need bags, low-cost air fares, or software that corners the market. All have resulted from creative strategic thinking about the possibilities within the consumer market. In the public sector it is perhaps not so easy to identify how creativity may underpin the development of strategy. But if we take diversity as an example—there are a number of ways in which creativity may need to be brought to bear.

> **EXERCISE**
>
> - How could a police service bring creativity to its strategy development?
> - What issues do you think require some creative thinking?

Some of the areas that require thinking to be creative might include:

- How to communicate with groups that may mistrust the police;
- How to effectively set up mechanisms to consult with such groups;
- How to influence police culture so that people can have confidence that it is inclusive rather than exclusive and therefore people will want to join;
- How to make the police an employer of choice;
- How to respond to, and work with the notion of 'private policing';
- How to respond to terrorism in such a way that certain communities do not lose trust and confidence in the police;
- How to make decisions about how scarce resources should be allocated;
- How to make training more effective.

The points above are just illustrations of how creativity might need to be brought to bear on the development of strategy in the police service. We noted under our discussion of the business case for diversity that one of the benefits of a diverse workforce is that a greater and richer variety of people will, in all probability, bring increased creativity and certainly different perspectives to the way things should be done. This needs to be harnessed.

6.2.2 **Drivers for strategy formulation**

The formulation and subsequent review of strategic goals will be influenced by many factors. These factors often act as drivers for strategy in that they cannot be ignored by the organization and therefore need to be responded to in strategic terms. The following points offer some examples of drivers for the development and review of police strategies in relation to diversity.

Response to changing social contexts

In social terms Britain has seen remarkable changes in the last half century. Such has been the impact of this social change that decades have become associated with the predominant themes. So for example we might talk about the 1960s as an era of 'flower power' and hippies. Such times were also characterized by significant policing issues in terms of drug use, pop festivals, and inter-gang violence between 'mods and rockers'. The rise of the skinhead culture with its associations with far right ideology was also a significant feature. Increased consumerism too has had a significant impact on police strategy with the advent of not only a vast range of new products, but also the opportunities to buy and own them and of course, steal them. There has also been a sea change in social attitudes, for example the decline of the idea of the nuclear family, increasing divorce rates, changes in patterns of working and the idea of long term careers, changed attitudes towards sexual orientation, and so on. All of this is set against a backdrop of a vastly increased flow of information to people, very often in real-time. Such changes in society need a response by the police in both operational and strategic terms. It is important always to remember that the police are not immune from these changes and themselves are representative of the society they serve. So officers who joined the police twenty-five years ago will often have a very different perspective on the world than those who have joined in more recent years. Attitudes and aspirations that we find in the prevailing culture will always be reflected in the police.

Response to changing ideas about policing

Often the words 'police' and 'policing' are used to mean the same thing. But there have been enormous changes in the last fifty years in ideas of what policing actually is. We have seen a rise in the 'diversities of policing'—the different ways in which the policing function is delivered. In 2006, for example, there are something in excess of 140,000 police officers in England and Wales. Set against this there are over 330,000 people involved in delivering security related services. So we have seen the rise of the idea of private policing, which refers to those bodies and agencies that are themselves involved in delivering a policing function. For example, many shopping malls and out of town outlets have their own policing arrangements. This is not restricted to the more traditional policing patrol functions. A further example would be the Highways Agency that has now taken over many of the responsibilities for roads policing, particularly on motorways. There are also large numbers of people involved in investigation activities and counter fraud such as HM Revenue & Customs, the National Health Service, the Department for Work and Pensions, and the Department for Trade and Industry all of whom have their own professional investigators who provide a focused policing function. All this combines to provide a challenge to the traditional police service, not only in the recognition that it no longer has a monopoly on policing, but also in terms of how it can work in partnership with such agencies. This leads to the assumption that the development of policing strategy in relation to diversity will need to take account of the diversities of policing as well.

Globalization

Britain now exists in a much more global society and we hear a great deal about the idea of globalization. This refers to the way in which the world has become subject to a number of interdependencies and the outcomes of this. Enhanced communications, enhanced travel networks and mobility, and the growth of multinational commercial enterprises have all combined to make the global scene far more interdependent. Large numbers of people do not necessarily see this as a good thing, and so civil disturbances have been seen to characterize meetings of the G8 Group of nations when they meet to discuss global issues. Multinational commercial activity has also attracted negative attention with many people believing that the power exercised by such companies is insufficiently accountable and counter-productive. Global activity has not of course been limited to legitimate commercial and political activity. The global society has also seen a rise in the globalization of criminality, particularly in the area of organized crime. This has led to a rise in international drugs and people trafficking, money laundering, and terrorism. Such phenomena present the police with new challenges particularly because such activities tend to disproportionately affect minority and more vulnerable groups.

Political agenda

Since coming to power in 1997, the New Labour Government has made responding to the diversity of society a priority in a number of areas. This has manifested itself in the concern of the Civil Service to be genuinely diverse and reflect the society it serves. In addition it was the New Labour Government that responded to calls for an inquiry into the circumstances surrounding the death and subsequent investigation of the murder of Stephen Lawrence. This led not only to many reforms in police operational and organizational approaches but also to changes in the law to try to bring about a society with greater freedom from prejudice and discrimination. The Race Relations (Amendment) Act 2000, for example, placed duties on all public authorities, not just the police, in their response to issues of race and diversity. There has also been a host of other legislation particularly in relation to the elimination of discrimination in employment which has all served to change the way that strategic priorities are set. Whilst Chief Officers of police do have independence in their role, they are answerable both to the local Police Authority and the Home Office in terms of accountability for their actions in addition to the communities they police. Strategy cannot be developed in isolation of the political agenda and this will be a significant driver.

Inquiries and reports

We have considered a number of inquires and reports in more detail in Chapter 4. It does need to be noted, however, that a number of these will need to be taken into account as drivers for the development and review of strategy. These will include factors such as:

- Recommendations in the Stephen Lawrence Inquiry
- Recommendations made in the various reports arising from inspections by the HMIC
- Reports by the Commission for Racial Equality
- Reports by the Association of Police Authorities.

6.2.3 **Why do some strategies fail?**

Even if the proper groundwork is done in the development of strategy in terms of analysis and creativity the truth is that some strategies will nevertheless fail. Jones (2005) argues that as many as 80 per cent of strategies fail for a number of reasons. In addition to the more classical reasons such as lack of effective communication and lack of analysis of the context in which the strategy is developed, these include the following.

Too ambitious

One of the songs that John Lennon is best remembered for is 'Imagine'. To paraphrase the words we are invited to imagine a world in which there is no religion, no ownership, no nationhood, and so on. This will, according to Lennon, lead to a united world that is at one with itself. The problem, of course, is that if such aspirations were to be expressed as strategic goals they would be far too ambitious and unlikely to be achieved. Diversity strategies can suffer from the same problem in that sometimes they set out to achieve too much. We have already seen that diversity and responding to it is far from a simple matter. There are many complicating factors and all organizations have to determine their strategy in the context of society at large. In addition, diversity strategies will need to rely on changes to the way people think and behave, what they value, and the development of attitudes that will support success. To attempt to do too much in this respect is doomed to fail.

Lack of buy-in from middle management

Strategies need to be effectively implemented in order to succeed. Very often strategy is formulated and led by the top levels of an organization but its implementation will be reliant on the commitment of the people on the ground. So for example in the police force, the implementation of a diversity strategy will reply on those who are in day-to-day contact with the public. This is where the role of middle management becomes critical. The HMIC have been consistently concerned to stress the importance of the role of middle management in supporting the implementation of strategy. Middle managers—sergeants, inspectors, and chief inspectors—have a critical part to play in interpreting the strategy and ensuring that it is implemented in the day-to-day work of the organization.

Strategic sabotage

It might be strange to think of a strategy being sabotaged in some way by members of the organization. There are a number of ways, however, in which a strategy can be sabotaged, wilfully, unwittingly, or through neglect. Wilful sabotage can occur when people with responsibility for the implementation of a strategy are not committed to the goals because they cannot see the need for it or are just opposed to it for personal reasons. This can particularly be the case in diversity. Where people are not committed to the need to respond to diversity, for reasons of racism, sexism, homophobia, or other manifestations of prejudice, then they may actively work to subvert the strategy. Strategies may also be subverted through an unwitting neglect. This, for example is the case where strategic goals are set clearly, but exist largely on paper and insufficient attention is paid to what needs to be done to ensure that they are properly implemented and reviewed. With the plethora of regulatory imperatives to 'do something' about diversity, organizations can all too easily fall into the trap of falling into a 'tick the box' mentality where the organization is doing something because it has to rather than because it genuinely accepts the need to.

Under and over project management

It is not unusual for the action plans falling out of the setting of strategic goals around diversity to be implemented as projects. In this regard we might define projects as the structured processes that lead to the achievement of an end goal. Projects however are prone to lack of success when they are either over or under managed. An over managed project will be characterized by an undue concern and attention to the process of the project, where the managing of the project becomes the all consuming preoccupation and the actual delivery of the goal or end state of change is lost sight of. On the other side of the coin projects may not be managed to the extent that they need to be in order to ensure success. Sometimes this will be due to the fact that insufficient resources are allocated to get the work done. Successful projects will be characterized by three things: being delivered on time, to budget, and to the required quality. It is important therefore that projects arising from diversity strategies meet these criteria.

Intervening variables

We have seen that the diversity scene is ever changing and fast moving. It is dynamic rather than static, and this can create problems in strategic terms. The context in which a particular diversity strategy is set will in all likelihood change year by year and there will be variables that will necessitate changes in the strategic thinking. Such variables may arise from a number of sources. These will include such factors as global events, local operational events, changes in legislation and regulations, and changes in budgets. Where there is insufficient flexibility built in to the strategic thinking the effect of these variables may well be to de-rail the strategy. It is important therefore that the strategy is reviewed on a regular basis to take account of changes so that it remains both responsive and relevant and in doing so remains achievable.

6.2.4 **Diversity strategy case study**

In the sections above we have looked at the nature of strategy, how it is developed, the drivers for its development and some reasons why strategies might fail. Figure 6.1 below represents just one example of a strategy. In this case it is the diversity strategy of Sussex Police. It is available on the Sussex Police website at the following address: <http://www.sussex.police.uk/about_us/race_diversity.asp#diversity>.

It has been chosen simply as an example, and by searching other police service websites you will be able to find many other such strategies. It should also be noted that Sussex Police, as with most of the diversity strategies, does not offer this in isolation to its other activities in relation to diversity. For example it needs to be considered in the light of the associated Race Equality Scheme. Having said that, it does provide an opportunity to examine it in the light of what we have been saying about the development of strategy.

EXERCISE

Study the diversity strategy of Sussex Police and consider the following questions:

- How explicit is the strategy in terms of its strategic goals?
- How ambitious is it?
- Is it explicit about how it will be implemented on the ground?
- What are the potential risks to its success?

Figure 6.1 Sussex Police Diversity Strategy

Sussex Police Diversity Strategy: Protect & Respect

Protect & Respect is the umbrella through which all race, equalities and diversity work is co-ordinated and delivered. This strategy is built upon the Human Rights Act and the Sussex Police Statement of Values, our commitment to a culture of anti-discrimination and the standard for all staff.

Article 14 of the European Convention on Human Rights

The enjoyment of the rights and freedoms set forth in this convention shall be secured without discrimination on any ground such as sex, race, colour, language, religion, political or other opinion, national or social origin, association with a national minority, property, birth, or other status.

The Sussex Police Statement of Values

We, the police officers, police staff and volunteers of Sussex Police, are dedicated to the values which underpin the police service: *integrity, fairness, equity, justice* and *courage*. We will actively build a culture in our force which is overtly hostile to those who discriminate on the grounds of race, religion, skin colour, sexual orientation, disability, gender, social class or any other inappropriate factor.

What does Protect & Respect mean?

It means upholding the law fairly and appropriately to protect, respect, help and reassure everyone in all communities.

Our job is to **protect** all lives and property. That comes with a responsibility to **respect** the human rights of the individual.

We will ensure that none of our policing activities has an unjustifiable impact on, or excludes anyone—regardless of situation or circumstance, background or religion.

This includes ourselves. Ensuring that everyone working with, or thinking of working with us can be confident in equality of opportunity and fair and equitable treatment.

Why are we doing this?

There are clear legal and professional reasons why this is important.

We must meet all of the current legislative requirements concerning human rights, race, disability and all employment law that relates to equality and diversity. Whilst welcoming these legislative requirements we cannot limit our aspirations, or our efforts, if we are to meet the needs of the diverse communities we serve. This strategy extends to all sections of the community.

Sussex Police is committed to turning words into actions. This strategy will ensure delivery of a consistent service that gains and maintains trust and confidence.

How does it work?

Scope. The strategy looks right across the organization and impacts at all levels—from corporate to individual. Everyone must have the confidence and knowledge to police the many communities of Sussex efficiently and effectively.

Task. There is a range of tasks that will need to be carried out over several years. The race & diversity scheme is designed to make sure Sussex Police does not improperly discriminate whether operationally or internally and promotes equality. There will be changes in the way we operate. Where we find our activities have the potential to impact adversely on different people in different parts of the community, they will be reviewed. This includes our internal working practices, such as training and development, recruitment and leadership style.

Structure. The force Confidence & Equality board, led by the Chief Constable, ensures that the work done drives change throughout the organization. It monitors progress to ensure that our service delivery strives to match the needs of the communities of Sussex and receives advice from a strategic independent advisory group (IAG) to assist it. Comprising members of the community, the IAG is reflective of groups and communities in Sussex. A network of independent advisory groups provides the mechanism for feedback and monitoring between central policy, divisional implementation and impacts on communities. The Protect & Respect board includes senior officers and employees together with representatives from staff groups, Unison, Sussex Police Authority and the strategic IAG.

Focus. The focus is to provide a service that recognises, understands and applies the experience and needs of all communities to our decision making and service delivery. An organization that promotes fair working practices. Officers and staff who protect and respect diversity.

6.3 **Policy Responses to Diversity**

6.3.1 **Introduction**

We have seen in the section above how strategy is developed and what influences it. If strategic goals represent the overall direction that the organization is headed then policy represents one of the ways in which the strategy is put into operation. Policies represent statements of intent and usually offer guidance to decision making in relation to a particular area. Many organizations (including the police) for example will have an 'equal opportunities' policy. This will typically be a statement of intent, which sets out the approach to fairness in employment practice. Most organizations in the public sector will make reference to such a policy in job advertisements. So policies will often reflect the values of the organization—the same is often true of political policy. Policies may also reflect the standards of behaviour that are expected of people. For example there may be a policy on bullying and harassment which will set out standards of acceptable and unacceptable behaviour. The police service is currently constituted in what is termed a tri-partite relationship, that is the Home Office, the Police Authorities, and the police forces themselves. Each part of the relationship will have an input to the development of policy in pursuit of the strategic goals. The Association of Chief Police Officers (ACPO) will very often take the lead in the development of policy in conjunction with the Home Office and the Association of Police Authorities but its implementation will be the responsibility of the individual Chief Officers.

6.3.2 **Policy impacting on diversity**

A great deal of policy has been formulated in response to the needs of policing a diverse society and in the next sub-sections we will briefly explore some of the developments that have addressed themselves to the idea of hate crime. Hall (2005: 9) notes that the word 'hate' is vaguely defined and can at times be distinctly unhelpful. 'Clearly, then, hate crime thus defined isn't really about hate, but about criminal behaviour motivated by prejudice, of which hate is just one small and extreme part'.

Racial incidents

A driving factor in defining the nature of racial incidents was the Stephen Lawrence Inquiry. Recommendations 12–14 of the Macpherson Report dealt with the definition of a racial incident. Recommendation 12 stated 'that the definition should be: A racist incident is any incident that is perceived to be racist by the victim or any other person'. This was to be understood to include both crimes and non-crimes in policing terms and it was recommended that the police, local government, and other relevant agencies adopt the definition. One of the intentions underlying this definition was to focus attention on incidents that hitherto might not have been taken seriously enough to warrant investigation and to recognize that many incidents that may not have fallen within normal crime reporting structures nevertheless had a seriously detrimental effect on the victim. The definition put forward by Macpherson changed the previously held approach to such motivation that had been in place since 1985. Previously police had used:

> Any incident in which it appears to the reporting or investigating officer that the complaint involves an element of racial motivation; or any incident which includes an allegation of racial motivation made by any person (ACPO 1985).

In this definition, there was a discretionary element in the definition where the reporting or investigating officer had the discretion to determine whether a report included the element of racial motivation. Macpherson found that the unwillingness of some officers to acknowledge the racially motivated element of some crime and non-crime reports was having the effect of discriminating against victims and therefore it was necessary to remove that element of discretion.

Hate crime

A further response to the motivation that underlies some crime and non-crime incidents has been in the area of hate crime generally. This broadened the concept to include a more generalized idea of hate as a motivational factor. ACPO in a policy document defined hate crime as: 'a crime where the perpetrator's prejudice against any identifiable group of people is a factor in determining who is victimised' (ACPO 2000: 13). In 2005, ACPO put forward a further definition of hate crime: 'Any incident which may or may not constitute a criminal offence, which is perceived by the victim or any other person, as being motivated by prejudice or hate' (ACPO 2005: 9). There had already been a further definition refined in respect of homophobic motivation with another definition: 'any incident that is perceived to be homophobic by the victim or any other person' (ACPO 2000: 13).

Definitions such as we have outlined above and the very nature of hate as a motivational factor in crime is not unproblematic. Rowe (2004: 102) for example, draws our attention to what he calls the 'conceptual ambiguities of hate crime'. Firstly, he notes that a fundamental criticism of the notion of hate crime is the nature of motivation itself and capturing that in legal terms. The law usually focuses on the intent or mens rea of a perpetrator not the motive which is a much more subjective factor. Secondly, others have commented that a concentration on motivation is likely to present a further attack on rights to free speech. It is argued that in effect policing is moving towards the policing of thought and expression. Thirdly, there may be a perverse sense in which the law originally intended to protect certain minority groups is actually used more to protect the majority. Rowe (2004) citing Clancy et al (2001) reports that the British Crime Survey conducted in 1999 found that 65 per cent of those who claimed to have been the victim of a racially motivated attack were in fact white.

6.4 **Diversity and Leadership**

6.4.1 **Introduction**

A consistent theme in the response to diversity is that of leadership. We will note later that the HMIC has commented a number of times on the importance of leadership in driving the diversity agenda forward. It is now common for organizations to appoint diversity managers and in some cases diversity 'champions'—those who are charged with a specific responsibility for developing the response to diversity. In this section we will be exploring the idea of leadership, particularly as it relates to diversity. There are many models of leadership in current thinking and we will review some of these with particular reference to how they might fit the needs of responding to diversity. The section will conclude with a consideration of the specific linkages between leadership and diversity.

6.4.2 **Who are leaders in diversity?**

It is worth making the point at the outset that it is important to take a broad view of who has the responsibility to lead on diversity.

REFLECT ON PRACTICE

- In your own area of professional practice who do you regard as leaders in diversity?

The common response to the above question would be those in senior management positions in an organization. As we have seen in the section on strategy however, strategic intentions which may have been the result of leadership from the top may be put at risk if those in middle management positions are not also leading on the changes required by the strategy. The need for leadership can also be traced to the day-to-day operational requirements of the job. When an officer is called to a situation which may, for example, involve sensitivity to the needs of the community, then it may be that individual officer who has to take a lead and he or she will be responsible for the correct application of policy that has arisen from the overall strategy.

Engagement with communities also brings us to the need to consider the idea of 'community leaders'. It is sometimes tempting to engage with people with the loudest or most strident voice who may be self-appointed as leaders in particular communities. But it is always prudent to consider the extent to which such people actually represent the interests of those on whose behalf they purport to speak. That said, leaders are not always elected or appointed, sometimes they emerge in response to a particular situation or issue.

6.4.3 **Models of leadership**

So what makes a good leader? Kandola and Fullerton (1996: 106 ff) in writing about the management of diversity offer some suggestions about how leadership should show through individual management styles. For example, they note that leaders need to examine their own attitudes, values, beliefs, and styles of behaviour. This seems to be a crucial starting point for a good leader and leads to the idea that leaders need to be good role models. In addition, leaders need to be able to take a variety of perspectives on issues. This goes to the heart of diversity which of its very nature will involve different people taking different perspectives on the world. Leadership is unlikely to be very effective coming from people who themselves are unable to take different perspectives. The ability to take a lead in challenging accepted norms and unacceptable behaviour and attitudes is also likely to feature highly as a desirable skill of leadership. Challenging behaviour is difficult enough, but challenging attitudes is even harder. People who are able to do this effectively are more likely to make good leaders.

6.4.4 **Leadership defined**

Rollinson, Broadfield, and Edwards (1998) identify two characteristics of leadership. Firstly, that leadership is a non-coercive activity that guides or directs people towards a goal, and secondly, that those who follow leaders perceive that the leader has attributes or characteristics that allow the leader to exercise influence over them. Embodied in these two characteristics is the idea that leadership is not a one-way process (as is often implied by some definitions). So the fact that leadership is non-coercive means that the authority to lead is actually conferred from those who follow. In addition, people need the confidence to participate in goal directed activity (on which the leader leads) and this too will be a process that involves not only the attributes and style of the leader, but the 'followers'' response to them. So to summarize, by drawing again on Rollinson, Broadfield, and Edwards (1998: 336) we can arrive at a definition of leader and leadership:

Leader is a role conferred on a person by followers:

> Leadership is (1) 'a process in which leader and followers interact such that the leader influences the actions of the followers towards the achievement of certain aims and objectives ... (2) a set of characteristics or attributes of the person occupying the leader role which enables him or her to exert influence on the behaviour of followers'.

We can now start to apply all this to the idea of a leader in the response to diversity. People must have confidence enough in the leader that they are willing to accept that person's influence over them in relation to issues that may be very sensitive namely attitudes, values, and beliefs. This makes it doubly important that leaders in diversity are seen to 'walk the talk' in the sense that their actions and behaviours are congruent with what they say. Diversity leaders also need to have a highly developed understanding of the issues that confront the police and that understanding needs to show through in what they say and do. This leads us to consider some of the theoretical frameworks that have influenced thinking about leadership. For a detailed introduction to these frameworks see, for example, Rayner and Adam-Smith (2005). Table 6.2 below sets out the most common theoretical approaches and their characteristics.

Table 6.2 Theoretical frameworks of leadership (based on Rayner and Adam-Smith (2005))

Qualities or traits approach	Focuses on the qualities of accepted great leaders (such as Churchill) with an attempt to identify and isolate the successful characteristics. Self-confidence and intelligence have featured in such research. Tends not to be responsive to cultural differences particularly in terms of what is valued in a particular society.
Functional approach	The focus is on what people do and achieve rather what or who they are. There is a concern to study the (positive and negative) outcomes of leadership. The implication is that such leadership can be acquired and trained rather than being innate in the person.
Leadership as behaviour	This approach seeks to make direct links between the behaviours of leaders and the outcomes of that behaviour particularly in respect of the effect on those led. As above, this approach allows for the development of leaders through training.
Leadership as a personal style	This approach looks at the styles of different leaders. Primarily the attitudes they exhibit towards those whom they lead and the effects that those attitudes have on the team. Examples of leadership style would be at one end of the spectrum autocratic, and at the other democratic.
Situational approach	This theoretical approach to leadership seeks to answer the question 'what leadership works best in what situation?'. Self-evidently the contexts in which leadership will occur will vary enormously and so the approach to leadership needs to be selected to suit the circumstances. May be delineated in general terms as telling, selling, participating, and delegating.
Transformational leadership	Transformational leaders through effective communication of a clear vision and values are able to generate high levels of motivation and commitment amongst those led (see also Alimo-Metcalfe (1995)).
Inspirational leadership	This focuses on the charisma of leaders—their ability to inspire, create, and communicate a vision, and through their own dynamism are able to engage the enthusiasm and energy of the team. Critics of this type of leadership have referred to the fact that such leaders may also exhibit a tendency to emotionally manipulate people and even bully them.

> **EXERCISE**
>
> Study the theoretical approaches to leadership outlined in Table 6.2 and consider how they might relate to leadership in responding to diversity.
>
> - Is there a single explanation of what makes a good diversity leader, or is there a combination of explanations?

I am indebted to my colleague John Grieve (a senior research fellow) who some years ago gave a presentation which outlined his perspective on leadership and which over the years has made a lot of sense in relation to the type of leadership that is needed for those who lead on diversity. He called them the seven 'Cs' of leadership:

- *Creating a vision*—the need to capture people's imagination in terms of how the world of policing would be if prejudice, unfairness, and discrimination could be eliminated.
- *Communication*—the need effectively to communicate the vision and also to see that communication is a two way process and involves listening to both colleagues and communities to establish their needs and aspirations.
- *Competence*—being competent both at the level of behaviour and at the level of understanding the issues. This will include competence in the use of language and competence in dealing with people in terms of interpersonal skills.
- *Caring about people*—recognizing that policing is a people oriented business and that people and their needs are the bottom line.
- *Confronting the issues*—not flinching from the difficult issues that need to be confronted. Not being afraid to speak up when bad attitudes or behaviour are observed and challenging people who need to be challenged, whatever their level in the organization.
- *Commitment to the business*—recognizing and leading on the fact that policing is about being committed to policing diversity. That being a good police officer is about being one who is concerned for fairness and justice.
- *Charisma*—having that added dimension of being able to secure and keep the trust and confidence not only of colleagues but also members of communities who may have a natural tendency to be mistrustful of the police.

REFLECT ON PRACTICE

You should be able to identify in the seven 'Cs' of leadership above a number of the elements of the more theoretical perspectives in Table 6.2. Use the seven Cs as a way of reflecting on your own leadership in relation to diversity.

- Where do your own strengths and weaknesses lie?

6.4.5 **Police leadership and diversity**

In this concluding section on leadership we will briefly explore some of the issues that have become apparent in the relevant literature particularly that arising from inspections by the HMIC. As we noted above, leadership on diversity in the police has been a consistent theme and has been the subject of much criticism. In 'Diversity Matters' (HMIC 2003: 54), the HMIC notes: 'In the years following the Scarman report, consecutive publications have espoused the need for commitment and robust unerring leadership'. Given that the Scarman report was published over twenty years ago, it is apparent that the issue of leadership (or rather the lack of it) has not gone away, and that at best, examples of good leadership are patchy across the police service in England and Wales.

The third chapter of 'Diversity Matters' is devoted to the idea of commitment and leadership in diversity. For example in relation to training:

> Good leadership not only provides focus and acceptability to race and diversity training it also champions and enforces its necessity, as an ideal required as part of organisational values. It involves leaders recognising the real difference that effective race and diversity training makes to individual, team and organisational performance and then making it happen. This is the responsibility of all police service leaders. (para 3.3, p 37).

The need to exhibit leadership is not of course restricted to training alone. The whole agenda of diversity needs to be its object. The HMIC further noted that good examples of leadership at BCU (basic command unit) level would be seen in such characteristics as:

- Role modelling;
- Visibility;
- Resource management;
- Active transference of policy into practice;
- Continual communication of the operational benefits of strong links with the community;
- Explicit articulation of standards expected and required, and achievable through training and development (p 47).

The theme of leadership had been previously picked up in 'Winning the Race: Embracing Diversity' (HMIC 2001). This was the third in a series of thematic inspections in which the importance of leadership became a recurring theme. The key issue that the HMIC raised was that leadership in CRR (community and race relations) and diversity must be both constant and consistent. Whilst the HMIC noted that there had been progress in this area, there was still insufficient evidence of those two factors. Constant leadership is important because the issues are of such importance. Fairness in policing delivery and fairness within the police organization are not optional extras, they are at the very core of what policing is about. So leadership in this area needs to be ongoing. It needs to be consistent both within police forces and between forces so that communities as well as the officers who serve them are able to enjoy the same level of service which is free from prejudice and discrimination.

6.5 **Chapter Summary**

- Our point of departure for this chapter was to look at strategy as a response to diversity. We reviewed the meaning of words that are often used in connection with the development of strategy and distinguished between such terms as mission, strategic goals, objectives, and strategy. We identified that analysis and creativity are two important factors in the development of effective strategy. A number of drivers for strategy formulation were discussed and these included the need to respond to changing social contexts, changing ideas about the nature of policing itself, the impact of globalization, the political agenda, and the impact of inquiries and reports. A number of factors that relate to why strategies might fail were discussed. These included the lack of buy-in by middle management, the idea of strategic sabotage, the need to manage projects effectively, and the array of intervening variables that might impinge on the achievement of strategic goals.
- Policy was identified as being one of the ways in which strategy is achieved and the chapter included a brief discussion of policy in relation to the idea of hate crime which has been the subject of much policy formulation and discussion since the Stephen Lawrence Inquiry. We noted racial incidents as being an example of such policy as well as the broader agenda of hate crime. Some of the problems in relation to a conceptualization of hate crime were discussed.
- The last section addressed the need for leadership in response to diversity. After considering the question 'who are leaders on diversity?', we went on both to define leadership and to examine models of leadership ranging from the qualities or traits approach to the idea of transformational and inspirational leadership. A model of leadership under the heading of seven 'Cs' was offered as a possible way of seeing the requirements of leaders in diversity. The section concluded with a mention of some of the issues in relation to leadership that have been identified by the HMIC.

7

Diversity—Hard Issues

7.1 **Chapter Outline**

By now it is likely that you have formed the opinion that diversity is by no means a straightforward concept and that policing a diverse society is therefore a complex matter. There is no general agreement as to what diversity is, and the very notion raises a number of issues that need to be resolved if society is to become cohesive (see Chapter 5 for a discussion of what cohesive means), whilst at the same time embracing difference—not merely tolerating it but regarding difference as a strength. It is some of these 'hard' issues raised that we now turn to in this chapter. We may regard them as hard issues in the sense that their resolution is by no means clear and the debates they raise are far from over. Some of the issues we will cover represent those that seem to create cognitive dissonance for people and we will be exploring that concept. In examining the implications particularly of cultural and religious difference we also need to draw on philosophy and briefly look at the way people claim things to be true and how this may bring them into conflict with others who believe that an alternative opposing view is also true. Bear in mind as you read, that there are strong links between this chapter and Chapter 9, in which we will be discussing the impact that global and domestic terrorism has had on issues relating to a diverse society. In this chapter then we will be covering the following ground:

- The idea of cognitive dissonance as a psychological way of understanding the way some people feel about some issues of diversity and in particular cultural difference.
- Issues of cultural difference are a recurring theme in thinking about the way we respond to diversity. Cultural difference can very often lead to conflict and misunderstanding. In some circumstances cultural difference is in conflict with the law. We will look at a number of examples of where this can happen and the issues it raises.
- Language and diversity. In this section we review a number of the issues that surround language, communication, and diversity. We will, for example, review how language relates to power and how humour is often a smokescreen for the expression of that power.
- Personal response to diversity in society is a key factor in the overall picture of how an organization is able to manage its approach to that diversity. In this section we will focus on the range and types of response, attitudes, and behaviour and the critical role that personal leadership has to play.
- Political correctness is a phenomenon that came to the fore in the last quarter of the twentieth century and if anything in 2006 is more strongly on the agenda than ever before. In many ways this is connected very closely with the debates that we have mentioned elsewhere about the freedom of thought and expression. We will look at the idea of political correctness and examine some of the ways in which it is a helpful concept and some of the ways in which it is not.

7.2 **Cognitive Dissonance**

7.2.1 **Cognitive dissonance defined**

It is not uncommon to find that when people are thinking about issues relating to diversity, they experience a certain amount of what we might call cognitive dissonance. Essentially the idea relates to situations in life where we are confronted with having to rethink things that we have held or believed to be true, but these things are then challenged. Hayes and Orrell (1993) note that throughout history there are examples of times when people have put forward ideas that have put them in direct conflict with the accepted ways of thinking. People have even been persecuted for such thinking, for example in suggesting that the earth was not flat and that it actually orbits the sun rather than the other way round. A more recent example would be the debate in the US about creation and evolution where the challenging of what has come to be generally accepted truth about evolution has led to conflict with those who take a different (creationist) view. Put simply, cognitive dissonance is a 'state in which one attitude contradicts another, leading to attitude change' (Hayes and Orrell 1993: 463).

The original study into this by Festinger et al involved a quasi-religious group who believed that the world would come to an end on a particular day. Needless to say this did not happen, but the study focused on the effect this new information (ie that the world did not end) had on the attitudes and beliefs of the religious group. In fact, although there was a clear dissonance between what they believed and what actually happened, members of the group did not substantially change their views. Instead they attributed the fact that the world did not end to their own actions. Hayes and Orrell (1993: 307) go on to describe the theory of cognitive dissonance that Festinger put forward in 1957. The theory argues that:

> if we come to recognise that one or more of our attitudes contradict each other, it puts us into an uncomfortable state of tension, and we will need to change one or other of those attitudes so that the dissonance disappears.

A simple example of this would be a person who is a smoker. Their attitude towards smoking might actually be quite favourable, in that they enjoy it and find it relieves their stress. On the other hand, they accept the evidence that smoking is bad for your health and that there is increasing antipathy toward smoking in public places. So the smoker has cognitive dissonance. They are favourably inclined towards smoking but at the same time experience resistance and a great deal of evidence to show that it is harmful. Eventually something will have to change to get rid of the dissonance. Usually of course this means that the smoker will need to give up.

7.2.2 **Practical implications of cognitive dissonance**

The main application of dissonance theory that is relevant to our discussion about diversity is in the area of attitude change. Gross (1996) notes that dissonance only seems to occur when volitional (or voluntary) behaviour is involved. If we behave or have attitudes of our own free will, then there can be psychological dissonance. If we believe we have no choice then there will be no dissonance. The reality for nearly all of us is that we do have choices both about the attitudes we hold and the behaviour we use to express them. If there were no choice about attitudes and behaviour then there would be no problem of discrimination because people would simply be programmed to behave in a certain way. So because we have choices, dissonance arises.

Look for the practical illustrations of dissonance theory as the chapter progresses particularly in terms of:

- Dissonance about cultural and religious diversity and difference;
- The relationship between attitudes and behaviour;
- Dissonance about rights and responsibilities.

7.3 **Cultural and Religious Difference**

7.3.1 **Introduction**

There tends to be an assumption amongst some commentators on diversity that the whole idea is unproblematic and that all difference is both a good thing and is not open to challenge. Such a view is far too simplistic and does not takes account of the intelligence of people to work out for themselves that in the so-called 'celebration of diversity', there are, in fact a number of issues that do not easily fall into this notion. I have seen a number of police trainers founder in this respect in the sense that they take a simplistic view of the issues and expect people to accept what they are told without question. In a lecture with students at my university, I asked them to identify issues arising out of thinking about diversity that they found problematic in some way. They were able to generate a considerable list of things that they felt needed to be explored further. Diversity does not mean that we have to accept all differences being good, neither does it mean that we can never question (albeit in a constructive way) things that we find difficult to accept. People are far more likely to respond positively to the diversity agenda if they feel they have a genuine opportunity both to challenge things they feel are not easy, and if they are given the opportunity to examine them. In the sections below I have selected a number of the issues that my students raised.

7.3.2 **Knowledge and truth claims**

What we know about the world and the truth we claim for that knowledge is not always as straightforward as it seems. The truth of something will often depend on a number of conditions not least the way we see and experience the world. Anyone who has given evidence in court will know that what at first appeared to be true can easily be tangled up by a clever lawyer into a construction that leaves us wondering whether we actually experienced or saw, or said what we thought we did at all! Where two people have seen the same event they may well subsequently describe it in very different ways such they could easily be talking about different things. Their background, standpoint, belief system, and a whole range of other factors will influence their perception of the truth of something.

So truth is not a straightforward concept. What is true for me may not necessarily be true for you. Why does this impact on diversity and make it a hard issue? One aspect of diversity in society is the diversity of religious opinion and affiliation that exists. People with a strong faith or religious conviction will often take a very different view of truth to the one we have outlined above. For them, truth far from being relative (as above) is absolute. Many Christians for example would believe that when Jesus in the Bible is reported as saying 'I am the way the truth and the life' this was being expressed in absolute terms. Where truth is regarded as absolute there is little room for the acceptance of a diversity of opinion. The same will be true (if we can use the word) of other religions, most of which make truth claims about themselves that do not leave room for manoeuvre. Why is this a problem in diversity? Firstly, there is clearly the potential for a clash of ideas amongst people from different faith groups, each of which believes they have the truth. Secondly, although some would claim still that in the UK we live in a predominantly Christian society, most would argue that the UK is now largely post-Christian and secular. In such a society people (who are not religiously affiliated) are far more likely to accept that truth is relative and situational and would adopt the position: 'If its true for you then that's fine but I don't believe it and you should not expect me to'. This makes it much harder to understand and empathize with those who take a more absolutist view of truth.

7.3.3 **Cultural and religious difference**

A hard issue in diversity arises when cultural and religiously based differences are either in conflict with the law on diversity or where they appear to prejudice people's human rights. Some of the cultural and religious differences that may be thrown into such conflict include:

- Forced marriages
- Arranged marriages
- Honour killings
- Honour crimes

- Female genital circumcision
- Attitudes towards homosexuality
- Dress and cultural identity

It is worth noting that some people will argue that the issues such as those listed above are only problematic because the human rights law and domestic law is constructed by developed countries who do not share the same history and cultural development and therefore do not understand the depth of feeling that underlies some of the practices and beliefs. This seems to be a fairly radical perspective however, and many individuals and organizations *within* the various communities affected have challenged the practices and beliefs as being incompatible with human rights.

7.3.4 **Practical implications for police**

Differences between cultural and religious belief is an area that becomes a hard issue for police as inevitably it will be the police who bear the brunt of dealing with such differences when they come into conflict with the law. There seem to be three key implications for the police. Firstly, all of the areas listed above are complex and need great sensitivity in dealing with them, not least because they are often issues that are deeply rooted in values and belief systems. Secondly, the police need to pay special attention to the need to engage effectively with communities and understand the complexity of their social fabric so there will be both a willingness to report crimes, and the police will be able effectively to investigate them. Thirdly, there needs to be a recognition that these are not solely domestic issues and that they must be tackled in the wider context of what is going on globally.

7.4 **Language and Diversity**

7.4.1 **Introduction**

George Orwell, the author of *1984*, once said: 'but if thought corrupts language, language can also corrupt thought'. Language is important in diversity because, as Orwell alluded to, it is one of the main ways in which our attitudes, values, and beliefs are revealed to those around us. What we say, and the way we say it, will have a tremendous impact on the people with whom we engage. This can go right down to the actual words we choose; some words, for example may *include* others, whilst other words will *exclude* them. Language in the sense that we mean it here however is not just about words it is also about the role that words have to play in the overall context of our communication. This will involve paralanguage—the actual delivery of the words (tone of voice, spaces between words, and so on) and the non-verbal communication that is used to reinforce or enrich what we say. Non-verbal communication is important to language because a great deal of what we communicate is not done by words at all, but by the posture we adopt, the extent to which we get and maintain eye contact, and the space we leave between ourselves and the listener. We may *say* that we are committed to diversity, but the way that we say it can reveal a very different attitude.

7.4.2 Cultural difference in communication

A great deal has been written about the cultural difference in communication and this will often form a part of diversity awareness training. The motive behind raising such issues is usually a positive one but it is a hard issue for diversity, in my view for three reasons. Firstly, as with other aspects of such 'cultural awareness', for example handbooks on the culture of minority groups, there is a great danger that we will fall into the trap of making gross stereotypes about people that may or *may not* be true. If a police officer has been taught that a person from a particular community or ethnic background is likely to communicate in a certain way then the fact that the person may not do this may be problematic for their understanding of what is going on and can even lead to misunderstanding. Secondly, even if knowledge of cultural difference in communication is important, the question is then raised as to what do we include and what do we leave out? There are many thousands of different ethnic backgrounds all of which have cultural nuances in terms of the way they may communicate in their language. In addition there are many thousands of actual languages and many people do not have English as their first language. Which ones do we address? It is not feasible to suggest that an individual police officer or person engaged in the business of policing could learn what would be needed to grasp all of the cultural differences in communication. Thirdly, this is a hard issue because it can have the potential to be a smokescreen for more important things. We saw in the chapter on diversity developments that in assessing the impact of the Stephen Lawrence inquiry, it was found that thankfully expressions of racist language are now very rare (although there are still instances of it). But does that mean that the underlying attitudes and values of people have actually changed, or has the use of language changed for other reasons, such as the fear of being caught out and disciplined? It is interesting that the same report found that there has not been a similar reduction in homophobic or sexist language. It could therefore be argued that tackling language is actually going about the issue the wrong way round. If people have positive and inclusive attitudes and values in respect of diversity then the language they choose and the way they communicate will almost inevitably follow suit as they become more sensitive to the need to show respect and dignity to people from all backgrounds.

7.4.3 **Language and humour**

When I became a police officer in the late 70s a common phrase in use was 'if you can't take a joke, you shouldn't have joined'. The culture at the time was shot through with humour and almost anything was fair game for a laugh. I remember dealing with a particularly nasty incident where an eight-year-old boy had gone missing. I was sent to meet the mother of the boy who was located near a tube station in North London. On the way to the tube station I received another call to say that there was a body on the line and that I was likely to be first on scene. I arrived and met the mother and then went down to the tube station and very quickly discovered that the missing boy was in fact the body on the line. Needless to say the situation was very traumatic for all concerned. The boy was dead and had been burned very badly by the electric current. Later in the day I was having my refreshments in the canteen with other members of my shift and they, to my absolute horror were making light of the whole situation by saying things such as 'do you want a crisp Phil?', 'he must have had an electrifying experience' and similar remarks. The whole episode made me feel physically sick. Now there is a strong psychological argument that such humour is merely a way of coping for people who deal with dangerous and traumatic situations. Taking such situations seriously is not the same as taking them personally. But many police officers I knew at the time were unable to see where to draw the line and there was a failure to recognize that not all police officers want to deal with their trauma by making jokes about it. Such was the strength of the culture that everything was fair game for humour, and much of it was inappropriate, so it extended from traumatic situations to racist, sexist, and homophobic humour and tended to reveal the true underlying attitudes and values of people.

I was only joking

The defence that is often used by people who engage in language and communication that is offensive is that 'I was only joking'. This defence tends to rely on the fact that others will therefore believe that there was no underlying motivation to offend the other person. The problem is, of course, that what is said is said, and what is implied is implied, and it is far more difficult to draw back from that situation than to not get into it in the first place. Take the example of racist humour. It is not the intention of the humour, whether well meant or whether it was actually meant to demean the other person, but the way that the other person perceives it that is important. So even if I make a joke that I genuinely don't intend to cause offence, if it *does* have that effect then I am liable. The whole issue of humour in our communication has been studied extensively and there is a considerable literature on it. In the next few sub-sections we draw on Hargie (1997) to illustrate some of the ways in which humour may be used, all of which have relevance to the student of diversity and the issue of language and communication.

Humour as a search for information

When we meet people for the first time, it is common to want to find out about the person and often this extends to wanting to find out about their attitudes and values. Of course police officers meet new people all of the time both inside the police in terms of colleagues, and outside meeting members of the public. Naturally, it is quite difficult to come at sensitive issues 'head on' and so humour will often be the mechanism used to help us probe what the other person's position may be on a certain issue. This is often the case when we are moving into an unfamiliar culture. We have argued for example that it is probably truer to speak of 'police cultures' rather than a single culture within the police. When an officer is transferred they will need to find out about that culture and in particular where the levels of tolerance lie. These tend to be different for different groups. Humour is a way of doing this. On the other side of the coin we may want to find out how other people see us and are therefore interested in the way they might respond to us. Again rather than address this directly, it is common to use humour as a way in.

Humour as a means of interpersonal control

Another use of humour is to use it to express the way we respond to others and to determine power structures. According to Hargie (1997: 266ff) humour signals three affective ingredients about its encoder: firstly, as a jovial person who is rewarding and fun to be with; secondly, as a sensitive person who has a friendly interest and willingness to enter relationships with others, and thirdly, as one who seeks, and probably wins, the approval of others. Police culture is very much about being accepted and being elevated to the status of being in the 'in-group'. Such acceptance is often seen as essential both socially and operationally, and people will often signal their willingness and desire to be accepted by engaging in and responding to the humour of the group they are seeking to join.

Humour can of course also be used to express dislike and hostility and this is often the underlying motivation for humour which is racist, sexist, or homophobic. To quote Hargie (p 266) again:

> . . . humour is one way, possibly the only socially acceptable way, of expressing personal antagonism. We are inclined to enjoy cruel forms of humour, obtaining amusement from incompetence and deformity and from the oddities and incongruities of others' behaviour.

So this becomes a hard issue for responding to diversity. People may know that it is no longer acceptable to denigrate or put down other groups, in fact as we have seen elsewhere there are increasingly harsh restrictions on the freedoms that people have to express their opinions. So humour may well become the vehicle that people feel they are forced to use to express negative opinions about others.

7.4.4 **Practical implications for policing**

There are a number of practical implications of all this for policing and police officers.

- Strategy, policy, and the way police do things is, of course, vital, but it is the language that is used both written and verbal that people see and hear that will be one manifestation of this. Overall, people in the police need to be seen to be 'switched on' to the issue in terms of the language that they use.
- It is vital that leaders in the police are seen to be using language that is sensitive. Sensitivity in language will come through when it expresses the fact that people's needs and aspiration are being taken account of. It will show that people have been listened to. It will also show sensitivity to people's sense of their own identity.
- Language should also be inclusive. This will ensure that people do not become and do not feel themselves to be marginalized. It is, for example not uncommon to hear senior people talking of police*men* as if there are no women in the police. This is just one example of language that is exclusive but there are many others.
- Humour is used for many reasons other than to 'get a laugh'. Above all, humour *is* used as a way of coping with situations, but it is important to remember that it is also used to denigrate others who may be identified by their difference. People at all levels in the police need to develop a sense of what humour is appropriate and what is not.
- Language is not just the words we use. It is perfectly possible to (intentionally or unintentionally) offend someone say, in a stop and search situation by using the correct words but making the person feel they are at best not liked and at worst despised by the accompanying non-verbal behaviour and tone of voice. People who have been stopped rarely complain that the correct procedure was not followed, their complaint can nearly always be traced back to the attitude of the officer that they experienced.

REFLECT ON PRACTICE

Thinking about your own experience.

- How do you experience language and humour in the police?
- Is it still true that 'if you can't take a joke, you shouldn't have joined'?

7.5 **Political Correctness**

7.5.1 **The phenomenon of political correctness**

It has been said that political correctness is neither 'political' nor 'correct', and it is probably true to say that the very idea has many detractors. Responses to political correctness seem to cover the full range of possibilities:

- It is a left-wing plot to ensure that issues of concern to ordinary people can never be debated.
- It is a right-wing plot to ensure that the socially minded are undermined.
- It is nothing more than a game played by participants who try to outdo each other with the most ridiculous words or phrases.
- It is a means of intellectual and social control over what people may say or do.

Such has been the influence and impact of the idea of political correctness that whole books have been written about its influence on certain professions. For example, Philpott (1999) edited a collection of contributions to the debate about political correctness and social work. In his introductory chapter, he argues, citing a collection of examples, that the term is often used 'imprecisely and meaninglessly' and very often seen 'as a synonym for dogma—as if those who are said to be politically correct have no philosophical, moral, practical or other argument for their actions or stance, but only some mysteriously arrived at act of faith' (p 7).

7.5.2 **The extent of political correctness**

The bulk of the debate about political correctness and much of its object is of course spoken language. But we can extend this for example to the visual representation of images and even further to the realms of policy and decision making. The label 'politically correct' is not of course solely restricted to issues of race and diversity. It is applied to many other spheres also, for example health. An interesting example of this is cited by Philpot (1999: 5) who recounts the story of the famous image of Isambard Kingdom Brunel, the great engineer, being used as part of an advertising campaign. Those of you who know anything about Brunel will know that like Sir Winston Churchill he was famous for sporting a large cigar almost wherever he went. The advertising agency airbrushed out the cigar and a representative of the agency was quoted as saying: 'in these days of political correctness we thought it inappropriate for a potential role model such as Brunel to be seen smoking'. So political correctness applies to issues other than those we normally associate with diversity. But there is another area where the label politically correct is applied, more often than not unhelpfully and that is in the area of policy and decision making. Sir Ian Blair, the Commissioner of the Metropolitan Police Service (appointed in 2005), attracted such attention for his leadership and direction. He had a reputation for focusing on and dealing with issues of race and diversity, and this led to a great deal of criticism of him and his so-called political correctness. It is not the purpose of this book to critique his leadership or priorities but it does serve to illustrate the way that the label politically correct may be applied not just to language but also to people and ideas. Where the term is used in this regard it seems to be referring to an exaggerated concern with issues (generally social) that others feel do not merit such attention.

7.5.3 **The impact on policing a diverse society**

When I joined the police service in 1978, the world in general and British society in particular was a very different place. By extension of course so was the social context in which policing took place. Openly racist or homophobic 'comedy' programmes were common on television. The language and humour in currency amongst police officer colleagues was of the type that thankfully in 2006 is a very rare (although not completely eliminated) phenomenon. In as much as political correctness focuses people's minds on what it is appropriate to do or say then it has had a successful outcome. Philpot (1999: 14) argues that the use of the term 'political correctness' should be banned: 'It is a camouflage, and obfuscation, an obstacle, a disguise, a red herring, an irritant, a diversion ... once we have abolished the words political correctness then battle can commence'. If we apply such thinking to the policing of a diverse society we might also conclude that the words (political correctness) themselves are getting in the way of the real issues. For example:

- To produce lists of words that people can or cannot say (as some police forces do) fails to go to the core of what matters and that is whether individuals have the knowledge, understanding, and attitudes towards diversity that would enable them to identify for themselves what is appropriate to say and what is not.
- Where individual officers, senior officers, even whole police forces are labelled 'politically correct' then the implication of that assessment is that they are not actually addressing the right priorities. Such an implication devalues the importance of recognizing that policing is, in fact, about policing a diverse society. Labelling people as 'politically correct' should never be a stick with which to beat those who are trying to do the right thing.
- Those who *are* trying to do the right thing (and probably therefore support the tenor of political correctness, if not the words) should take care that this is expressed in rational, measured, and sensible terms. It does more harm than good when people take on a morally superior attitude and take upon themselves the right to challenge the tiniest (politically incorrect) word when they themselves could be challenged on much larger issues.

I can illustrate this last point from my own experience. I once used the term 'good egg' in relation to a colleague. Working as I did in a fairly sensitive environment, I was immediately challenged by a colleague that my language was racist. I apologized and chose not to pick this as a particular battle. What I found particularly difficult to accept, however, was that the colleague who challenged me *frequently* used the words 'Jesus' and 'Christ' as expletives and this was despite my having brought this to his attention on many occasions. Incidentally if you are wondering what the potential problem with 'good egg' is, there is an argument that it comes from Cockney rhyming slang 'egg and spoon'—'coon', which was a term of abuse applied to black people and was in currency particularly in the 1960s and 1970s. Some would say that the argument (as it currently appears to me) is actually urban myth.

EXERCISE

In this section we have thought about the way in which the words 'political correctness' are used as a label that may actually obscure an important concern to do the right thing.

- What is your own position on political correctness?

7.6 Personal Response to Diversity

People in general (and police officers are no different) respond to diversity in different ways. Issues that are easy for some are hard to accept for others, some people will have prejudice in some areas and not others and vice versa. Organizations are made up of individuals and it is the sum of those individual responses that will tend to make an organization either successful or not in its attempts to respond effectively to diversity. This is particularly important in the police where the interface with the public is more often than not at the level of the individual. That person will be acting as a representative of the police service and their behaviour and attitudes will be crucial in the way the person sees the police service as a whole.

7.6.1 The range of responses

Over a number of years of observation of the way that people respond to diversity training, it seems that the range of responses can be at one end of the scale a type of unthinking acceptance, at the other end, an outright hostility, and in the middle the person who thinks about the issues and will make a reasoned judgement about the way they are going to respond. It seems to me that this last group represents both the majority and probably the most effective response. Taking these in turn:

Unthinking acceptance

Typically such people would be quite responsive to the issues they are presented with. They would be receptive to new ideas but come at these with a fairly uncritical stance. It is difficult to tell whether they are really engaging with what they are learning or whether they are in reality playing the game in order to get a tick in the box that says they have received their training. There is a sense that they are in agreement with the issues merely as a strategy for an easy life. They are unlikely to be able to articulate their own case for why responding effectively to diversity is important.

Outright hostility

At the other end of the scale there are people who are hostile to the notion of diversity. They might seek to give the trainer a hard time and will be unsupportive of those in a group who are making genuine efforts to learn. They will be unwilling to disclose much about their own views although they will focus on all the negative aspects that they can think of and take the position that diversity is a problem not a solution. In the management training I have conducted, people such as this will constantly look for ways to get round the rules and will often use 'them and us' type expressions when they speak. They will often challenge the trainer's right to ask them about their attitudes and values, and they may also tend to make assumptions about being in a white majority as well as making assumptions about minority groups.

Reasoned judgement

The third general grouping of personal responses to diversity is those who are willing to think about the issues and make considered judgements about their own position. These people may well appear as challenging to a trainer because they will be willing to disclose their own prejudices with a view to learning about them and will want to ask questions. They will also want to challenge what is said to make certain that they can intellectually sign up to it. They are normally willing to be challenged both by a trainer and other colleagues in the group. They will normally be good at thinking through the hard issues and will be able to make their own case for why responding to diversity is a good thing.

REFLECT ON PRACTICE

On the assumption that the three descriptions above are valid—where would you place yourself?

One explanation of the behaviours outlined above may lie in some work that was done by Jones, Newburn, and Smith (1994). They identified three 'rules' by which police officers may work. *Working rules* become the guiding principles of day-to-day work which have been internalized by individual officers. *Inhibitory rules* are those which police officers will take cognisance of when deciding when and how to act. Such rules tend not to be internalized and they are more likely to discourage officers from adopting certain behaviours from fear of being detected and disciplined.

Presentational rules are intended to provide a perception that things are being done and that cooperation (of the police) can be assumed. It is of course the working rules that will have the most significant impact on how police officers respond to diversity. Where principles such as integrity, fairness, justice, and anti-discrimination become internalized then they become second nature. On the other hand, where a member of the police service is acting only out of fear of discipline (inhibitory rules) or by giving the impression that they are in favour of responding to diversity (presentational rules) then that person is at risk of being exposed when the pressure comes on.

7.6.2 Freedom of thought and expression

Freedom of thought and expression is never far away from the diversity agenda and one area in which it manifests itself is closely linked to what we have been saying above. The key issue that is hard to resolve is the way in which individuals may easily gain the perception that whilst they are expected to accept the diversity of society and respond to it in a positive way, this is actually achieved by a straightjacket around the way that people may think or express themselves. This is particularly acute when issues are presented as if they are beyond discussion where people may feel with some justification that there is actually a dogma to be subscribed to rather than a free exchange of ideas. We can illustrate this with a recent example. Sir Iqbal Sacranie has been the Secretary-General of the Muslim Council of Britain (MCB) since 2002 and has been honoured with an OBE and a Knighthood for his work in community relations. In a BBC Radio 4 programme in January 2006 he made some comments in answer to a question about homosexuality that were expressing mainstream Muslim views of the issue. In response to a complaint by a member of the public, what he said was investigated by the Metropolitan Police and the Crown Prosecution Service (CPS) became involved. Eventually the CPS advised that there should be no further action taken. A release by the MCB commented 'to be honest we thought it somewhat surprising when we heard that Sir Iqbal was being investigated by the police for merely articulating the mainstream Islamic viewpoint about homosexuality' (BBC 2006). The hard issue for responding to diversity here is striking the right balance between legitimate freedom of expression and the possibility of offending someone. If too much restriction is placed on what people may legitimately discuss then people will be forced into the 'unthinking acceptance' position we noted above, and what will happen in reality is that people are more likely to lash out against the idea of diversity, seeing it as dogmatic and coercive rather than a matter of free choice.

7.6.3 Changing attitudes and behaviour

Responding to diversity at the personal level, as we have seen earlier, is a matter of attitudes, values, beliefs, and behaviour. People's values are often very deeply rooted and hard to change. This is why it is critical that the police service recruits people into the extended police family who hold values that are congruent with those of the police service. Beliefs, attitudes, and behaviour are all much more susceptible to change. The hard issue about changing attitudes and behaviour however is which should come first? There is a view that says if you can change a person's behaviour then the attitudes and values will follow. There is some strength in this argument and it largely lies in the fact that, it is argued, it is behaviour that matters in terms of the interface with the public. Provided an officer is behaving correctly, what does it matter what their attitudes and values are, surely the officer's attitudes and values are personal to them and not the business of anyone else? The whole issue of attitudes and behaviour, then, is a hard one to address in diversity for a number of reasons:

- Some people will make a very convincing case that their attitudes and values are their business and that provided they are behaving in accordance with policy and the law then that should be the end of it and others do not have the right to probe any deeper. This is a hard issue though because it goes with an underlying assumption that there is no linkage between attitudes and values, and behaviour. Such people believe that they can 'bolt down' their attitudes and values in a way that will not affect their behaviour.
- Whilst this may be true some of the time, it raises two problems. Firstly, that when confronted with a stressful situation, then it is much more likely that the attitudes will surface and have an affect on behaviour. Secondly, how does it impact on the idea of trust and confidence? Is it really tenable to suggest, for example, that a member of a minority ethnic group can have trust and confidence in an officer who, in terms of their attitudes and values is racist, but *claims* that this in no way affects their behaviour?
- Thirdly, organizations that have statements of their values and aspirations as do the police, have a right to expect that people being paid by the organization will exhibit values and attitudes which are congruent with those of the organization. It is not sufficient for people to claim that their values are their own and no business of anyone else.

7.6.4 **Personal leadership**

In this final section on the personal response to diversity, we will just consider a few points in relation to the idea of personal leadership. This is also closely linked to the idea of rights and responsibilities. We all have rights and should all be able to expect to enjoy the human rights that are afforded to others, and there should be no discrimination in the enjoyment of those rights. Rights are also accompanied by responsibilities, however, and that also needs to be a clear two-way responsibility between police and the communities they serve. As the partner in the relationship with the most power of course, it is likely that the onus will be on the police to take the lead in the establishment of the relationship and that lead is not just the actions of senior officers, it is the leadership shown by everybody. Police work in occupational terms is fairly unique in that individual officers of constable rank may well be first on scene at almost any type of incident and have to take a lead until backup arrives. The 7 July 2005 bombings in London would be a striking example of this. So leadership in the police can, or at least should be, detected at all levels. We have seen the important relationship between a successful response to diversity and leadership. Therefore it can be argued that such leadership needs to be evident at all levels and that all in the service have a responsibility to lead in forwarding the diversity agenda.

7.7 **Chapter Summary**

Diversity or, more accurately, responding to diversity is by no means a straightforward thing. Diversity raises many 'hard issues' which are best confronted rather that brushed under the carpet. In this chapter we identified a few of these hard issues, but you will probably be able to think of many others.

- Our point of departure in this chapter was to consider the idea of cognitive dissonance. This seeks to explain what happens when two attitudes that we hold may be in contradiction to each other. This will set up a state of tension in our minds and can only really be resolved when one or other of the attitudes changes. Dissonance usually only occurs when we have a free choice about something and if there is no choice, then there is likely to be no dissonance. But we do have choices about our attitudes and behaviour and so there are many examples of how cognitive dissonance may appear in relation to diversity. A common one is where a person has a positive attitude towards human rights and the need not to discriminate, but at the same time holds a prejudice about a particular group. This is likely to set up cognitive dissonance for them and they will either need to change their attitude towards the universality of the principles of human rights and fairness, or they will need to change their attitude towards the particular group.

- In the second section which looked at the idea of cultural and religious difference as a hard issue for diversity. We noted that the idea of 'truth' is not as straightforward as it might seem and that religious groups in particular may regard truth as absolute. Where that 'truth' is in opposition then there will be difficulty and this will manifest itself not only in the strength of the argument but also in the way others may not understand the depth of feeling that can underpin an adherence to absolute truth. We also briefly noted a range of cultural differences that would all be regarded as coming under the umbrella of diversity but may of themselves be either against the law or be against Western conceptions of human rights.

- Language and diversity was introduced as a hard issue. We noted the significance of cultural differences in communication and in particular why this is problematic if it is regarded as a training issue. We then went on to explore some of the issues that arise from language when it is used as a medium for humour. Humour is ingrained in police culture and one explanation for this is that humour is a way of people coping with difficult and sometimes traumatic situations. There are, or at least should be, limits on the use of humour though and the defence of 'I was only joking' will not stand up when someone is genuinely offended by the inappropriate use of humour. We also noted that humour may be used in the search for information, and as a means of interpersonal control.

- Linked to the idea of language is the issue of political correctness. This is a hard issue for responding to diversity because more often than not the term is used as a pejorative label and this masks the ways in which the idea can actually be helpful, because at the core of political correctness is the idea of 'doing the right thing' both in terms of the way we speak (which as we saw in the language section is important) and also in the way that we act.

- The last hard issue that we identified was that responding to diversity is not just a matter of strategy or policy, nor is it a matter of what organizations may do, it is about personal responses, not least because organizations are actually collectives of people. We noted that there seems to be a range of responses to diversity from unthinking acceptance to outright hostility. A position in the middle of these two extremes is likely to be the most effective in responding to diversity. We took a very brief look at the freedom of thought and expression as it relates to individuals and noted that it is important that people are not left with the impression that their own freedom to think for themselves is being taken away from them. Diversity needs to accommodate diversity of opinion as well. This section concluded with a consideration of the relationship between attitudes and values and behaviour and the need for personal leadership at all levels.

Responding to Diversity—Training and Education

8.1 **Chapter Outline**

In Chapter 6 we reviewed police responses to a diverse society in terms of strategy, policy, and operations. A further response that has acknowledged the increasing importance of responding to a diverse society has been the explosion of initiatives aimed at training and education. The Macpherson Inquiry (1999) made a number of recommendations in relation to how the issues arising from the report should be addressed through training initiatives in the police service. In this chapter, we will explore a number of the issues that surround attempts to help people, and in particular police officers, learn about diversity. We will cover the following issues:

- Learning to learn about diversity. This will address the idea of learning and awareness, the way in which diversity may be considered to be a special case, and the idea of mainstreaming or embedding diversity into training programmes;
- The issues surrounding a competence based approach to training;
- The relative merits of training and education;
- The findings of the HMIC in relation to diversity training initiatives in the police;
- A consideration of 'what works' based on research that was conducted shortly after the Stephen Lawrence Inquiry was published.

The chapter will conclude with a summary of the key issues.

8.2 **Learning to Learn About Diversity**

8.2.1 **Learning and awareness**

As we have already seen, in the last quarter of the twentieth century, two reports stood out as being of huge significance to the British police in terms of its relations with the minority groups to which it delivers its service: the Scarman Report (1981) and the Report of the Inquiry into the Death of Stephen Lawrence (Macpherson 1999). Both of these reports identified the need for effective police training in community and race relations (CRR). Although many changes to the police curriculum were made after Scarman, criticisms made by the Macpherson Report published some eighteen years later suggested that substantial progress had not been made. Other literature (for example HMIC 1993, 1996, 1997, 1999, 2000) also charts the patchy progress made by the police in training for equal opportunities, community and race relations, and latterly diversity.

The idea of 'awareness' emerges as a common theme in various recommendations about police officers' need for training. For example, of the seventy recommendations that Macpherson made, three related directly to police training:

48. That there should be an immediate review and revision of *racism awareness* training within the Police Service to ensure:-

   a. that there exists a consistent strategy to deliver appropriate training within all police services based on the value of our cultural diversity;
   b. that training courses are designed and delivered in order to develop the full understanding that good community relations are essential to good policing and that a racist officer is an incompetent officer.

49. That all police officers including CID and civilian staff, should be trained in racism awareness and valuing cultural diversity.

50. That police training and practical experience in the field of racism awareness and valuing cultural diversity should regularly be conducted at local level. And that it should be recognised that local minority ethnic communities should be involved in such training and experience. (Macpherson 1999: 332)

EXERCISE

- What do you understand by the term awareness?
- How far does the term go in capturing what a police officer may need in terms of training in race and diversity?

A key problem is that awareness means different things to different people. At best it is a vague term. In addition, people may experience awareness of the same thing in different ways. Very often awareness is associated with a fairly low level and simple way of experiencing something. For example as you read this book you will be aware of the context in which you are reading it, you will be aware of who else is in the room, you will have awareness of the temperature, lighting levels and many other factors. But in what sense can you say that you are learning about these things? In what sense are they changing you as a person? The answer is probably not much. So what does awareness mean? Marton (1994) describes how a person may experience the same object in different ways according to the context in which it is experienced. Awareness is often taken to be synonymous with knowledge, both internal to the individual, usually their attitudes, values, beliefs, and prejudices, and external issues such as culture. Awareness may also develop out of personal experience or hearing about the experience of others.

So we come to the problem of suggesting that the goal of race awareness or diversity training (as for example recommended in Macpherson) should be 'training in racism awareness and valuing cultural diversity' (1999: 332). Is simply raising awareness of racism sufficient? It needs to go much further than that. For example, a police officer may be aware of cultural diversity but that says nothing about how he or she may respond to that awareness. Crucially the officer may become 'aware' that he or she has feelings of prejudice or may even become aware of racism that hitherto had been undisclosed to them. The

157

learning needs to go further and will require a change in the way that person sees the world if they are to function effectively as a police officer.

8.2.2 **Diversity as a special case**

Many attempts have been made to argue that diversity training should be integrated and mainstreamed into other generic police training. The main thrust of the argument is that as policing itself is essentially about policing a diverse society then it makes sense to deal with diversity as integrated, even synthesized into all that a police officer might learn about the business of policing. Indeed more than just making sense, it is argued, it goes to show that diversity is not regarded as a mere optional extra but is something that goes to the heart of the training curriculum. Both these arguments are powerful, but a note of caution needs to be sounded. Experience shows that whilst it is easy to talk about such notions as embedding, mainstreaming, a golden thread, or even a golden tapestry, the reality is harder to achieve. A few of the reasons for this difficulty are outlined here:

- Far from avoiding 'bolting-on' and tokenism, the reality of much of the police curriculum is that attempts to integrate or embed diversity have led to exactly that. Where, for example a training designer has a strict brief to make sure that diversity is integrated into all aspects of the training, this can all too easily lead to a shallow representation of the issues and a mere paying of lip service to them, for example assuming that putting a few Asian (or whatever) sounding names to the characters in a case study will be sufficient to make the learning 'diversity proof'.
- We have already seen in the introduction to the book that for a real appreciation of diverse society and all the issues that raises, a deep understanding of the issues is needed. A further objection to the idea of mainstreaming and embedding is that the detailed consideration and reflection that is needed is unlikely to happen in a curriculum where diversity is not dealt with as an issue in its own right.
- A third objection involves the attributes and skills of the trainers. Clements and Jones (2002) cite research conducted that identified a number of skills and attributes that effective diversity trainers need. These are shown in Table 8.1 below.

The question that needs to be asked is whether all trainers have the necessary skills and attributes effectively either to integrate diversity into the curriculum or even to deal with it as a specialist subject. The fact remains that a high level of personal awareness and skill is needed for a trainer to effectively engage with the issues. The issue is too important to leave it in the hands of trainers who are not up to the job.

Table 8.1 The skills and attributes of diversity trainers

Skills	Attributes
Makes appropriate interventions	Resilience
Conflict management	Belief in the task
Able to ask tough questions	Mental agility
Flexible	Positive outlook
Able to manage group dynamics	Recognizes own limits
Knowledge of the relevant law	Been through the process
Able to manage resistance strategies	Sincerity
Knowledge of policy issues	Sensitive to people's needs and concerns
Knowledge of own prejudice	'Walks the talk'
	Motivation to change
	Experienced in diversity

8.2.3 Authority to engage

In my own experience as a diversity trainer a frequent comment from police officers engaged in diversity training was 'what right do you have to challenge me about my attitudes, values and beliefs'? To be effective, learning about diversity will inevitably involve a certain amount of challenge to people and taking them out of their comfort zone. But where trainers are challenged as to their moral or institutional right to do this many are not sure of the ground on which they stand.

EXERCISE

• If you were a trainer receiving such a challenge—what would you say?

When organizations want to develop a training or educationally based response to diversity the issue of the authority which the organization, or in this case the trainer (as an agent of the organization), has to engage with the values, attitudes, and beliefs of the people it employs will inevitably come to light.

In my own research in this area (Clements 2000), twenty-two trainers (out of a sample of thirty) talked about the authority (or lack of it) they had to engage with learners particularly in relation to raising their awareness about diversity issues and in encouraging the learners to engage in reflection on their attitudes, values, and beliefs. Some key points which emerged from this are useful to note as they illustrate several of the things that need to be considered in developing diversity programmes:

• Thinking reflectively about attitudes, values, and beliefs in respect of diversity issues is likely to cause discomfort for the learner. An interesting by-product

159

of this is that on many courses in diversity I have run, there has been the traditional end of course evaluation (sometimes referred to as 'happy sheets'), and it is not uncommon for some students to note on the sheet that they did not find the course enjoyable. There is a strong sense in which this could be an expression of the success of the course—being confronted and having to face attitudes and values that are inappropriate will not always be a comfortable or enjoyable experience.

- Some trainers (and managers) feel that they are *mandated* by the organization to challenge learners or staff and take them into areas where they may feel uncomfortable. They feel that they have the authority of the organization behind them and are willing therefore to challenge people's attitudes, values, and beliefs (particularly if these are inappropriate in a culture which values diversity).

- Other trainers are much less certain of their ground. An alternative view that the research revealed is that if a learner does not want to take part in a process that challenges their attitudes, values, and beliefs, then the trainer would accept that no further progress could or should be made. This reluctance to attempt to change a person's way of seeing something may, for the trainer, become an ethical or moral barrier to progress.

It is important therefore that where attitudes, values, and beliefs are addressed, trainers and participants together know the authority under which this is being conducted and that both are properly supported. One way in which some organizations have addressed this is to ensure that courses on diversity are 'opened' by a senior member of the organization who will make a statement regarding the commitment of the organization to the training and the authority that the trainer has to work on behalf of the organization. My experience when this has happened, is that such interventions are helpful in establishing the authority to engage with learners.

8.3 The Issues Surrounding a Competence Based Approach to Training

8.3.1 Introduction

The competence movement has gained increasing penetration into all aspects of the police curriculum. We have already discussed the National Learning Requirement for police officers in respect of diversity and the pivotal role that the National Occupational Standards and associated knowledge and understanding requirements have to play in learning and development. My own experience as a police trainer over a decade of delivering equal opportunities and race and diversity training to both operational police officers and trainers, is that the development of competence based approaches to training and performance in the police has led to the false belief that this is an adequate approach to effective training.

Scant attention has been paid to the issues raised by the question what does it take for a police officer to 'learn' diversity? Bowden and Marton (1998) identified a need to re-couple an understanding of 'learning' with what is learned in universities. The same applies to what and how police officers learn, or achieve the outcomes that are defined in competence terms for the police.

8.3.2 Behaviourist approaches to learning

In the years that I was involved, behaviourism was the main conceptual underpinning of police training, and, despite a move in the mid to late 1980s towards more cognitive, adult centred approaches, the pendulum has now swung back to behaviourism in response to the demands of the competency movement. Expected outcomes for diversity training are very often expressed in terms of observable competence. The focus is on what people can do as opposed to what they know, think, feel, or believe. It is of course very important, even critical, that police officers have the competence to do the job correctly and within the law. This applies to the ability to engage with a diverse society as much as any other aspect of policing. But skills and competence are never adequately developed in a vacuum. There needs to be an underpinning knowledge, understanding *which is coupled with appropriate attitudes*. The object of learning diversity needs to be a changed capability for police officers to engage in the 'principled policing' advocated by Alderson (1998). This can only really effectively be achieved where attitudes and beliefs are congruent with the behaviour that is expected.

REFLECT ON PRACTICE

Think about a police officer you know whose attitudes towards diversity are negative.

- How confident are you that those attitudes will never be exhibited in the officer's behaviour?
- Can you think of examples of when attitudes have been expressed in behaviour?

8.3.3 Attitudes, values, and beliefs in training

It is inevitable that any effective programme of 'learning' diversity will need to address attitudes, values, and beliefs and we have already noted that an issue surrounding this is the extent to which any organization and the people representing it have the authority to delve into and challenge people's attitudes. Undoubtedly, religion and belief is a major factor in a diverse society and many people have strong beliefs and values in that regard. Harvey and Allard (1995:

161

151) observe that the 'impact of religion at the level of core values and beliefs is strong'. Diversity by its nature then will include the diversity of religious belief and many attitudes and values will be involved. Both Christianity and Islam, for example, hold the idea of work as a core value; in Hinduism duty is regarded as one means of salvation. These combine together to illustrate that such values need to be respected, nurtured, and catered for in police service delivery. What then are the practical implications for the training curriculum?

Harvey and Allard (1995:151) describe the issues in terms of layers, but it is perhaps more helpful to see them as stemming from the core of an individual's value system. Figure 8.1 below gives just some examples of some of the challenging issues that may need to be addressed—you will, in all likelihood be able to think of others.

Figure 8.1 The interconnection of religious and cultural belief

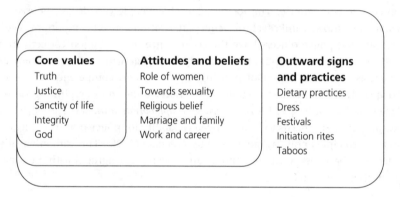

Core values	Attitudes and beliefs	Outward signs and practices
Truth	Role of women	Dietary practices
Justice	Towards sexuality	Dress
Sanctity of life	Religious belief	Festivals
Integrity	Marriage and family	Initiation rites
God	Work and career	Taboos

You should be able to see that learning about all this is not merely a question of what a police officer can do, it will also involve a fairly deep knowledge and understanding and response to the issues at varying levels. Approaching this from a competence perspective alone will not be adequate.

8.3.4 **Strengths and weaknesses of competence approaches**

All the above leads us to consider the strengths and weaknesses of a competence approach to training. Table 8.2 below indicates what some of these are.

To sum up, we have explored the idea that learning about diversity is more than just about what people can do. Where training approaches this learning solely from the perspective of competence it is unlikely to capture all that a police officer needs to learn to deliver a good service to a diverse society. This takes us to the next section in which we discuss the relative merits of training and education as ways of helping police officers to learn about diversity.

Table 8.2 Strengths and weaknesses of a competence based approach

Strengths	Weaknesses
Competence is vital in all professions—being able to do the job well is central to this.	All professions including the police have knowledge and understanding requirements—these may not receive due attention with a focus solely on what people can do.
Competence frameworks attempt to define what needs to be done and the standards expected.	Policing is complex—how can we be certain that everything required of a police officer is defined adequately?
Competence approaches help define learning outcomes in terms of what a police officer needs to do.	Whilst outcomes in terms of what a person can do are important, we also need outcomes in terms of a police officer's knowledge, understanding attitudes, values, and beliefs.
Competence frameworks provide a benchmark for people outside of the police service to make judgements about performance.	Where competence outcomes are defined, there is often no accompanying definition of the way in which something might be done.
Competence frameworks provide a way of identifying training needs.	But do they address attitudes, values, and beliefs?

8.4 Training and Education

8.4.1 Compared and contrasted

Diversity is a given; what is important is how people in organizations such as the police service respond to it, and in this regard whether this should be a matter of training or education becomes important. There is a real and not just semantic difference between education and training as paradigms (ways of approaching) of learning. Learning that is acquired through training is often characterized as the acquisition of new knowledge and associated skills and 'includes any activity with a clearly defined performance improvement outcome' (HMIC 1999b: 153). Few would argue that people in organizations do need to acquire the necessary knowledge and skills to do the job, but such a restrictive understanding in terms of training fails to recognize two crucial features of what needs to be learned in regard to the response to diversity.

The first is that virtually all the skills police officers need to learn relate to their interactions with people, the second is that the consistent focus on the skills required to underpin performance often fails to recognize that where training traditionally and by *its very nature* seeks to reduce skill actions to their simple components, in fact the socio-political context in which police officers will exercise their skill is highly complex.

Models of training such as those put forward by Bee and Bee (1994) and Bramley (1986) have a number of elements in common in that they are object-ives driven and focus on inputs and behavioural outputs. Overarching these aspects is the presumption that the training event must be aimed at improv-ing operational effectiveness (Bramley 1986) or business needs (Bee and Bee 1994). Significantly, the presumption does not extend to higher-level goals asso-ciated with education—understanding, application of that understanding, and the generalized ability to solve problems in a range of different contexts.

Education in classical thinking has altogether different goals. Kenney and Reid (1986) identify the key areas of difference as being process, orientation, method, content, and the degree of precision involved. In regard to the latter, for example, education crucially involves the development of transferable and generalizable ability to apply learning to a range of circumstances rather than relying on the precisely defined outcomes that would be associated with training. The type of learning associated with education (as opposed to training) may be reduced to the simple notion that learning is change (Marton and Booth 1997). That change will be in the areas of what an individual knows, understands, and can do, but will not (and probably cannot be) restricted to narrowly defined behavioural outcomes. The type, or perhaps more correctly the object of learning in the sense of learning about diversity, is characterized as an activity in which we come to know and understand ourselves both in relation to our life context, the complex nature of that life context, and the complex nature of the organization in which we conduct our professional life. Responding to diversity represents that very complexity that people need to learn about.

EXERCISE

- Is the context in which policing takes place becoming more or less complex?

8.4.2 **The role of higher education**

So how are the police to engage in this type of learning? Just one of the answers for example, lies in the opportunity for police officers to engage in study at degree level in the same way as other professions. For example, in line with the Government's drive to widen access to higher education and provide a means of accrediting study which is essentially vocationally based and oriented, many higher education institutions now offer foundation degrees. These are typically two to three years of study at degree level and are offered in a wide range of vocational contexts such as early years education, engineering, and para-medical sciences.

The first Foundation Degree in Police Studies of this type was launched at the University of Portsmouth in October 2002. This degree programme in common with other foundation degrees was designed in conjunction with stakeholders from the police sector, including Skills for Justice, the organization charged with responsibility for defining the National Occupational Standards of policing in the UK. The Home Office, the Association of Chief Police Officers, and the HMIC also had involvement in the design and have had oversight of the programme. The foundation degree programme for police officers currently has many police officers, with a wide geographic, length of service, and age range studying such topics as the 'Social Context of Policing', 'Police Operations and Policing Processes', 'Research Skills', and 'Crime Disorder and Justice' The knowledge and understanding gained from studying these units is then applied to a Professional Practice in Policing Project which will focus on an issue or problem in the officer's local work-based context. The degree is studied by distance learning and makes heavy use of online learning as a means of delivery and engaging with the students, and by providing a means for the students to discuss together in a 'virtual' environment.

The virtual environment has been used to track students' perceptions of the value added they feel is represented by their learning. For example, the question 'What difference might being on the degree make to the way you perceive your role as a police officer?' produced responses of which the following are a sample.

> I understand how my role fits into current strategy and initiatives. By understanding this it enables me to be more focused. But I also understand that the answer is not as simple as many think. The role of the modern police officer is to perform so many different tasks that it is difficult to please everyone as there are many factors to consider.

> I feel that I am better placed to understand senior management decision making processes and I have found that I am more confident in explaining why policies etc have been developed and how my shift and I can have a positive impact on them.

> The degree makes me question more the processes and policy I use. Not always a positive experience.

> Knowledge is power and this new knowledge has given me greater confidence in my role. I think it has been important to appreciate the wider role of a police officer in society and to understand the impact that we can have. However we must also appreciate the limitations of the role.

The comments of these students represent a number of 'learning' issues that would typically be more associated with education rather than training. For example, an understanding of the role, and its relation to the complexity of society, the ability to understand the development and application of policy and higher level decision making, the ability to question and critically assess practices and procedures and confidence, particularly in the area of understanding the importance and impact of policing on society. Current police training programmes typically pay scant attention to such issues, and it is questionable whether police trainers, given the preparation they have for the role, would be in a position to deliver a meaningful learning experience in relation to the more complex social and political issues.

There seems to be, then, a need to break out of the training cycle mentality. Typically systematic approaches to training will follow a cycle of identifying a need, designing a training intervention, delivering that intervention, and then evaluating its effectiveness. Where deficit is found the solution almost always lies in designing a different training intervention and typically never involves consideration of whether training itself is the appropriate medium of learning. Where training is seen to be ineffective for the requirement, what is needed is to re-conceptualize the whole paradigm in a way that allows for a different approach.

8.5 Reviews by the HMIC

In Chapter 4 we reviewed some of the HMIC findings in relation to diversity generally in the police. In this section we will focus our attention on what the HMIC has said about the progress in the police service on training in relation to race and diversity. Our point of departure is a report published in 1993 which serves to show the way things were just over ten years ago. This is followed by a discussion of two other reports that illuminate some of the issues we have discussed in the chapter so far. The following section seeks only to pick out some of the issues that we have been discussing. You are encouraged to read the full reports which are all published on the HMIC website: <http://inspectorates.homeoffice.gov.uk/hmic/> where you need to follow the links to the thematic inspections.

8.5.1 Equal Opportunities in the Police Service (1993)

This was the report of a thematic inspection carried out in 1992. Twelve forces were inspected with two being drawn from each of the six Inspectorate areas, and the purpose of the inspection was to '... ensure that forces have implemented or are actively implementing equal opportunities policies ... in line with Home Office Circular 87/1989' (HMIC 1993: 1). Interviews were held with police officers and support staff of all ranks and grades. A number of themes emerged but two are of particular interest for the purpose of this literature review, namely training issues, and the 'culture of equal opportunities'.

The report noted that the training provision ranged from none at all in two of the forces to 'a major commitment' of one or more days' training for all staff in others. In terms of abstraction from the work place, a full day's training for every staff member is a major commitment for any organization. In training delivery terms, particularly if the training is to be highly participative in nature, it is decidedly questionable what could actually be achieved in a day. Nevertheless the report does remark that in the forces where there was no awareness raising, the negative and inappropriate language that was used in discussions was noticeable.

The HMIC noted its concern about the wide variation in the knowledge of equal opportunities issues. Some of those interviewed said that they had no knowledge at all. This may, according to the report, have been in part due to the fact that it was policy in probationer training that issues of equality be threaded through the entire curriculum. Instructors were expected to weave this thread into all aspects of what they did. The HMIC concluded that *'sadly the policy appears to be failing'*. The way the then District Training Centres were regimented and run may also have been influential in sending negative messages, and some of the standing orders may in themselves have been discriminatory. It was also found that there was a paucity of provision for those moving into supervisory and managerial ranks.

In terms of developing a culture of equal opportunities, the report noted that progress is made faster when the chief officers and senior management openly express their commitment and support. Some of those interviewed during the research expressed their cynicism and scepticism about their forces' commitment to equal opportunities. Three elements of traditional culture were recurring themes in the interviews. They revolved around the relationship between police officers and support staff, the acceptance of racial stereotyping, and the treatment of women police officers. It was noted that language in its role as a vehicle for communicating attitudes has a critical part to play in that it is an expression of cultures itself. An underlying level of racist banter signalled the need for first line supervisors to challenge inappropriate behaviour. Another worrying feature identified by the report was that there seemed to be a persistent low-level harassment of women in the forces inspected. It was not uncommon for the language of senior officers to appear exclusionary.

This report painted a fairly bleak picture of the situation as it was then. Bear in mind though that this was six years before the Stephen Lawrence Inquiry and the police service had yet to be confronted with the issues that raised.

8.5.2 Developing Diversity in the Police Service (1996)

This inspection built on the work done in 1992 and this time thirteen forces were inspected including four from the 1992 inspection. In the preamble to the report a number of significant observations were made. It was noted for example that the 1992 report found that many could not see the value of an equal opportunities policy:

> Many people do not yet understand how or why managing diverse groups of people is a crucial concept in the effective policing of society now and in the future. (HMIC 1996: 10).

Another significant observation in the report was the acknowledgement that mechanisms designed to improve equality of opportunity would be ineffective in the long term if they were not accompanied by a general shift in attitudes and culture. 'Lip service' and 'tokenism' were seen as masking subtle yet continuing discriminatory behaviour and practices.

In reporting on training, the HMIC curiously, in the light of the 1993 criticism of such a strategy, opens the section with the proposition that DIVERSITY training needs to run like a 'golden thread' (HMIC 1996: 45) through all training programmes, so that equal opportunity is seen as essential to any human resource strategy. In commenting on the need for evaluation, however, the report outlines the problems that are associated with the 'integration' principle. There was, and still is, a serious lack of quality control and evaluation of training in the police service generally (HMIC 2005). This being the case, the HMIC noted that it was all too easy where integration was expected for it to be marginalized or even ignored completely.

Interviews also covered perceptions of equal opportunities and the responses to this were varied. Some saw equal opportunities as a statement of the obvious, others saw it as a mechanism to transfer responsibility from senior to junior staff, still others saw the possibility of claiming compensation for their own bad experiences. An interesting and useful conclusion by the HMIC was that 'Too often the training set equal opportunities in the context of race or gender rather than in fairness and the value of diversity' (HMIC 1996: 45). This is a very important comment that should not be lost. In designing a training programme to tackle issues of equality of opportunity it is all too easy to lose the wood for the trees. Few would suggest that the aims of training in equal opportunities should be restricted to dealing with black people, women, or gay issues. The aim should be to enable police officers to develop a view of the world which encompasses the attitudes and skills needed to treat *all* human beings as individuals and with fairness dignity and respect. The Articles contained within the European Convention on Human Rights 1950 are all grounded in the inclusive term 'everyone'. In my own experience of equal opportunities training, many police officers feel themselves to be unfairly treated whether from within the organization or by the attitudes of some towards it, notably the media. This can be a huge barrier to learning and needs to be addressed if it is not to have a deleterious effect on the training outcomes.

The report goes on to note that staff trainers have a tendency to become the focus for attacks by some students who see the equal opportunities training as the opportunity to air their grievances. It was not uncommon to find that trainers involved in equal opportunities training delivery would go sick with stress. It appeared that some senior management had not appreciated the commitment required to be an equal opportunities trainer.

As with the 1993 Report, it was noted that without evaluation there could be no judgement about the effectiveness of training. It was noted that where there had been a substantial investment in equal opportunities training, the benefits from this could have been increased if the training had been professionally evaluated. Subsequent costs could be reduced if this had been done. Other training issues identified by the 1996 Report include:

- The need to include support staff.
- The need to recognize that equal opportunities training should be inclusive rather than exclusive and that specific courses on race or gender tended to give them a status of bolt-on extras.
- It was noted that distance learning packs can be effective for disseminating information to people who want to learn, but they cannot in themselves be relied upon to bring about cultural change.
- When the cultural change is taking place, new lessons that are learned will need to be reinforced on a regular basis. This implies that for any training strategy arrangements need to be made for follow up work to be done.

8.5.3 Diversity Matters (2003)

This was a comprehensive inspection of what had by this time come to be known as diversity training (as opposed to the earlier use of 'equal opportunities').

In terms of the progress on race and diversity training, one of the most worrying findings of the HMIC was that 'overall the current training appears to be driven solely by a desire to meet targets' (HMIC 2003: 102). This seems to suggest that some forces at least are not concerned with actually improving performance or building better relationships with the communities they serve, but are succumbing to a 'tick the box' syndrome where they can show that they are doing something but in fact are only paying lip service to the need. Picking up on the theme we identified above, the HMIC also identified that the training is mostly of short duration and 'cannot be expected to change attitudes or behaviour'. A further set of barriers to effective training were identified (p 102):

- When designing training, the Service lacks a national model of guidance on how to involve the community at all stages of the training cycle;
- Training delivery methods are too often carelessly selected and are often unstructured;
- Training content is neither holistic nor set to national standards;
- The environment, in which the training is delivered, is not by design always one in which safe learning can take place;
- External partners and contributors are too often mismanaged or made to feel vulnerable or unwelcome;
- Many police staff, in the absence of an organizational learning culture and a clearly articulated rationale, neither welcome nor support the concept of race and diversity training.

The last bullet point above resonates with the experience of many police trainers and others who are involved in police training. It is not uncommon to find that participants in training events are resistant or unwilling to engage. This reflects the discussion above about the authority to engage. If attitudes are to be addressed effectively there must be a clear understanding of the reasons for the training and the fact that the organization reserves the right to challenge inappropriate attitudes and also has the right to expect that having been confronted with them people will not only reflect but also demonstrate a willingness to change.

The report also made comments about the outcomes of race and diversity training and some of the findings resonate with what we were saying above in regard to the limitations on competency approaches to training. The HMIC noted:

> Race and diversity training cannot and must not be measured in terms of learner satisfaction alone, particularly if the desired or planned outcomes do not encourage individuals to:
> • Examine and challenge their own practice as well as that of others;
> • Acknowledge discriminatory practices exist;
> • Seek alternative, more considered approaches to their operational decisions where necessary (and the key is knowing where). (p 133).

It seems that critical to learning about the issues is to reflectively and critically reflect on practice, to be open to the fact that prejudice and discrimination still manifest themselves both personally and institutionally, and to be willing to change. Again a disturbing outcome of the inspection was that many police officers who had been through race and diversity training were unable to demonstrate a meaningful understanding of institutional racism or institutional discrimination. This perhaps illustrates best of all that a competence outcome approach is not adequate on its own and that education in its truest sense of critical reflection, knowledge, and understanding has a crucial role to play.

8.6 What Works in Diversity Training

Research has been conducted into many of the issues that we have discussed in this chapter with a specific focus on what works for police officers in learning diversity. The research is reported in Clements (2000) and is summarized below. Based primarily on interview data and literature four components of 'good' training were identified as: the objects, the act, and the process of the training, and the trainers themselves. In the following sections we will identify the key features that were identified.

8.6.1 The objects of the training

Aims and objectives (the terms often used in training) and learning outcomes (used more frequently in education) can sometimes give the illusion that there is clarity of purpose, when in fact they may create a dissonance between what is specified for trainers to achieve and what they (trainers) believe they should be aiming at. They do have a role to play in helping to make training accountable to the many stakeholders in it but they may not be entirely helpful to instructors or learners where the processes and outcomes of training may not be so easy to express, certainly in pure behavioural terms. In vocational training paid for out of public funds, there must be a concern for accountability, but this does not have to get in the way of specifying training which works with learners at a deeper and more meaningful level than merely aiming at behavioural competencies. An understanding of the nature of awareness is important because of the frequency with which the word 'awareness' is used in connection with diversity training (see the discussion on awareness in 8.2.1 above). One of the objects of good diversity training will therefore be to engage with the different ways in which people experience the issues. This of course has implications for the way diversity trainers should be taught.

Another object, which is strongly related to awareness, is knowledge. This is not just knowledge of things outside of the individual such as law, policy, and so on, but will also be things internal to the individual such as prejudice, attitudes, and values. Good diversity training therefore needs to embody knowledge of self as well.

One of the specific objects of diversity training should be prejudice. Addressing people's personal value systems may be a way into helping them identify their prejudices. It will help in the training if there is an acceptance that everyone has prejudices of one form or another. Trainers need to have worked through their own prejudices before they engage in this training and it will be helpful if they offer some personal self-disclosure to the learners. Some training situations may be more difficult if people do not accept that they have any prejudices. Figure 8.2 presents these points in diagrammatic form.

8.6.2 The act of diversity training

This is about what the learner is doing when he or she engages in diversity training, in other words it refers to how the learner is personally engaging in the process to achieve the objects. Understanding is key to this as well as seeing the world in different ways, reflection, and realization. All these 'acts' will need to be encouraged to facilitate the deeper level of exploration that is implied by the 'self-knowledge' objects referred to above.

Seeing things in different ways is very important as we need to recognize that others may see the world quite differently to the way we see it because, as we have seen above, their way of experiencing a certain aspect of the world might be quite different. Our assumptions tend to be built upon our own way of experiencing and therefore all our assumptions need to be challenged. Coming to see the world differently and having our assumptions challenged is very likely to be an uncomfortable, even painful, process and this needs to be taken account of. Coming to see things in a different way may or may not be a sudden experience

Figure 8.2 The objects of good diversity training

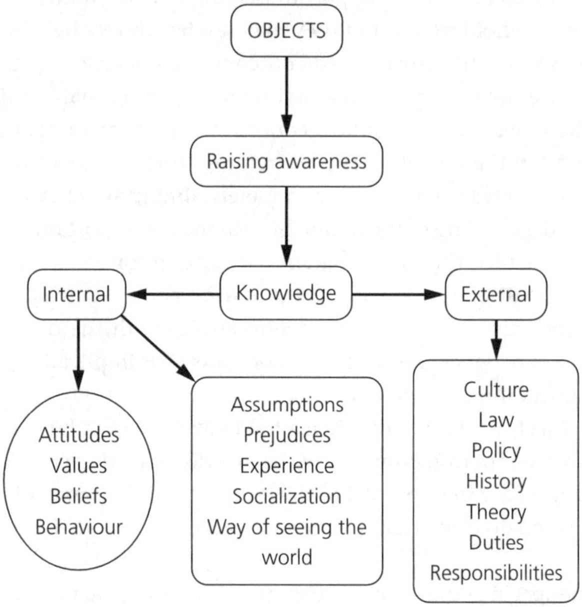

for the learner, but however it happens a process of exploration will precede it, and this exploration will be either external or internal in that it may be knowledge of issues or knowledge of self.

Reflection is also an important 'act' in diversity training, but there can be variation in the way 'reflection' is understood. For example, there is the 'reflective practitioner' described by Schön (1983), but 'reflection' may also be used variously to mean 'reflect back' in the sense of mirror, 'think about', 'dwell on', or think about in a way that leads to some change, during, after, or some time after the training event.

REFLECT ON PRACTICE

It is timely to ask you to stop and reflect on reflection!

- What does the word mean to you?
- How do you do it?
- How often do you do it?
- Do you regard it as necessary for the way you learn?

Truthful and honest reflection on the part of the learner may result in them becoming 'consciously aware'. This can be seen as an act of 'realization'. The outcome of realization is also expressed as a state of 'heightened awareness'. The timing of realization runs in parallel to the act of reflection described above. Realization may happen suddenly in the context of a classroom session where for some this will be like a light switching on and may be connected with experiencing a new way of seeing something. These points are shown in Figure 8.3 below.

Figure 8.3 The act of diversity training

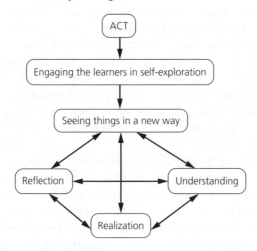

8.6.3 **The process of diversity training**

The process of diversity training is an element of the model that has themes from the data which are neither objects nor the specific act of training but relate either to the conditions under which the training is taking place or some qualitative aspect of it. So this element includes an assessment of issues about authority to engage with the learners at other than merely a cognitive level, and the way in which diversity training is likely to involve an element of discomfort or pain for the learner (and sometimes the trainer). Several trainers made an analogy between diversity training and 'being on a journey'.

As we discussed above, some trainers are confident that they are mandated by the organization to challenge learners and take them into areas where they may feel uncomfortable. An alternative view in the research data is that if a learner does not want to take part in the process then the trainer would have to accept that. A further way of seeing the problem is that trainers feel that they want to engage with learners in a way that challenges them to explore their attitudes, values, and beliefs because they know this makes for effective diversity training, but they are reluctant to do so as they do not feel they have either organizational sanction or the moral right to do so. Clearly a model of good diversity training cannot embody all three approaches. Given what has been built up so far in terms of the object and act of diversity training, it becomes apparent that to adopt a position which expresses reluctance to engage with learners is to approach the training from a standpoint that is unlikely to succeed. Trainers need to be clear that they are mandated by the organization to deliver this training, that organizational values embody the expectation that the employees will share in them, and that learners who are unwilling to engage in the process are effectively distancing themselves from the values that they should be espousing.

A model of good diversity training will recognize that when people engage in an exploration of their attitudes, values, and beliefs, this may be an uncomfortable process. For some they will find things about themselves that will cause them emotional pain, and often the tension in the learner will be how they should respond. This discomfort may be a necessary factor in personal growth in diversity training terms and, rather than shy away from it or try to avoid it, the process should be constructed in a way that discomfort can take place in a secure and supportive environment. This will involve skill on the part of the trainer, and carefully thought through issues of confidentiality and group contract. Trainers need to recognize that the way some learners will respond to discomfort may include discrediting the course, avoiding the process, and retreating into a safety-net/comfort zone. Ironically this may be taken as an indicator of successful process, and that the person is being effectively challenged.

The analogy of the journey is one frequently used by trainers to describe the overall process of diversity training. It is a powerful one and has a number of qualities that may be carried forward in to a model. The analogy stresses, for example, the need for the training to be learner centred, in the sense that each person's journey will be an individual one and will have a different starting point. The learner must complete the journey in a model of good diversity training. So it would not be good training to exit just at the point of increased knowledge. The learner needs to go further in a process of self-exploration to achieve the objects in the first element, such as understanding, seeing the world in different ways so that they feel they can sit comfortably with the purpose and values of the organization. Through reflection, realization, and understanding the journey will be one of exploration—things will be discovered that may not have been planned for, and each person will experience the exploration in different ways. A successful outcome of the journey would be where the student had been empowered to make his or her own choices, and that those choices were then congruent with the values of the organization.

REFLECT ON PRACTICE

If you have engaged in diversity training—to what extent could you describe your own experience as being on a journey?

• What was your point of departure—where are you now?

Being on a journey *with* the trainer may have the effect of making the training less threatening, and will help to engage the learner's interest. The journey should be made in the context of the individual's life experience. Trainers have an important role to play in acting in the role of guide and will have metaphorically gathered together the equipment needed for a journey of exploration. Figure 8.4 gathers these strands together in diagrammatic form.

Figure 8.4 The process of diversity training

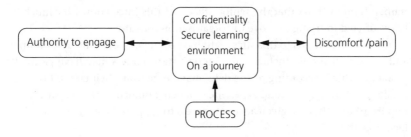

8.6.4 **The trainers involved in diversity training**

The final element concerns themes about the trainers themselves. This includes the skills that diversity trainers need, and their own knowledge, understanding, and acceptance of the issues. The skills and attributes needed by trainers can be identified and these are summarized in Table 8.1 above. Trainers need to be able to facilitate effectively because they need to work with learners at a level that is much more than one of knowledge transmission. They have to be clear about what they are trying to do and how they will do it, but at the same time will need to be flexible to adapt to changing circumstances in the classroom. Trainers who do not have the appropriate skill to work in sensitive and emotional areas may actually cause psychological damage to learners.

Trainers should not engage in diversity training until they have identified their own prejudices, worked through their positions in relation to CRR issues, and had their attitudes exposed. This will be important for a number of reasons. Firstly, they need to be sincere and committed to what they are doing and will need to know how they personally respond to the issues around which they will be facilitating. They need to have attitudes, values, beliefs, and behaviour that are congruent with what they are training and therefore also need to have had the opportunity to work through the areas of difficulty for them as individuals.

Trainers need to recognize that if they are to engage in this type of training, stress can be a problem. This can range from feeling devalued to feeling that they are not getting anywhere. Some classroom situations will be very emotionally charged and challenging to deal with and they need to be able to cope with such situations. Working at a level which is effective will involve the discomfort

175

and pain, even trauma, that self-exploration may involve. To deal with this the trainer will need to be not only a skilled facilitator, but also resilient, sensitive, flexible, able to read body language, skilled in recognizing and responding to group dynamics and confident to lead learners on a journey which may be difficult.

Diversity trainers may find they suffer stress quite unlike the stresses involved in training other topics. The phenomenon is not new and is reported in literature outside the police context (Kandola 1991, Garrett and Taylor 1993). The HMIC Report (1996: 45) contains a telling statement from a female diversity trainer: 'I don't think that the senior officers of this force know how much we have suffered in trying to move the organisation forward'.

One of the solutions to this stress is to have a support mechanism for trainers and the model should include this. Support staff trainers may have particular problems which, according to the data, may range from their credibility being challenged through to actual experiences of being bullied. It will be particularly important that they are given adequate access to support. Figure 8.5 draws these ideas together.

Figure 8.5 The trainers engaged in diversity training

8.7 **Chapter Summary**

In this chapter we have considered the issues surrounding how people learn about diversity.

- In terms of learning to learn about diversity we looked at some of the ways in which people approach learning about the issues. We noted particularly that raised 'awareness' is frequently mentioned as one of the key learning outcomes, but that it is important to be clear about what awareness means. There is a strong sense in which diversity can be seen as a special case and that where it is assumed to be 'mainstreamed' this can sometimes have the effect of tokenism or watering down the issues.
- We saw that competence based approaches to training have now penetrated all aspects of the police training curriculum. Whilst we acknowledged that there is no doubt that police officers need to be competent, competence alone will not reflect fully what the professional police

officer needs. Competence needs to be supported or enshrined in a set of attitudes, values, and beliefs that are congruent with policing a diverse society.

- There is an ongoing debate about the relative merits of training and education as approaches to learning and whilst training is the natural bedfellow of competence, education has a vital part to play in terms of the development of an understanding of the bigger picture. Where training of necessity tries to break down complex issues into simple components, education encourages the taking of a broader view and importantly challenges learners to see the world differently. This is vital for effective diversity training.

- We noted some of the key outcomes of inspections by the HMIC in relation to diversity training initiatives in the police. Whilst there are many examples of good practice we saw that the HMIC has consistently offered constructive criticism of the way the police service has responded to its duty in relation to training diversity.

- We concluded the discussion of training responses to diversity with consideration of 'what works'. We noted that there are four components of a model of good training which are:

  - the objects of the training: these need to express not only knowledge and understanding of what is external to the learner but also a dimension of self-knowledge;

  - the act of the training: which includes important issues such as realization and reflection;

  - the process of the training: which can be compared to being on a journey where the trainer acts as a guide;

  - the trainers themselves, who need to be competent to facilitate difficult issues, have a high level of self awareness, and be sure of the authority that they have to engage learners with the more difficult issues.

Diversity and the Impact
of Terrorism

9.1 **Chapter Outline**

As we have seen throughout the book, diversity in society and the response to that diversity by the police and other agencies is far from a simple and uncomplicated matter. That complication has been made even stronger by events in the UK and the world at large which have their roots in terrorist activity. In this concluding chapter, we will briefly consider how terrorism and terrorist activity have directly and indirectly impacted on thinking about and responding to diversity in society. We will cover the following ground:

- A brief résumé of major events that have sparked debates about diversity;
- Islamophobia, increasing suspicion of Islam, stereotyping of, and prejudice towards Muslims, including a marked increase in racially and religiously motivated crime;
- Stop and search and finding the balance between protecting against terrorism and the need to avoid alienating communities;
- The Government's response to terrorism and the concern to avoid the erosion of liberty and human rights;
- The response to new threats such as suicide bombings and what this means for the police in terms of firearms policy, the use of lethal force, and the potential to erode trust in the police service and its policy;
- The increased fear of crime amongst communities of all kinds, including no-go areas, and a general raising of perceptions of personal security including the fuelling of moral panic where people merely wearing puffed jackets or rucksacks may easily become suspects.

9.2 **Terrorist Events**

There have, regrettably, been numerous instances of terrorist activity over the past five years that have been aimed mainly, but not exclusively at the West. The purpose of the discussion is not to dwell on the personal motivations underlying these attacks or their strategic intentions, which where they exist are complex. Rather, our purpose is to consider the effect of the so-called 'war on terrorism' and identify ways in which an already complex situation in relation to diversity in society has been made more so by bringing to the fore a number of difficult issues. We will briefly review three key events, in the US, Madrid, and London as examples of activity that has provoked discussion, debate, and feelings of vulnerability among some religious and ethnic groups. It needs to be acknowledged of course that feelings of vulnerability extend to all members of a society which may feel itself to be under the threat of attack. That said, the potential and reality of a backlash against members of particular minority groups is one that must be of great concern to those who believe in a fair, equitable society where cultural, religious, and ethnic diversity is valued.

9.2.1 **The attacks in the US**

At 8.38am on 11 September 2001, the American Federal Aviation Administration alerted the North American Defence Command that American Airlines flight 11 had been hijacked. Just eight minutes later the aircraft hit the north tower of the World Trade Center in New York. By this time the media had been alerted and in full view of the television cameras another passenger plane, United Airlines flight 175 crashed into the south tower of the World Trade Center. By 9.30am both the towers in which up to 50,000 people could be expected to be working, were ablaze. This was followed some seven minutes later by another plane, American Airlines flight 77 crashing into the Pentagon, the headquarters of the US military, in Washington. Part of the structure of the building collapsed. At 10.03am a further aircraft—a United Airlines flight bound for San Francisco, crashed 80 miles from Pittsburgh having been hijacked. By 10.30, both towers of the World Trade Center had collapsed causing massive loss of life. According to the subsequent 9/11 Commission Report in the US more than 2,600 people died at the World Trade Center, 125 died at the Pentagon, and 256 died in the four aircraft. Al Qaeda was identified as the responsible group but to quote from the Commission's report:

> The enemy is not just 'terrorism'. It is the threat posed specifically by Islamist terrorism, by Bin Ladin and others who draw on a long tradition of extreme intolerance within a minority strain of Islam that does not distinguish politics from religion, and distorts both. The enemy is not Islam, the great world faith, but a perversion of Islam. The enemy goes beyond al Qaeda to include the radical ideological movement, inspired in part by al Qaeda, that has spawned other terrorist groups and violence. (9/11 Commission Report July 2004—Executive Summary: 16ff)

The implications, particularly for religious diversity became evident in that although it made was clear and acknowledged that the radical ideology represented by Al Qaeda was not representative of mainstream Islam, the possibility that people would conflate the two existed. The experience of many Muslims has shown this to be the case.

9.2.2 **The attacks on Madrid**

On 11 March 2004, there were a number of attacks on commuter trains in Madrid, Spain. Ten bombs were exploded on four trains causing the deaths of 191 people. The perpetrators of the attacks were believed to be from groups linked to Al Qaeda. The significance of these attacks was that it became clear that terrorist activity was now targeting European States and that there was a clear need to coordinate the response to this at a European level. Just over a year later the terrorist activity moved to the UK.

9.2.3 **The attacks in London**

On 7 July 2005, 52 people were killed and over 700 injured in a series of terrorist attacks on the transport system in London. At 8.50am three bombs exploded on underground trains. Two of the trains were near stations at Edgware Road and Liverpool Street, and the third was in a tunnel between King's Cross and Russell Square. About an hour later a bomb exploded on a bus in Tavistock Square. Apart from the injury and loss of life, a particularly devastating aspect of the attack was that for the first time in the UK, suicide bombers had perpetrated a terrorist outrage. These were quickly identified as Hasib Hussain, Mohammad Sidiq Khan, Germaine Lindsay, and Shehzad Tanwir. All of them were British citizens who hitherto had apparently led unremarkable lives. For example, Hasib Hussain was just 18, had left school with seven GCSEs and had left his family devastated by the knowledge that he had been responsible for the bus bombing that killed thirteen people in Tavistock Square.

9.3 **Islamophobia**

A striking outcome of the terrorist activity that has been described above is that of the increased antipathy, prejudice, and discrimination experienced by Muslims who are stereotyped on the basis of what an extremely small number of terrorists have done. Islamophobia is the term that has come to be used as a way of understanding and describing the root causes of this prejudice and discrimination. It is important to note that the notion of Islamophobia has not merely arisen since 11 September. The issue of prejudice and discrimination against Muslims goes much further back than that. For example, in 1997 the Runnymede Trust produced a report entitled 'Islamophobia: A Challenge to Us All'. The report built on a consultation process that had been undertaken and sought to highlight the consequences and outcomes of Islamophobia throughout society. A number of police forces were involved in that consultation.

9.3.1 **Islamophobia defined**

Reduced to its most basic level, Islamophobia can be defined as hostility towards Islam and Muslims. It is not a new phenomenon although its label is relatively recent in origin. The Commission on British Muslims and Islamophobia (<http://www.insted.co.uk>) notes that Islamophobia, hostility towards Islam and Muslims, has been present in European societies since the eighth century of the Common Era. It is a phenomenon that has many parallels with racism and since the 1960s key factors in its development have included:

• The presence of some 15 million Muslims in European States;
• The increased influence of oil rich states, many of which are Islamic in their culture and traditions;

- The abuse of human rights by repressive regimes that claim to be motivated by Muslim beliefs;
- The emergence of ideologically driven movements that use terrorism as an instrument to achieve often unclear aims.

In Britain, as well as in the wider European community, there have been frequent examples of the manifestations of hostility towards Muslims and Islam. These include:

- Verbal and physical attacks;
- Attacks on mosques and the desecration of Muslim cemeteries;
- Widespread negative stereotyping in the media;
- Discrimination in recruitment and employment practices and in workplace culture and customs;
- Bureaucratic delay in responding to Muslim requests for cultural sensitivity in education and healthcare and planning applications for mosques;
- Lack of attention to the disproportionate nature of social exclusion and poverty experienced by Muslims;
- Anomalies in public order legislation where Muslims do not enjoy similar protection from incitement to hatred as other religious groups (notably Jews and Sikhs). (<http://www.insted.co.uk/relations.html#top>)

In its report 'Islamophobia: A Challenge for Us All', the Runnymede Trust (1997) outlines a number of the issues that are raised with closed and open views of Islam. The distinction between closed and open views is useful in that they provide a good benchmark against which personal and organizational responses to Islam can be checked. Study the table below and make an assessment as to how closed or open your views are in relation to Islam. The results are likely to be heavily influenced by your own background, values, attitudes, and beliefs.

9.3.2 **Muslims in Britain**

Vertovic (2002) charts the presence of Muslims in Britain and notes that they have been here for many centuries but that:

> it was only during the years following the (Second World) war that a large, permanent, visible predominantly South Asian, and eventually politically active Muslim population grew in Britain.

It is now estimated that there are between 1.5 and 3 million Muslims in Britain in 2006. What is not in doubt is that Muslims form the largest religious minority. From the 1970s onwards, there has been an expansion of the number of Muslim organizations and institutions and a large growth in the number of mosques, the spiritual focal points for Muslims. The disparate nature of the growth of Muslim associations and institutions had an impact on the coherence of the Muslim voice in Britain and consequently had an impact on the recognition of such a significant minority in the population generally. Again Vertovic (2002) argues that the establishment of the Muslim Council of Britain (MCB), which was inaugurated in November 1977, represented a great deal of progress in Muslim unification. The MCB is an umbrella organization of several hundred associations at local, regional and national level.

EXERCISE

- Visit the Muslim Council of Britain's website <http://www.mcb.org.uk> and explore the work of the Council.

The aims of the MCB are:

1. To promote cooperation, consensus and unity on Muslim affairs in the UK.
2. To encourage and strengthen all existing efforts being made for the benefit of the Muslim community.
3. To work for a more enlightened appreciation of Islam and Muslims in the wider society.
4. To establish a position for the Muslim community within British society that is fair and based on due rights.
5. To work for the eradication of disadvantages and forms of discrimination faced by Muslims.
6. To foster better community relations and work for the good of society as a whole.

It is interesting to compare these aims with the issues raised in Table 9.1 below. They are far more congruent with the open views than the closed and represent a greater inclusiveness than would be suggested by a closed view of Islam. This for example is represented by the aim (6) to work for the good of society as a whole and recognizes that Muslims are part of society and not apart from it.

9.3.3 The consequences of Islamophobia

We have already seen that Islamophobia has a long history and that a great deal needs to be done to eradicate it. Acts of terrorism by individuals who claim Islam as their justification and who do not represent mainstream moderate views have served to provide fuel for the fire of Islamophobia. This has not been helped by the way in which some sections of the media have stereotyped all Muslims as being somehow involved even though it is not true. The effect has been that many Muslims in Britain have experienced increased levels of prejudice, discrimination, exclusion, and even violence as Islamophobia has taken an even firmer grip in society.

The Runnymede Trust (1997: 11) report provides a diagram that charts the effect of Islamophobia. Bearing in mind that the report was published before the

Table 9.1 Open and closed views of Islam

Distinctions	Closed views of Islam	Open views of Islam
1. Monolithic/diverse	Islam seen as a single monolithic bloc, static and unresponsive to new realities	Islam seen as diverse and progressive with internal debates and development
2. Separate/interacting	Islam seen as separate and other (a) not having any aims or values in common with other cultures, (b) not affected by them, (c) not influencing them	Islam seen as interdependent with other faiths and cultures (a) having certain shared values and aims, (b) affected by them, (c) enriching them
3. Inferior/different	Islam seen as inferior to the West—barbaric, irrational, primitive, sexist	Islam seen as distinctly different, but not deficient, and as equally worthy of respect
4. Enemy/partner	Islam seen as violent, aggressive, threatening, supportive of terrorism, engaged in a 'clash of civilisations'	Islam seen as an actual or potential partner in joint cooperative enterprises in the solution of shared problems
5. Manipulative/sincere	Islam seen as a political ideology, used for political or military advantage	Islam seen as a genuine religious faith practiced sincerely by its adherents
6. Criticism of West rejected/considered	Criticisms made by Islam of 'the West' rejected out of hand	Criticism of the West and other cultures are considered and debated.
7. Discrimination defended/criticized	Hostility towards Islam used to justify discriminatory practices towards Muslims and the exclusion of Muslims from mainstream society	Debates and disagreements with Islam do not diminish efforts to combat discrimination and exclusion
8. Islamophobia seen as natural/problematic	Anti-Muslim hostility accepted as natural and normal	Critical views of Islam are themselves subjected to critique, lest they be inaccurate and unfair

Source: Runnymede Trust 1997: 5 used with permission.

events of 11 September 2001 and 7 July 2005 I have included some additional effects.

REFLECT ON PRACTICE

- What is your experience of the manifestation of Islamophobia in your own area of professional practice?
- What is being done to counter it?

Figure 9.1 Islamophobia a Visual Summary

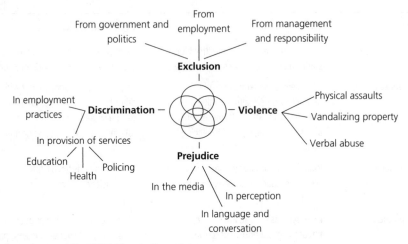

Source: Runnymede Trust 1997: 11 used with permission.

9.3.4 **Implications for policing**

In the aftermath of the attacks on the London Transport system on 7 July 2005 there were 269 religiously motivated hate crimes reported compared to 40 in the same period in 2004 (BBC 4 August 2005). Whilst most of these were verbal abuse and minor assaults, there was also damage to mosques and other property and the emotional impact on the Muslim population was enormous.

Islamophobia is motivated by hate as much as any other type of hate motivated crime and needs to feature strongly on the police agenda for tackling such type of crime. There are implications for policing that need to be considered, but some of the most significant are outlined below:

- *Recognizing the issue.* A constant frustration of many minority groups, including minority religious groups, is that the authorities of the state pay insufficient attention to their plight. The response of the police in the wake of 7 July was rightly to recognize that there would need to be considerable efforts put in place to protect the Muslim minority from what was seen as an inevitable backlash. In responding to comments made in this vein by Metropolitan Police Assistant Commissioner Tariq Ghaffur, a spokesperson for the Muslim Safety Forum, Tahir Butt, welcomed the fact that a senior police officer had voiced such sentiments. It is a vital component of good police community relations that the issues are both recognized and seen to be recognized.
- *Sensitivity.* The issue of terrorism and its motivation and causes are complex and police need to show great sensitivity in the strategic and operational response. They are at particular risk of gross stereotyping and need to be

sensitive to the fact that the vast majority of Muslims condemn terrorist acts as much as anyone else.

- *Enabling reporting.* It has been estimated that as much as 90 per cent of hate motivated crime goes unreported. Almost self-evidently the implications of this are that a true picture of the extent of the problem will never emerge. Efforts need to be put in place to enable as much reporting of hate motivated crime as possible. This links with the point about recognition above. Where particular groups feel that the issue has been publicly recognized, then that will go a long way to encouraging people to report crime of this nature. Of course there needs to be confidence that such a report will not only be taken seriously but that it will be followed through with a proper investigation and offenders prosecuted. Where such confidence in the police and other parts of the judicial system is lacking then the problem will only be exacerbated. The introduction of opportunities for third party reporting have served to allevi- ate this to some extent, but the ideal position is where people feel confident enough to approach the police direct to report crime motivated by religious hatred.

- *Gathering intelligence.* We noted in Chapter 3 that intelligence gathering is a particularly sensitive issue for some communities. This stems from the suspi- cion that the motivation for good community relations is merely grounded in the desire to gather intelligence from that community. Having said that, the gathering of high quality intelligence is a vital component of the operational police response to combating crime in general and terrorism in particular. If Islamophobia is allowed to function without challenge by the police then it is far more likely that Muslim communities will be reluctant to cooperate with the police in their efforts to gain intelligence. This aspect has taken on a par- ticular significance given that the bombers on 7 July were all of British origin.

- *Listening to and understanding communities.* It is therefore important that in all this the police are seen to be listening, responding to, and understanding Muslims. If you glance again at Table 9.1 you should be able to see that open views of Islam on the part of the police are far more likely to produce a con- structive dialogue that an orientation that is characterized by suspicion and antipathy. The relationship needs to be one where Islam is seen as an actual or potential partner in joint cooperative enterprises in the solution of shared problems.

9.4 **Stop and Search**

9.4.1 **Introduction**

A particularly controversial police power is that of stop and search, both the powers under the Police and Criminal Evidence Act 1984 and the powers under prevention of terrorism legislation. A consideration of stop and search power in relation to the effects of terrorism has been included in this chapter because the discussion that has been generated in relation to stop and search as a counter-terrorist measure has highlighted the main concerns that surrounded the power before terrorism was so high up the agenda. The codes of practice that were introduced to regulate the use and application of stop and search powers were intended to ensure that the power could be used without detriment to public confidence in the police. Where there is a suspicion that the police are actively or even unwittingly exercising discrimination against certain groups in society, then the power to stop and search can easily be seen as an instrument to express that discrimination. With the advent of terrorism that can be traced to Islamic extremism, the potential to lose the trust and support of Middle Eastern, Asian, and other Muslim communities is enormous. This clearly has a significant impact on the policing of a diverse society. In this section we will firstly evaluate stop and search as a power in the police operational toolkit. This will be followed by a discussion of the implications of stop and search that have become apparent since there has been a greater focus on the need to respond to the terrorist threat.

9.4.2 Strengths, weaknesses, opportunities, and threats

Whilst stop and search is a controversial power, it is useful to briefly analyse it using the SWOT analysis technique. This is a way of identifying the Strengths, Weaknesses, Opportunities, and Threats that are revealed in the use of the power.

EXERCISE

Reflect on what you consider to be the strengths, weaknesses, opportunities and threats of powers to stop and search.

Most of the identified features that are presented below are drawn from Neyroud and Beckley (2001: 162) others have been added.

Strengths

- Up to 12 per cent of all arrests result from stop and search powers, particularly those for going equipped and offensive weapons (Fitzgerald 1999).
- Many more result in intelligence that contributes to detection.
- Targeted policing using stop and search has been identified as an effective policing strategy (Home Office 1998).
- Stop and search enables proactive policing operations.

Weaknesses

- There is a disproportionate use of the power against black and Asian young men (Brown 1997).
- There is an adverse impact on police community relations (Holdaway 1996).
- There is evidence of unlawful use of the powers to gather intelligence or for 'social control' (Fitzgerald 1999).
- Searches in public have a wider impact on those who observe police actions (Fitzgerald 1999).

Opportunities

- To achieve more effective use of police resources by better targeting and professional skills (Quinton and Bland 1999).
- Better training and situational skills (Fitzgerald 1999).
- Better supervision of discretion (Quinton and Bland 1999).
- To deal with minor street crimes, such as personal possession of cannabis by informal action and no arrest (Fitzgerald 1999).
- Lay and community involvement in the strategy, target setting, and evaluation of stop and search (Quinton and Bland 1999).

Threats

- Article 14 challenges under the Human Rights Act (the enjoyment of rights and freedoms under the European Convention on Human Rights without discrimination).
- Breach of provisions of the Race Relations Act.
- Insecurity and low morale of officers concerned about complaints, civil claims, and actions under the Human Rights Act—reducing the effective application of stop and search (Fitzgerald 1999).
- Criminalizing of young black and Asian men (Fitzgerald 1999).

9.4.3 General issues surrounding stop and search

General concerns

A study into the use of stop and search conducted by Fitzgerald (1999) revealed a number of general concerns relating to the use of the power. For example, regardless of whether the officer had the reasonable grounds for the search there was likely to be ill feeling in relation to the way that the officer conducted the search. The impact particularly on young people was likely to be profound, and might form a lasting impression given that they would likely have little other types of contact with the police. The attitude of the officer will be a significant factor in the way the stop and search is perceived by the individual being stopped.

The grounds on which the power is used

Where people are already known to the police, particularly those with a criminal record, evidence was found to support the notion that such people were being stopped as a way of disrupting their (potential) criminal activity. The absence of reasonable grounds to support a particular stop and search is unjustifiable under the Police and Criminal Evidence Act 1984 and leads to the assumption that the power is merely being used as a form of social control.

Criminalizing groups

The Fitzgerald study also identified numerous instances where the use of the power to stop and search may have the effect of criminalizing particular groups. The congregation of groups may make them appear to be more threatening and are therefore more likely to attract the attention of police. In a study into Recommendation 61 of the Macpherson Report (recording stops) the 1990 Trust (2004), it was found that most respondents who were stopped and searched reported a negative experience. Of those who rated their encounter as satisfactory, a major contributory factor was that they had been given credible reasons for the stop. Of those who reported a negative experience, the contributory factors were a perception of a wilful and unnecessary intrusion of privacy which was exacerbated by the encounter being poorly managed by the police officer. Some reported rudeness and bullying and in some cases they reported being assaulted by the police officer. Of the whole sample in the study, 16 per cent found that the stop was satisfactory, 43 per cent said that they found the experience intimidating, 28 per cent found the experience to be a negative one, and 13 per cent were unmoved by the experience. Of those who had a negative experience the most common feeling was one of humiliation. Even though 86 per cent of the respondents had been given a reason for their stop 56 per cent thought that the reason they had been given was false. An unconvincing reason for a stop was likely to produce as much anger and frustration as being given no reason at all.

Action to improve public confidence

The three major threats to public confidence in stops and searches are reported by the 1990 Trust (2004: 47) as:

- The continuing or accelerating disproportionate rate of stops and searches of those from minority ethnic backgrounds;
- Poor management of encounters by police officers; and
- Inadequate explanations by officers to those stopped or searched.

REFLECT ON PRACTICE

- Given the three factors above, do you think there are any other factors that get in the way of public trust and confidence in relation to stops and searches?

In terms of how to improve public trust and confidence the report (p 49) notes: '... Police performance, behaviour and a demonstrable understanding of the community were seen as the most likely avenues to improving public confidence in the police'. One way of achieving this is for the police to become more involved in the community. This includes such activities as working more proactively in the community, listening to the community more (talking instead of assuming guilt), and more patrols. This should be supported by a more professional approach, which was characterized in the report as 'polite, honest and respectful'. Some respondents also noted that a greater representation of minority groups in the police would be beneficial.

9.5 **Government Response to Terrorism**

9.5.1 **Introduction**

In this section we will consider four of the issues that have been hotly debated in the media and in political circles, both of which impact on the policing of a diverse society. Both are related directly to human rights and in essence the debates have been around the perceived erosion of those rights. We have noted elsewhere the important relationship between human rights and the freedoms that people should be able to enjoy in a diverse society that is free from discrimination. When terrorism impacts on society a number of factors become inevitable. Firstly, there will be an expectation from people that the Government will engage in some kind of action to counter both the threat and the reality of terrorist attacks. Secondly, in responding to the threat there will need to be a balancing of rights and responsibilities on citizens given that one of the usual responses is to strengthen the law in some way. Thirdly, there will be disagreement about what should be done. For example, many people in Britain moved from a position of being uncomfortable about the war in Iraq to outright opposition, particularly in the light of the fact that so-called weapons of mass destruction were not found and that had been the initial reason for military action. Lastly, there will be an impact on the diverse society in Britain because of the perceived threat from particular terrorist groups. After the bombings of 7 July it became apparent to the Government that the detention period under anti-terrorist legislation for suspected terrorists should be increased to ninety days. In addition the increased incidence of religiously motivated hate crime led the Government to propose legislation to outlaw incitement to religious hatred.

In both cases the Government has had to accept that the proposed legislation be watered down to accommodate those who argue that the erosion of individual rights is too great a step to take. In the next sections we will briefly review some of the key issues that have been debated. It will be for you the reader to make up your mind if you have not already done so where you stand on the issue.

9.5.2 Incitement to religious hatred

A particularly contentious proposed amendment to the Public Order Act 1986 surrounds the issues of incitement to religious hatred. Employment regulations now cover the issue of discrimination in the workplace on the grounds of religious belief and many regarded this as a welcome strengthening of the law in relation to people's rights at work. Outside of the workplace, the Public Order Act 1986 already outlaws incitement to hatred on racial grounds. In other case law it had been found that Jews and Sikhs could legitimately be covered by this legislation as they could also be identified as racial groups in their own right. The situation was not the same with other religious groups however because in these there was not unique ethnic identity. So Muslims, Christians, and Hindus for example would not be covered by legislation intended to outlaw hatred on racial grounds. In the wake of 9/11 and 7/7 it became clear that Islamophobia—hostility towards Islam and Muslims—was such a significant problem that the Government decided to put forward legislation to protect these groups in the same way as religious groups with a racial identity.

So the original Religious Hatred Bill was intended to outlaw the stirring up of hatred on grounds of religion. This was intended to include threatening, abusive, and insulting behaviour but it was this that caused so much heat in the argument. Whilst few, if any opponents were actually suggesting that incitement to hatred on religious grounds was acceptable, many argued that the proposed law was too restrictive on the freedom of thought and expression. The opposition to the Bill brought together a strange alliance of people, for example, Christians, atheists, and comedians all of whom in their own way felt that the law would put ordinary people at risk of breaching it. The Christian argument centred on the notion of legitimate criticism and debate. Clearly there are significant differences between what Christians and for example Muslims believe. The question would be whether debate and criticism of these differences would be in breach of the law. Many were not convinced that they would not be. Likewise, people from show business were concerned that the restriction on the ability to poke fun at a particular religion (which might have been construed as insulting or abusive) would be a step too far in the restriction on the freedom of thought and expression which is enshrined in the Human Rights Act.

Attempts to reframe the law to limit its effect were also opposed in Parliament. The outcome was that the New Labour Government for only the second time in its period of office lost a crucial vote in the Commons. The Bill now merely outlaws threatening words or behaviour which are intended to stir up racial hatred.

9.5.3 **Glorification of terrorism**

A further provision of the proposals to combat terrorism was to legislate to outlaw the 'glorification of terrorism'. This was intended to put a stop to those who make public pronouncements supporting terrorist acts and glorifying those who perpetrated them. In a debate in the House of Lords, Baroness Scotland of Asthal, the Home Office Minister, told peers:

> The Government does not believe it acceptable that people should be allowed to make statements which glorify terrorism and in doing so make it more likely their audience will themselves commit acts of terrorism.

Many criticisms of the proposed legislation were made in the debate however. For example, it was argued that such a measure was unnecessary, that it contravened Article 10 of the European Convention on Human Rights in relation to the freedom of thought and expression, and that it would be damaging to community relations. A particularly difficult outcome of such a law would be the definition of what glorification means—how would a jury be able to decide?

9.5.4 **Identity cards**

As part of the overall response to terrorism, the Government has made a case for people to carry identity cards. This is not new in this country, in fact during the Second World War people were required to carry cards and the scheme was not withdrawn until the 1950s when tensions between the police and citizens led to them being abandoned. Although the details of a new scheme are not yet known, it is likely that the cards will make use of the latest technology and will be expensive not only to the individual, but the scheme including the National Identity register will also cost many millions of pounds to run. The cards would bear the individual's photograph, name, address, date of birth, and gender. Biometric information would be held on a microchip on the card—possibly fingerprints, facial scan, or iris scan. People would not be compelled to carry the cards routinely, but would be required to produce them on request.

Arguments in favour of the scheme tend to centre on the potential impact that identity cards could have on crime and terrorism. In addition they would help to combat fraud such as social security fraud and other abuse of access to public services. Proponents of identity cards often point to other countries where they are routinely held and are much less contentious.

The arguments against are grounded in the concern that identity cards would be a further erosion of civil liberties and that in any case, if the ownership or carrying of such a card is not compulsory then many of the arguments in favour fall away. In terms of policing a diverse society there is the concern that an identity card scheme would further complicate relations between police and the public. Although the use and production of cards would not be exclusively in the domain of policing, it will be significant. Where people already feel alienated from the police, it is quite possible that the situation would be made even worse. It has been argued that this would be particularly so in the case of stop and search where the friction that this power causes between police and communities would be exacerbated by another requirement to produce identity. It has also been argued that groups such as illegal immigrants who could not legitimately obtain a card would simply be driven underground.

REFLECT ON PRACTICE

- How would identity cards both help and hinder police officers in their work?

9.5.5 **Detention without charge**

In November 2005, after much debate MPs finally voted to increase the length of time a terrorist suspect could be held from fourteen to twenty-eight days. There has been considerable debate over the length of time that suspects should be held and the police had put forward a period of ninety days which was originally supported by the Government. During the debate many MPs and Lords expressed deep concern that the period amounted to imprisonment without trial and that it was serious infliction on human rights. Some minority groups, including Muslims, argued that such detention would further damage community relations. In favour of the proposal it was argued that with the complexity of the investigation of terrorist offences much more time was needed to gather the evidence necessary to support a charge. This was particularly so in cases where police were acting on information that needed to be verified and followed up. People who were suspected of terrorist activity needed to be detained to disrupt their activity, even though such activity might only be in the planning stages. In terms of achieving this aim it is questionable whether the compromise of twenty-eight days that was reached was sufficient.

The real issues underlying this which relate to our consideration of policing diversity are that:

- The fight against terrorism must be tempered by a concern for the type of society that people want. For centuries there has been a fundamental principle in British law that people have a right not to be detained without being charged and without subsequently being brought before a court to answer the allegations made against them. Even though an extended period of detention is intended only to affect a very small number of people, it does represent an erosion of the civil liberties that people can expect to enjoy.
- A number of suspects have been held and have never been charged or brought before a court. The assumption must be that there is insufficient evidence to

bring charges against them. This effectively means that an innocent person can be detained by the state.

- Due to the nature of the terrorist threat, it is far more likely that such suspects will be from minority groups. This will have an inevitable impact on the way that such groups perceive themselves to be singled out for special treatment by the state.
- Apart from the obvious devastating effect on individuals and their families when they become victims of terrorist activity, one of the threats that society perceives is to the liberal democracy that is currently enjoyed. There is a sense therefore that when the response to terrorism becomes ever more draconian that inevitably has a damaging effect on the very society that it is intended to protect.

9.5.6 Summary

In the above section we took a look at some of the ways in which the Government has been attempting to respond to terrorism. What does need to be considered by way of summary is the impact that all this might have for the police.

Firstly, for many years in this country relations between the police and the communities they serve have been the subject of much attention and as we have seen elsewhere in the book, such relationships have not always been good. Particularly since the publication of the Macpherson Report in 1999, the police have made demonstrable efforts to reach out to communities and to do what they can to improve the nature and quality of the relationship. It would be hard to argue that there is not still a great deal more that could be done, but many public commentators have commended the police for their efforts. The response to terrorism has placed a great burden on the police in terms of the use of resources and in many ways they are now grappling with an unknown quantity. The response to terrorism has also called for a much more overt paramilitary style of policing and this can only give the impression that the style of policing is moving towards one of coercion rather than consensus. The police are charged with the responsibility of protecting the public. It is important in a liberal democracy that this protection is not only from an unquantifiable terrorist threat but also the protection of the human rights of British citizens. Where laws are made to protect society from attack that impinge on those rights, however necessary they might appear to be, it is vital that the balance between individual freedom and the protection of society is not lost.

9.6 **Responding to New Terrorist Threats**

9.6.1 **The changing context**

An interview with Sir Ian Blair, Commissioner of the Metropolitan Police published in *The Guardian* (16 November 2005) highlighted the way the Commissioner was thinking about the effect that the events of 7 July 2005 have had on perceptions of policing. The theme of the Richard Dimbleby Lecture that the Commissioner gave that day was 'what kind of police service do we want?'. He drew a stark contrast between 'a July 6th police service'—the unarmed, light-touch, community based police that was part of London's successful 2012 Olympic bid—and the armed counter-terrorist 'July 7th police service' mobilized to deal with the bomb attacks on London. The assumption is that the public want a 6 July police service and not a 7 July police service:

> However it is now clear that we cannot have that to which July 6th aspired without understanding July 7th. That means … that national security is dependent on neighbourhood security. (*The Guardian* 16 November 2005)

REFLECT ON PRACTICE

- In your experience how true would you say it is that policing is facing tough questions about policing styles pre and post 7 July 2005?
- To what extent do you consider that national security is dependent on neighbourhood security?

The fight against terrorism in this country can only be successful if the consensus and cooperation of communities is maintained. This will mean that all the other factors that relate to policing a diverse society that we have explored in the previous chapters of this book will become even more important. Policing in a liberal democracy can only be carried out with the consent of the people. This will mean that the police need to operate within a sound ethical framework that recognizes the diversity of communities and the diverse needs that those communities have. In doing this, the police are far more likely to enjoy the cooperation of those communities. With the evidence now that terrorists have emanated from communities within Britain such cooperation must be an essential element of the strategy.

9.6.2 **Police firearms policy**

On 21 July 2005, there were further attempts to attack the transport system in London. Tension was extremely high and the police were in a state of high alert. On 22 July, a Brazilian electrician living in London, Jean Charles de Menezes, was shot at Stockwell tube station as a suspect. Metropolitan Police Commissioner

Sir Ian Blair told a news conference: 'As I understand the situation, the man was challenged and refused to obey police instructions.' The Yard said his 'clothing and behaviour at the station added to their suspicions' (BBC 22 July 2005). It rapidly became clear that de Menezes was, in fact, an innocent victim and that he had nothing to do with the previous day's events and was the victim of mistaken identity. The shooting was placed in the hands of the Independent Police Complaints Commission to be investigated. At the time of writing, the IPCC report was not in the public domain but what is interesting for this debate is the bigger question of police firearms policy in relation to the response to terrorism. It is important to consider, because police policy and the way it is implemented can do enormous damage to relations with communities. Deaths in custody or deaths caused by police officers have not surprisingly been flashpoints in the past for the complete breakdown of police community relations.

9.6.3 Operation Kratos

Named after the Greek god of strength, Operation Kratos was developed by the Metropolitan Police in London after the attacks in the US on 11 September 2001. According to the Metropolitan Police, Kratos does not represent a so-called 'shoot to kill' policy, and it reaffirmed that even though it was addressing a new type of terrorist threat (in the West) in the form of suicide bombing, police firearms officers still need to operate within the law, particularly referring to s 3 of the Criminal Law Act 1967 which gives the power to use force, deadly if necessary in self defence or in the protection of others. The underlying principle of Kratos is that the police must work within the law on behalf of the public and in their protection. In a report to the Metropolitan Police Authority dated 27 October 2005 (MPA 2005), the Commissioner of the Metropolitan Police again reiterated that Kratos was not a shoot to kill policy, but that the nature of the threat of suicide bombing was such that such an outcome was likely given two key factors. The first being that suicide bombers are known to have detonated their explosives having been identified, and secondly that the use of force must take into account the possibility that any intervention (for example shooting) may have the effect of detonation of the explosives. The more usual and well-tried tactic of containment would be unlikely to work effectively. An important aspect of all this is the recognition that with the need to change tactics there would also be an impact on relations with the community. Whilst proponents of Kratos are at pains to point out that there is no single profile of a suicide bomber it is acknowledged that the effect on some groups in terms of their feeling of vulnerability would be greater than others. The shooting of Jean Charles de Menezes served to highlight this fear. In the report, the Metropolitan Police was keen to ensure that effective communications with particularly vulnerable groups should be maintained and that they should be involved in reviews of police tactics.

9.7 **Moral Panic**

Our final consideration in terms of the effect of terrorism on the policing of a diverse society is to consider the idea of moral panic. This is a term associated more usually with criminology and in many ways sums up what we have been saying in this chapter about the impact of terrorism. Murji (2006) offers a definition of moral panic as:

> Disproportional and hostile social reaction to a condition, person or group defined as a threat to societal values, involving stereotypical media representations and leading to demands for greater social control and creating a spiral of reaction.

EXERCISE

Study the definition of moral panic above and consider how this is manifest in response to terrorism and what impact it might have on policing diversity.

Cohen (1972), who first outlined ideas on moral panic, noted that the response to moral panic will involve an increase in social control and that this control culture has three elements:

- Diffusion—where events in other places are interconnected with the initial event. Although the bombings on 7 July 2005 occurred in London, there was quickly a spread on interconnections to many other parts of the country as the origin of bombers was traced.
- Escalation—where there are increasingly strident calls for strong action to be taken to counter the threat. We have seen above in the Government response to terrorism that there were just such calls for tough action and many of these have started to impinge on basic human rights.
- Innovation—where the police and courts are granted increased powers to deal with the threat. Again we have seen that this has been taking place in relation to terrorism.

Whilst there are many arguments against the very idea of moral panic we can see that the characteristics of the phenomenon are evident in a Britain which is trying to come to terms with a new form of terrorist threat. Goode and Ben-Yehuda (1994 in Murji 2006: 252) identify five characteristics of moral panic:

- Disproportional reaction;
- Concern about the threat;
- Hostility to the objects of the panic;
- Widespread agreement that the threat is real;
- Volatility in the sense that the scale and intensity of the panic are unpredictable.

EXERCISE

Considering the characteristics of moral panic identified by Goode and Ben Yehuda, to what extent do you think they are relevant to the response to terrorism and its effect in a diverse society?

There is clear evidence of the concern about the threat and widespread agreement about the fact that the threat is real and is unlikely to go away in the near future. In terms of disproportional reaction, this will very much depend on individual perspectives. People caught up in bombings and those affected, such as families and friends, may well justifiably feel that it would be hard to react disproportionately. But the Government and the police need to take a longer perspective and ensure that the balance between reaction and freedom is maintained. It is the characteristic of hostility to the objects of the panic that must be of greatest concern however. As we have seen above, there is no single profile of a terrorist bomber and every effort needs to be made to avoid the type of gross and unjustifiable stereotyping of particular groups that leads to increased prejudice and discrimination.

9.8 Chapter Summary

In this chapter we have outlined some of the effects that terrorism has had on policing a diverse society.

- We noted that in the aftermath of terrorist activity in both the US and Europe there has been a marked increase in Islamophobia—hostility towards Islam and Muslims. The idea that views of Islam may be either open or closed was introduced and it was suggested that this is a good benchmark for evaluating both organizational and individual perspectives. We noted that the Muslim Council of Britain is an organization that has provided an umbrella for a range of Islamic associations and institutions and that one of its aims is to foster better community relations and work for the good of society as a whole. The consequences of Islamophobia were identified in terms of exclusion, violence, discrimination, and prejudice. The implications for policing were identified as the need to recognize the issues faced by minority communities, the need for sensitivity, making arrangements for people to feel safe to report crimes motivated by hate, gathering intelligence, and the need to understand and listen to communities.
- We outlined the impact of stop and search and considered the strengths weaknesses, opportunities, and threats that are apparent in the use of the power by the police. We discussed some negative outcomes of the power

to stop and search and highlighted some of the things the police need to do to improve public confidence. A key to this as with many other aspects of policing diversity is to engage more fully with communities.

- We briefly examined the Government's response to terrorism and identified issues that have been debated hotly in terms of their impact on human rights and potential to damage community relations and relations with the police. This included the proposed introduction of identity cards, incitement to hatred on religious grounds, and the issue of detention without charge. An overriding issue in the debate is the need, in a liberal democracy, to balance the need to protect people from terrorist action with the maintenance of individual rights and freedoms.

- We considered the changing context of policing that has been brought about by terrorism and noted Sir Ian Blair's comments about the impact that the attacks of 7 July were having on policing styles. In connection with this the potential effect of police firearms policy was explored and we noted that this can have the effect of making already vulnerable groups feel even more threatened.

- The chapter concluded with an introduction to the idea of moral panic, a concept drawn from criminology. We explored the way in which the response to terrorism can be seen as one which generates moral panic and the way that this has implications for policing.

References

Ackerman, N. and Jahoda, M. (1950), *Anti-Semitism and Emotional Disorder: A Psycho-analytic Interpretation* (New York, Harper and Brothers).

Alimo-Metcalfe, B. (1995), 'An Investigation of Female and Male Constructs of Leadership and Empowerment' 10(2) *Women in Management Review* 3.

Alderson, J. (1998), *Principled Policing* (Winchester, Waterside Press).

Allport, G., Vernon, P., and Lindzey, G. (1951), *Study of Values* (Boston, Houghton-Mifflin).

Allport, G. W. (1954), *The Nature of Prejudice* (Reading MA, Addison Wesley).

Ashcroft, K., Bigger, S., and Coates, D. (1996), *Researching into Equal Opportunities in Colleges and Universities* (London, Kogan Page).

Association of Chief Police Officers (1985), *Guiding Principles Concerning Racial Attacks* (London, ACPO).

—— (2000), *ACPO Guide to Identifying and Combating Hate Crime* (London, ACPO)

—— (2005), *Hate Crime, Delivering a Quality Service (Good Practice and Tactical Guidance)* (London, ACPO).

Baron, R. A. and Byrne, D. (1994), *Social Psychology: Understanding Human Interaction* (Boston, Allyn and Bacon).

BBC (2006), 'Muslim chief will not face charge' <http://news.bbc.co.uk/1/hi/uk/4081208.stm> accessed 24 February 2006.

Bee, F. and Bee, R. (1994), *Training Needs Analysis and Evaluation* (London, McGraw-Hill).

Bennett, T. (1994), 'Recent Developments in Community Policing', in Stephens, M. and Becker, S. (eds), *Police Force, Police Service* (London, Macmillan) 107–29.

Bobo, L. (1983), 'Whites Opposition to Bussing: Symbolic Racism or Realistic Conflict?' 45 *Journal of Personality and Social Psychology* 1196–210.

Bowden, J. A. and Marton, F. (1998), *The University of Learning* (London, Kogan Page).

Bramley, P. (1986), *Evaluation Training—A Practical Guide* (London, British Association for Commercial and Industrial Training).

Brown, R. (1995), *Prejudice* (Blackwell, Oxford).

Brown, D. (1997), *PACE Ten Years On: A Review of the Research* (Home Office Research Study 115, London, Home Office).

Bullock, A. and Trombley, S. (eds) (1999), *The New Fontana Dictionary of Modern Thought* (London, Harper Collins).

Chan, J. (1997), 'Changing Police Culture' 36 *British Journal of Criminology* 109–34.

Chanan, G. (2005), 'What is Community Engagement?' Presentation to Community Engagement Good Practice Seminar <http://www.crimereduction.gov.uk/gpce01.htm> accessed 27 March 2006.

Clancy, A., Hough, M., Aust, R., and Kershaw, C. (2001), 'Crime, Policing and Justice: The Experience of Ethnic Minorities: Findings for the 2000 British Crime Survey'

(Research Study 223, London, Home Office), in Rowe, M. (2004), *Policing, Race and Racism* (Collumpton, Willan).

Clark, K. E. and Miller G. A. (eds) (1970), *Psychology: The Behavioural and Social Science Survey* (Prentice Hall, New Jersey).

Clements, P. (2000), *Fair Enough? Improving the Teaching and Learning of Equal Opportunities in the British Police Service* (London, Home Office Police Research Award Scheme).

——and Jones, J. (2002), *The Diversity Training Handbook* (London, Kogan Page).

Cohen, S. (1972), *Folk Devils and Moral Panics* (London, MacGibbon and Kee).

Cohen, A. P. (1985), *The Symbolic Construction of Community* (London, Tavistock).

Commission for Racial Equality (1985), *Birmingham Local Education Authority and Schools: Referrals and Suspensions* (London, Commission for Racial Equality).

——(2005a), *The Police Service in England and Wales : Final Report of a Formal Investigation by the Commission for Racial Equality* (London, Commission for Racial Equality).

——(2005b), *The Police Service in England and Wales: Full List of Recommendations of a Formal Investigation by the Commission for Racial Equality* (London, Commission for Racial Equality).

De Lint, W. (1998), 'New Managerialism and Canadian Police Training Reform' 7 *Social and Legal Studies* 2.

Drummond, D. (1976), *Police Culture* (Beverley Hills, Sage Publications).

Elliott, R. and Nicholls, J. (1996), *It's Good to Talk: Lessons in Public Consultation and Feedback* (Police Research Series Paper 22, Home Office Police Research Group) (London, Home Office).

Fahy, P. (2005), 'Professional Diversity' in *Policing Professional*, issue 34. August 2005.

Fielding, N. (1994), 'Cop Canteen Culture', in Newburn, T. and Stanko, E. (eds), *Just Boys Doing the Business; Men, Masculinity and Crime* (London, Routledge).

Fishbein, M. and Ajzen, I. (1975), *Belief, Attitude, Intention and Behaviour: An Introduction to Theory and Research* (Reading MA, Addison-Wesley).

Fitzgerald, M. (1999), 'Final Report into Stop and Search' <www.met.police.uk/police/mps/stop.htm>.

Forrest, R. and Kearns, A. (2000), 'Social Cohesion, Social Capital and the Neighbourhood'. Paper presented to ESRC Cities Programme Neighbourhoods Colloquium, Liverpool, 5–6 June.

Foster, J., Newburn, T., and Souhami, A. (2005), *Assessing the Impact of the Stephen Lawrence Inquiry* (Home Office Research Study 294) (London, Home Office Research and Statistics Directorate).

Frewin, K. and Tuffin, K. (1998), 'Police Status, Conformity and Internal Pressure: A Discursive Analysis of Police Culture' 9 *Discourse and Society* 2.

Galagan, P. A. (1991), 'Tapping the Power of a Diverse Workforce' 45(3) *Training and Development Journal* 38–44.

Garrett, H. and Taylor, J. (1993), *How to Design and deliver Equal Opportunities Training* (London, Kogan Page).

Goldsmith, A. (1990), 'Taking Police Culture Seriously: Police Discretion and the Limits of Law' 1 *Policing and Society* 2.

Goode, E. and Ben Yehuda, N. (1994), *Moral Panics: The Social Construction of Deviance* (Oxford, Blackwell).

Gross, R. (1996), *Psychology: The Science of Mind and Behaviour* (London, Hodder and Stoughton).

Hall, N. (2005), *Hate Crime* (Collumpton, Willan).

Hammond, T. R. and Kleiner, B. H. (1992), 'Managing Multicultural Work Environments' 11(2) *Equal Opportunities International* 6–9.

Hargie, O. (1997) (ed), *The Handbook of Communication Skills* (2nd edn, London, Routledge).

Harvey, C. and Allard, M., *Understanding and Managing Diversity* (2nd edn, Upper Saddle River, NJ, Prentice Hall).

Hayes, N. and Orrell, S. (1993), *Psychology: An Introduction* (London, Longman).

HMIC (1993), *Equal Opportunities in the Police Service* (London, Home Office).

—— (1996), *Developing Diversity in the Police Service* (London, Home Office).

—— (1997), *Winning the Race. Policing Plural Communities* (London, Home Office).

—— (1999a), *Winning the Race Revisited* (London, Home Office).

—— (1999b), *Managing Learning* (London, Home Office).

—— (2000), *Policing London: 'Winning Consent'* (London, Home Office).

—— (2001), *Winning the Race: Embracing Diversity* (London, Home Office).

—— (2003), *Diversity Matters* (London, Home Office).

—— (2005), *Value Matters* (London, Home Office).

HM Government (1999), *Modernising Government: A Diverse Civil Service* <www.cabinet-office.gov.uk/civilservice/21st century>.

Holdaway, S. (1983), *Inside the British Police: A Force at Work* (Oxford, Blackwell).

—— (1996), *The Racialisation of British Policing* (Basingstoke, Macmillan).

Home Office (1998), *Reducing Offending: An Assessment of the Research Evidence on Ways of Dealing with Offending Behaviour* (Home Office Research Study 187) (London, Home Office).

—— (2002), *Community Cohesion: A Report of the Independent Review Team*, chaired by Ted Cantle (London, Home Office).

—— (2004a), *Building Communities, Beating Crime: A Better Police Service for the 21st Century* (London, Home Office).

—— (2004b), *National Evaluation of Community Support Officers*, Interim Report December 2004 (London, Home Office).

—— (2005a), *Race and Diversity National Learning Requirement* (London, Home Office).

—— (2005b), *National Community Safety Plan 2006–2009* (London, Home Office).

—— (2005c), *Community Support Officers Strength as at 30th June 2005 by Basic Command Unit* <http://police.homeoffice.gov.uk/news-and-publications/publication/community-policing/CSO_numbers_June_2005.pdf> accessed 27 March 2006.

—— (2005d), *Emerging Findings and Good Practice Form the Community Support Officer Evaluation* (London, Home Office).

—— (2005e), *Police Service Strength 2005*, Statistical Bulletin 12/05 (London, Home Office).

Hovland, C. and Sears, R. R. (1940), 'Minor Studies in Aggression: Correlation of Lynching with Economic Indices' 9 *Journal of Psychology* 301–10.

Independent Police Complaints Commission (2006), *Confidence in the Police Complaints System: A Survey of the General Population*, IPCC Research and Statistics Series, Paper 2 (London, IPCC).

Jamieson, D. and O'Mara, J. (1991), *Managing Workforce 2000: Gaining the Diversity Advantage* (San Francisco, Jossey-Bass).

Johnston, L. (2000), *Policing Britain: Risk, Security and Governance* (London, Longman).

Jones, T., Newburn, T., and Smith, D. G. (1994), *Democracy in Policing* (London, Policy Studies Institute).

—— and Newburn, T. (2001), *Widening Access: Improving Police Relations with Hard to Reach Groups* (Police Research Series Paper 138) (London, Home Office Policing and Crime Reduction Unit).

Kandola, R. S. (1991), *Equal Opportunities Can Damage Your Health!* (Oxford, Pearn Kandola Downs).

Kandola, R., and Fullerton, J. (1996), *Diversity in Action* (London, Institute of Personnel and Development).

Kenny, J. and Reid, M. (1986), *Training Interventions* (London, Institute of Personnel Management).

✳ Kettle, M. (2005), 'What Type of Policing Do We Want?' Interview with Sir Ian Blair, *The Guardian*, 16 November 2005.

Lee, D. and Newby, H. (1983), *The Problem of Sociology: An Introduction to the Discipline* (London, Unwin Hyman).

Macpherson, W. (1999), *The Stephen Lawrence Inquiry—Report* (London, HMSO).

Marlow, A. and Loveday, B. (2000), 'Race, Policing and the Need for Leadership', in *After Macpherson: Policing after the Stephen Lawrence Inquiry* (Lyme Regis, Russell House Publishing).

Marton, F. (1994), 'Phenomenography', in Husen, T. and Postlethwaite, N. (eds.), *The International Encyclopaedia of Education* (Oxford, Pergamon).

Marton, F. and Booth, S. (1997), *Learning and Awareness* (Mahwah, NJ, L. Erlbaum Associates).

Metropolitan Police Authority (2003), *Extended Police Family*, Report 13, 25 September 2003.

—— (2004), *The Case for Change: People in the Metropolitan Police Service* (London, Metropolitan Police Authority).

—— (2005), *Suicide Terrorism*, Report 13, 27 October 2005 <http://www.mpa.gov.uk/committees/mpa/2005/051027/13.htm>.

Murji, K. (2006), 'Moral Panic', in *Sage Dictionary of Criminology* (London, Sage).

Newburn, T. (2003) (ed), *Handbook of Policing* (Collumpton, Willan).

National Black Police Association (2006), *Mission Statement* <http://www.nationalbpa.com/index.php?option=com_content&task=view&id=18&Itemid=49> accessed 27 March 2006.

Neyroud, P. and Beckley, A. (2001), *Policing, Ethics and Human Rights* (Collumpton, Willan).

Nine Eleven Commission Report (2004), *Final Report of the National Commission on Terrorist Attacks on the United States*.

Phillips, T. (2005), 'After 7/7: Sleepwalking to Segregation', Speech made to the Manchester Council for Community Relations 22 September 2005 <http://www.cre.gov.uk/Default.aspx?LocID=0hgnew07s&RefLocID=0hg00900c002&Lang=EN&pr=true> accessed 27 March 2006.

Philpott, T. (1999) (ed), *Political Correctness and Social Work*, IEA Health and Welfare Unit, Choice in Welfare No 54 (London, IEA).

Quinton, P. and Bland, N. (1999), *Modernising the Tactic: Improving the Use of Stop and Search* (London, Home Office, Policing and Reducing Crime Unit).

Rayner, C. and Adam-Smith, D. (2005) (eds), *Managing and Leading People* (London, Chartered Institute of Personnel and Development).

Reber, A. S. and Reber, I. (2001), *The Penguin Dictionary of Psychology* (Penguin, Harmondsworth).

Reiner, R. (1992), *The Politics of the Police*. London: Harvester Wheatsheaf.

—— (2000), *The Politics of the Police* (3rd edn, London, Harvester Wheatsheaf).

Rokeach, M. (1968), *Beliefs, Attitudes and Values* (San Francisco, Jossey-Bass).

Rollinson, D., Broadfield, A., and Edwards, D. (1998), *Organisational Behaviour and Analysis* (London, Addison-Wesley).

Rowe, M. (2004), *Policing, Race and Racism* (Collumpton, Willan).

Runnymede Trust (1997), *Islamophobia: A Challenge for Us All*, Report of the Commis- ⨽ sion on British Muslims and Islamophobia, chaired by Gordon Conway (London, Runnymede) <http://www.runnymedetrust.org/publications/pdfs/islamophobia.pdf>.

—— (2000), *The Future of Multi-Ethnic Britain*, Report of the Commission on the Future of Multi-Ethnic Britain (London, Runnymede Trust).

Scarman, Lord (1982), *The Scarman Report* (Harmondsworth, Penguin Books).

Scripture, A. (1997), 'The Sources of Police Culture: Demographic or Environmental Variables?' 7 *Policing and Society* 3.

Security Industries Association (2005), *The Extended Police Family* <http://www.the-sia.org.uk/home/security/police_family.htm> accessed 27 March 2006.

Schein, E. (1984), 'Coming to a New Awareness of Organizational Culture', *Sloan Management Review*, Winter.

Schön, D. A. (1983), *The Reflective Practitioner* (US, Harper Collins).

Skills for Justice (2005), *National Occupational Standards* <www.skillsforjustice.com> accessed 27 March 2006.

Skolnick, J. (1966), *Justice Without Trial* (New York, John Wiley).

Smith, M. K. (2001), 'Community' in *The Encyclopaedia of Informal Education* <http://www.infed.org/community/community.htm> last updated 28 January 2005.

Smith, D. and Gray, J. (1983), *Police and People in London. Volume 4, The Police in Action* (London, Policy Studies Institute).

Schneider, R. (2001), 'Diversity and Competitive Advantage', in *People Management*, 3 May 2001.

Tajfel, H. (1982), 'Social Psychology and Intergroup Relations' *Annual Review of Psychology* 33.1.

The 1990 Trust (2004), *Stop and Search: A Community Evaluation of Recommendation 61 in the London Borough of Hackney* (London, MPA).

Vertovec, S. (2002), 'Islamophobia and Muslim Recognition in Britain,' in Y. Haddad (ed), *Muslims in the West: From Sojourners to Citizens* (New York, Oxford University Press).

Waddington, P. (1999a), 'Police (Canteen) Culture', 39 *British Journal of Criminology* 2.

—— (1999b), *Policing Citizens* (London, UCL Press).

References

Walklate, S. (1996), 'Equal Opportunities and the Future of Policing', in Leishman, F., Loveday, B., and Savage, S. (eds), *Core Issues in Policing* (London, Longman).

White, R. K. (1977), 'Misperception in the Arab-Israeli Conflict', 33 *Journal of Social Issues* 190–221.

Wright, A. (2002), *Policing: An Introduction to Concepts and Practice* (Collumpton, Willan).

Index